No Longer Bound

No Longer Bound

A Theology of Reading and Preaching

JAMES HENRY HARRIS

CASCADE *Books* • Eugene, Oregon

NO LONGER BOUND
A Theology of Reading and Preaching

Cascade Books
An Imprint of Wipf and Stock Publishers
199 W. 8th Ave., Suite 3
Eugene, OR 97401

www.wipfandstock.com

ISBN 13: 978–1-62032–290-1

Cataloging-in-Publication data:

Harris, James Henry.

No longer bound : a theology of reading and preaching / James Henry Harris.

x + 230 p. 23 cm. Includes bibliographical data and indexes.

ISBN 13: 978–1-62032–290-1

1. African American preaching. 2. Black theology. 1. Title.

BV4211.2 H285 2013

Manufactured in the U.S.A.

To the diaconate, trustees, members, and friends of
Second Baptist Church, Richmond, VA
And my wife Demetrius who taught our sons
James Corey and Cameron Christopher how to read

And Professors Harold E. and Loretta M. Braxton

And to my deceased parents:
Richard and Carrie Anna Jones Harris who both loved to read

Contents

Acknowledgments

I AM THANKFUL FOR the opportunity to see another book come to fruition because of the generous help of so many. For this, I am indebted to a host of individuals and institutions. The staff and members of Second Baptist Church, Richmond, Virginia have been more helpful than they know. The leadership team led by Paula Watson, Gregory Turner, Sr., Lucy Jones, John Allen, Henry Tucker, and Julius Richardson has made my life easier by taking on more and more responsibility for the operations of the church, thus enabling me to read, study and write sermons and books. Paula Watson has typed and retyped this manuscript more than we want to remember. She deserves much credit in helping to get this book in the form that the editors and publisher require. The L. Douglas Wilder Library at Virginia Union provided me with space to think and to study. The late Dr. Delores Pretlow and Mr. Ronald Shelton deserve special thanks for providing me access to a study room that I could use seven days a week. My editor at Cascade Books, Rodney Clapp, deserves special thanks for his help in bringing this book to publication.

The editorial and theological acumen of Paul Gleason helped to give the manuscript linearity and logical progression. I am grateful for the time and expertise he devoted to reading and evaluating every word, sentence, and paragraph. Larry Bouchard has been more than kind and generous with his analysis as a theologian, ethicist, and literary scholar. I cannot thank him enough for his expertise in ethics, philosophical hermeneutics, and the relationship between theology and literature—all of which helped to strengthen this book. Larry provided a thorough and systematic critique of the manuscript from beginning to end—even during a portion of his sabbatical. He deserves my highest praise and thanks. Peter Ochs, the consummate intellectual, also read the entire manuscript and encouraged me all along the way with his searing analysis and understanding of what

I am trying to convey. His unsurpassed personal and spiritual compassion coupled with his expertise in scripture interpretation and philosophical theology contributed immensely to the clarity of this book.

Paul Scott Wilson, Ronald J. Allen, and Tom Long read the manuscript and provided valuable assistance, critique, insight, and encouragement which aided in bringing this piece to publication. Also, my biblical scholar colleague Boykin Sanders' keen and novel analysis of scripture texts has helped and challenged me all along the way. He has been a trusted friend and brother ever since we shared an office together nearly twenty years ago.

I must thank the current and former students in the Graduate School of Theology, Virginia Union University for their critiques and interest in this book. Also, my advisory group, the Dialectical and Literary Society, a student led reading and study group at our school has allowed me to present portions of this book during the 2010-11 academic year. Moreover, portions of this work were also presented to a work group at the Academy of Homiletics meeting in Austin, Texas in 2011. Thanks to Dean John Kinney and the faculty and students at the School of Theology for asking me to do The Ellison-Jones Lectures on Preaching during the 2012 John Malcus Ellison and Miles Jerome Jones Convocation at the School of Theology, Virginia Union University. Many extraordinarily gifted and talented people have helped to make this book what it is; however, I alone am responsible for its shortcomings and weaknesses. I pray that the reader will accept this submission as the best that I have to offer at this particular time.

I am grateful to Patricia Perry, Marcel Cornis-Pope, and Terry Oggel with whom I studied African American literature and pedagogy, literary criticism and textuality, and Mark Twain's works *Adventures of Huckleberry Finn* and *Life on the Mississippi*. All of my academic studies are in service to the practice of preaching and theology in the dual contexts of the congregation and the seminary/university.

Finally thanks to my wife Dee Harris and sons James Corey and Cameron Christopher for their continued support of my preaching, research, teaching, and writing—especially since I have made education and learning a life-long process.

Introduction

Practical, Narrative, and Sermonic Theology

"All beginnings contain an element of recollection."
—Paul Connerton

"Oh, Freedom! Oh, freedom, Oh, freedom over me!
And before I'd be a slave, I'll be buried in my grave,
And go home to my Lord and be free ..."
—Negro Spiritual

I was born in the grip of the South, nurtured by the memory of slavery, segregation, and the sign language of a blatantly racial dialectic—a South unpurged after war and a century of bloodshed. It was nearly one hundred years after slavery, and yet I felt so much suffering and pain while living on land that seeped with the blood of my ancestors. It is a blood that gives new meaning to the red clay hills of Georgia, the Carolinas, and Virginia. The red clay dirt itself conjures violent memories, in which I envision the hangings and the beatings of Black brothers and sisters, their blood spilling deep into the soil.

The symbolism of the red clay provokes a feeling of kinship to the land that until lately was unclear to me. But thankfully, it is a part of my personal memory and the memory of my ancestors. It is the collective memory that we share as an oppressed community of believers. My individual memory is a part of this collectivity of experiences, thoughts, ideas and faith. The memory is sedimented in my body through the practice of actually eating this red clay dirt that my aunts would bring back from their visits back home to Oxford, North Carolina.[1] This was something my siblings and cousins did and looked forward to. Why I loved to eat the dirt, I don't claim to know—except that upon reflection, it was a ritualistic act whose meaning is gradually becoming clear some fifty years later. Event and meaning perdures, as I will explain in the next few chapters. This red clay dirt—gathered from the land of my ancestors and brought back to our little house in Virginia to be shared with children and adults alike—has become a "collective symbolic text,"[2] which I interpret with the same methods and strategies I use to interpret a biblical text or a poem by Adrienne Rich or a film by Eddie Murphy. In other words, I am always trying to determine what this earthy text, this event means. The "bodily practice" of eating this red clay as a child was done habitually, and the memory of it as a symbol, a gesture or a communal practice, means more to me now than it did then. Thus the meaning of an event is not bound by time. For example, people come to me asking to be rebaptized because "I didn't understand what I was doing; I was too young." I explain to them that now that they have an understanding of their first baptism, there is no need to be rebaptized. It is understanding the event that is critical whenever and however that understanding occurs. This applies to all rituals and sacraments, such as marriage and the Lord's supper/holy communion.

W. E. B. Du Bois in his essay "Of the Dawn of Freedom" recalls the vestiges of slavery in the effort to establish the Freedmen's Bureau years after the Civil War. The Freedmen's Bureau was supposed to be a way of providing some modicum of economic and social freedom. Yet there was no freedom to be found, not even in the Freedmen's Bureau. Du Bois says "there was scarcely a white man in the South who did not honestly regard Emancipation as a crime, and its practical nullification a duty . . . Thus Negro suffrage ended a civil war by beginning a race feud."[3]

1. Connerton, *How Societies Remember*. Also, I have vivid memories of the taste of the dirt. It was a starchy gritty compost that we treasured as children.

2. Ibid., 53.

3. Du Bois, *The Souls of Black Folk*, 132.

I think the race feud started long before the Civil War ended, and the suffering continues one hundred and fifty years later. The feud over the idea of freedom for Blacks in America was a primal cause of the war. During this period in American history Blacks were pervasively referred to as "niggers." The term "Black" is a recent and insurgent term, resulting from the struggles of the civil rights movement and a new-found self-esteem among Americans of African descent. Both Stokeley Carmichael and the Godfather of Soul music, James Brown, helped to transform the word into a positive expression of racial identity: "Say it loud, I'm Black and I'm proud." A few years earlier Stokely Carmichael had been the first young Black leader to use the language of "Black Power" at a freedom rally in Greenwood, Mississippi—just a few miles from where Emmett Till was murdered.

One goal throughout this book is to acknowledge a fleeting appreciation of the hermeneutics of Heidegger, Bultmann, Gerhard Ebeling, and Ernst Fuchs. But I do not wish to foreground their theories because I believe that my own thoughts and the thoughts of W. E. B. Du Bois, James Cone, Gayraud Wilmore, and Dwight Hopkins are more culturally attuned to my own experience and the experience of the poor and oppressed. Even more important are the thoughts, ideas, and experiences of ordinary Black church folk whose struggles simulate and reflect my own. We share a common inner history that makes our stories commensurate and our sorrows shared. Again, this primal kinship is what makes Black religion so powerful and the Black church so critical to understanding a theology of freedom from the bottom up, or from the underside of culture. We share a common experience and a common language—a language that speaks of freedom even if it is coded like the spirituals and the blues, the sorrow songs of the Black experience in America.

The desire for freedom is even more primal than spoken language. Spoken language is critical to sermonic discourse. And yet sermonic discourse precedes and supercedes spoken language with its rhetorical flair that we love and cherish as a people. It is gestural, moanful, and eruptive. The quest for freedom often cannot be spoken, but it can be felt and demonstrated by the moans and groans of a desire for freedom "too deep for words" (see Rom 8:26, NRSV). However, when that desire is spoken as sermonic discourse, it ushers in a new understanding and experience of freedom both in form and substance. The sermon in the Black church experience harbors the meaning of the gospel of freedom and offers transformation for those whose existential situation is one of bondage and oppression. This is the "good news" in the face of evil and its concomitants of hate and injustice.

INTERDISCIPLINARITY IN PREACHING AND THEOLOGY

This entire project combines a longtime interest in interpretation theory with an even longer practice of sermonic discourse, otherwise known as Black preaching. The project is grounded in texts and textuality as well as in performance theory. Sermonic discourse itself is inherently interdisciplinary, involving language, speech, texts, contexts, communications (written, oral, and visual), etc. There are also moments of social and cultural critique throughout the book's practical, narrative, and sermonic elements. Textual analysis and hermeneutics have been integral to both Jewish and Christian traditions for over two thousand years beginning with the ancient rabbis and with the oral nature of stories, myths, and legends that remain a part of the literary and scriptural canons.

More precisely, the interdisciplinary nature of sermonic discourse is evidenced by its mingling of texts and contexts, the preacher as text and sermonic discourse as a textual and performative event. In Black preaching "call and response" is comparable to audience participation in theater; however, it is a much more hermeneutical enterprise because it helps to determine the direction of the particular sermonic discourse, meaning that the sermon will change depending on the response. Worship in the Black church harbors many elements of performance: choirs that rehearse *ad nauseam*, praise dancers, mime artists, scripture readers and preachers are all a part of the cast every Sunday. And the sermon is a masterful form of communication (utilizing voice, gestures, tonality, syncopation, and so forth) that has stood the test of time. It is grounded in the "call of God" that rests upon the heart, mind and soul of the preacher. The pulpit is a type of stage, and every preacher, no matter how stoic and restrained, has an element of entertainment buried deep in his/her soul, waiting for an opportunity to display itself. The preacher's use of the body in the preaching process is highly correlated with theater's characterization of the performing body as text.[4] Black preaching is an act of gestural, spiritual, physical,

---

4. See New Con/texts: "*Wrecks and Other Plays*" 1st edition. (New York: Farrar, Straus and Giroux, 2007) (Neil La Bute); "The Performing Body as Text." Excerpts from Aaron Anderson and Jonathan Becker presentation during The Masks of Transformation Conference at Southern Illinois University, Carbondale, 2005.

and mental freedom that contributes to the meaning and interpretation of scriptural texts and everyday experiences.

This book recognizes that multimedia now permeate sermonic discourse with the use of the Internet, Facebook, television, and so forth. They are means of getting the message heard. Some of this media usage results in communicative distortion because television media, for example, is what Marshall McLuhan called a [cool] medium and radio is a hot medium. The point is that the content is not the message. It is not what is said on television by the preacher, but its being on television that produces certain effects.[5] Likewise, the pulpit is a cool medium, it is a stage, architecturally elevated and centrally located so that the audience can have a direct line of vision to the central cast, usually the preacher and the choir. The image and the symbolism are more important than anything being said. There are ushers at every entrance directing persons to their seats, just as in the theater. So, to me, the subject matter here is completely commensurate with the goal of interdisciplinarity. It must involve cultural, communicative, dramaturgy, and textual analysis. Sermonic discourse is a performative and interpretive act.

WHAT IS A BLACK CHURCH THEOLOGY?

This book on sermonic discourse is searching for a new direction of thought for a Black church theology of freedom. The direction it seeks is grounded in textuality, not topicality. It starts from the textual nature of scripture and flows toward contemporary topics, not vice versa. I am suggesting that Black church theology and freedom is a textual event, such that a new focus on scriptural meaning and interpretation is the means by which the preacher can make a difference in the lives of those in the church and community. How is this so? Freedom is grounded in creativity—and the creative elements inherent in Black sermon construction and delivery are emblematic of this freedom. Not only is freedom

5. Cf. Marshall McLuhan's idiomatic expression that "the medium is the message" suggesting that the message of television is a medium of entertainment and to keep one's high ratings, entertainment has to be the basic core message of programming whether drama, comedy or television religion. See McLuhan and Quentin Fiore, *The Medium Is the Message*. Larry Bouchard of the University of Virginia has helped me with this concept, explaining: "that the medium itself has an import and social sigificance so powerful as to overshadow or change any actual message. Examples: 'even bad publicity is good pubilicity,' or how television must 'dumb down' complex news, or how the fact that a TV preacher is on TV says more than anything he might actually be saying." Also, see McLuhan's *Understanding Media*.

grounded in creative action, but the impetus for such action is the imagination which harbors both good and evil. And, it goes without saying that sin and evil are the negative concomitants of freedom. However, my interest lies more in the positive elements of freedom, such as hope and the grace of God—inherent elements in Black sermonic discourse from slavery to the present postmodern period. Yet postmodernity with its emphasis on the present and the collapse of grand narratives does not describe Black practical theology, which privileges the history and suffering of African Americans. We have known evil and ugliness on a grand scale because we have had four hundred years of it in our experience, from the struggles of the Middle Passage to the current quest for freedom in all walks of life. The modern era began with a horrific collective act of terror. The first experience Africans had of modernity was one of terror; slavery was how modernity began for them. That's what the Middle Passage was all about—a modern project in terrorism.

In spite of this oppression, Black people have survived because of their strength and ability to imagine a day of freedom expressed through their songs and sermons. The sermon is the systematic and philosophical theology of the Black church, and the preacher was and still is the people's most acclaimed theologian and philosopher. The preacher takes seriously the call to preach and the responsibility to communicate a vision of freedom to the people, believing that "Where there is no vision, the people perish" (Prov 29:18). I am not a romanticist who believes in the glorious and beautiful past; however, I do believe that we learn from the struggles and the wisdom of our ancestors with the hope of not allowing the sins and the evils of the past to be brushed aside and forgotten.

Freedom begins with the unbinding power of the imagination. Our slave foreparents imagined a world where there would be no more chains and no more slavocracy. Freedom begins when the imagination concretely demands a response to bondage, when it says "All things are possible for those who believe" (Mark 9:23). Freedom is the ability to tell my story in a way that encourages others with hope and love. It is also the ability to offer a critique of self and others that will advance and expand the meaning of love and the meaning of freedom itself. Moreover, freedom had to be invented by the hopes and dreams of a people who were unwilling to accept slavery as the *telos* of existence or quite frankly as the will of God.

Black freedom has been born of dissension, not consensus because as Jean-Francois Lyotard points out "invention is always born of dissension . . ."[6] Moreover, "consensus is an act of violence against heterogeneity and against freedom and truth."[7] If Gabriel Prosser, Denmark Vesey, and Nat Turner had sought and demanded consensus among their Black brothers and sisters, there would never have been a single insurrection. And, more importantly, people have a right to their own beliefs and ideas of freedom and their ultimate freedom is to express their objection to the notion of univocity.

My focus here is on both the social self and the religious, spiritual self—which in some ways is a part of the self in the church and world. This is better expressed as the community of saints or the communion of saints (*communio sanctorum*) as reflected in Black church culture. The thesis here is that there is a positive correlation between Black sermonic discourse as communication, personal narratives as texts, and a Black practical theology of freedom as the necessary hermeneutic for interpreting the cultural, economic, social, and political lives of Black people. The relevant question is: What does confession mean, i.e., what role does an articulation of one's individual story play in Black church preaching and theology? We know that Augustine's fourth-century *Confessions* and Malcolm X's twentieth-century autobiography, Sojourner Truth's defiant ontological speech "Ain't I a Woman," and Monica A. Coleman's postmodern experience of Black women in shelters for battered women are all narrative reflections, memories, and confessions. In other words, how do individual narratives function in the development of a Black theology of freedom? For me, the practical and the theoretical are not antithetical but complementary and overlapping. However, I want to assert that in theology all roads, in one way or another, lead to and from preaching and practice, whether that practice is on the street corner, on television, in the classroom, hospital room, chapel, church sanctuary, chancel, or pulpit. While practical theology remains a stepchild in a significant number of theological schools and universities, it is gradually gaining respect and status in the curriculum, because the postmodern world no longer privileges the academy over the church. However, postmodernity privileges the media, especially in its news, educational, and entertainment modes. Hence, the value of the local church community, the individual, and the importance of the individual narrative in the construction of theological and sermonic discourse.

Systematic theology struggles to be relevant because of its lack of focus on the poor and oppressed. It has historically been a theology of

6. Lyotard, *The Postmodern Condition*, 25.
7. Ibid.

privilege, grounded in the dogma and rulemaking of the social, political, and academic elites, from philosophers such as Immanuel Kant and G. W. F. Hegel, to liberal theologians from Albrecht Ritschl to Ernst Troeltsch. In other words, German and North American liberal theology was systematically exclusionary of the poor and the oppressed, especially Blacks and women. The very people who have been left out are the ones that I want to include as those who not only constitute the body of Christ, *Soma Christou,* but also those whose voices give meaning to theological discourse as it is experienced by those whose feet are firmly placed on the ground. Black church-based theology is freedom theology and freedom theology is practical theology manifested in the everyday rituals and actions of the Black church. And preaching is the most public manifestation of theological discourse as praxis. Moreover, practical theology is philosophical theology because theory and practice are entwined in the Black church, where preaching reigns supreme regardless of its postmodern carnivalesque, imitative, and televisionistic form. There is no doxological activity or ritual that rivals the preached word in the Black church even when that word is a shameful exercise in the advancement of the personality traits of the preacher, a masquerade of a sermon. The purpose of the New Testament is to advance the preached word—the kerygma. Therefore the preacher must interpret this word and interpret it rightly in order to communicate the gospel of freedom and love in the Black community. These are not the intellectuals privileged by Du Bois, but the common folk who keep the church doors open seven days a week. These are the grunt workers of Black religion—not the elites, but the ordinary folk who continue to pack the pews every Sunday morning—not just on Easter Sunday and Homecoming Sunday.

I seek to show that autobiography and self-understanding are critical to sermonic discourse and the practice of communicating the gospel in the Black church. I continue by emphasizing the dominance of race in American religion and use my own history of being exposed to the ubiquitous, vile racial epithet "nigger" at a very early age as a critical tool for my understanding and interpretation of lived theology and its quest for freedom. Ernst Troeltsch's claim that to "identify the essence of Christianity means to shape it afresh"[8] describes what I seek to do throughout this book. My goal is to shape sermonic discourse afresh such that it becomes an act of love as well as a sign and symbol of love in service to the people and the Word of God. This is the "new hermeneutic" for a Black church

8. Troeltsch, *Ernst Troeltsch and Liberal Theology*, 218.

theology of preaching and freedom. In talking about sermonic discourse in the Black church I am shaping and reshaping what it means to be Black and Christian in America against the media images we see on television and in movies. Unfortunately, being Black in America is a bifurcated state of existence grounded in what W. E. B. Du Bois called "double consciousness." In other words, Black consciousness is ontologically double sided or dialectic because the issue of race in America is signified and symbolized by the historical nature and effect of centuries of chattel slavery. My inner history is the story of most Black folk and this story is also their story. It represents the common experiences of the oppressed and constitutes the uniqueness of Black religion and the Black Church. The Black Church in America remains the only institution owned and operated by Blacks. It has no economic, social, political, or religious equal, though it has many rivals.

My experience in the Black church suggests that personal narratives as texts help to cohere and constitute the community of believers. The Black church is constituted by the faith-stories of individuals that cohere to form an identifiable social, cultural, and ecclesial community full of memory that is never devoid of past and present struggles, joys, sorrows and experiences. This means that philosophers, theologians and preachers should take heed of "thick descriptions" of black church and community life, whether they appear in social science analysis, historical report, autobiographical reflection, cultural criticism, gender studies, etc. Through these overlapping (interdisciplinary) genres the self and community seek to at least speak in a quasi-unitary voice.

Each chapter concludes with a sermon that allows the reader to use her imagination to make connections between the theological discourse and the sermonic discourse. It also encourages filling in the perceived gaps that may exist in the text of sermons and the themes of chapters. The reader is asked to be creative in reading and in understanding the text.

Finally, preaching or sermon preparation is a theological act. More precisely, I agree with David Buttrick who claims that preaching is theology. And, I also agree with Karl Barth who claimed that theology is nothing other than sermon preparation. The sermon is a prophetic manifestation of philosophic theology.

Chapter 1

Teaching Preaching
Scriptural Texts and Textuality

"Am I not free?"

—1 Corinthians 9:1a

*"When we let freedom ring, when we let it ring from every village
and every hamlet, from every state and every city, we will be able to
speed up that day when all of God's children . . . Jews and Gentiles,
Protestants and Catholics will be able to join hands and sing in the
words of the Old Negro Spiritual, "Free at Last! Free at last! Thank
God almighty, we are free at last!"*

—Martin Luther King Jr.

BORN TO READ:
A PRELUDE TO TEACHING PREACHING

Reading is life. Each word and sentence instantiates the breath of God
in us, enabling us to live. In other words, learning to read is to learn to

live. Reading is a life and death enterprise because to read is to be born again, to be reborn, to be born of the Spirit. It is to be transformed and made anew.[1] This means that I love words—big words, small words, hard words, and easy words. As a preacher, one of the most powerful tools in my arsenal is the use of words. I love to use words to paint a picture, to make a clear claim, and to speak truth. I love to write and to speak words.

When I was growing up, we didn't have many books in our house. The only books we had were textbooks from school and a Bible with some pages missing. We were too poor to buy books on our own. While we knew love, we were too poor to really know what poverty was and too proud to admit it. To tell the truth, I had to go to school to learn about how poor we really were.

Our house had no electricity and no running water. It had no indoor plumbing and no central heat. We used to draw water from the well at the big house and carry it in buckets to our house, along the back path about a quarter mile away. The big house was my grandmother's, an old plantation house in the center of a 100-acre farm. It was a pretty deep well, about twenty to twenty-five feet. I used to lean over it and look down into the cavernous dark hole. Sometimes, I'd drop a rock into the well and wait to hear it reach the bottom. Its echo sounded so distant; I imagined what it would feel like to slip and fall over into the abyss. Each bucket carried about five gallons, and most of the time two or three of us would draw water using the four buckets we had at the house. The water was thick-tasting and pretty dirty. Often it contained the grit and bugs that inhabited the well. But we drank the water and never got sick from it. Since water was scarce, bathing was a luxury. During the week, we would wash up in the wash pan with about a half gallon of water. Taking a bath was a once-a-week activity so we would be fresh and clean for church on Sundays. A bath was an exercise in splurging or splashing that was supposed to last all week.

What we called the outhouse sat about fifty yards from the back door of the little house that Daddy built. At night we used a chamber pot or slop jar if we needed it. Most of the time we would hold it until morning. The outdoor toilet was a big hole in the ground with a little two foot by four foot house covering it. In later years, water also came from a well not too far from the outhouse. I'm not sure that waste water and drinking water weren't pretty much the same. They were no more than two hundred feet apart. There was no process of chlorination or filtration system to purify

1. Derrida, *Learning to Live Finally*, 30–31.

the water and kill bacteria. Still, it didn't kill us then, and we're not dead yet.

We used to do our homework by the light of the kerosene lamp. Most of time this meant that when the sun went down, we went to bed. And we got up when the sun came up—at sunrise.

I always had a head cold or sinus infection that lasted most of the winter. Nose running or congested. Head and stomach aches. No health insurance, which meant no doctor visits, unless you were sick unto death. The first time I went to the dentist, I was in the eleventh grade, sixteen years old. I wouldn't have gone then, either, if any of Daddy's concoctions had worked. Daddy was a jackleg in everything. He was both doctor and pharmacist, whose only credential was what he called "mother-wit."

We would sleep with three or four to a bed—often two at the head and two at the foot. We covered the thin blanket with coats and old clothes to keep warm, because the winters were often quite frigid. Any joy of winter lay only in the knowledge that spring was around the corner, but I often felt that it took forever to arrive. I started thinking of spring the day after Christmas. Spring was greater than Christmas because it was a gift of warmth and sunshine. It was the promise and hope of God's long and sweet-smelling summer. I could hardly wait for springtime and summertime. No shoes needed. No coats or hats. No freezing from the wisp of the wind or the snow blowing in from the north. Summer was like the joy of heaven. It was a dream fulfilled every single year, and I loved every minute of it.

What a joy to walk around in summertime with bare feet and scanty clothes. The years were 1958 through 1965, and I was so eager to start school. I couldn't wait to demonstrate my reading knowledge and my ability to comprehend. I have been able to read and spell big words for as long as I can remember. Truthfully, I cannot remember a time when I could not read. This is not hubris or delusion; it is simply the truth as I remember it. Anything put before me: the English Bible, the newspaper, the dictionary, picture books, word books, the *Weekly Reader*, magazines, and, yes, the romance novels my oldest sister Maria left on the couch. She was a romantic.

I was born reading; I was gifted with the word. In his memoir *Father and Son,* Edmund Gosse's words about himself also apply to me: "I one day drew towards me a volume, and said, 'book' with startling distinctness . . . I cannot recollect a time when a printed page of English was closed to me."[2] Reading and writing were critical to understanding and excelling in school. I was good at both. So I was a young scholar throughout elementary school. Aside from the nightly visits to the big house, we had no distractions. That's part of the reason I could excel in school. I loved school so much that I feel even now that I was born to go to school both as a learner and a teacher. Most of my life has been centered around school. Education is my passion.

Ever since I was a child, I have had a love for school and a thirst for knowledge. I could learn anything that was put before me—especially reading and writing. It was my gift to learn and to teach others. In the summertime, when school was out, I ran my own school and tutorials. My students were my parents and my brothers and sisters. There were ten of us children, so I had a small class where I taught reading, writing, social studies, and arithmetic. I started this when I was eight years old and I have been teaching and preaching ever since. In elementary school, I became the teacher's pet because I always wanted to please. My teachers were like goddesses. Gurus. Gandhi was indeed right in saying that true knowledge is impossible without a guru. They were all very attractive women. So, I think I was in love with my teachers as well as with the opportunity to learn. I wanted to display good conduct and excel academically. Whenever I was called upon to go to the blackboard to solve a math problem, spell a word, conjugate a verb, or write a sentence, I was eager to do it. I seldom missed a day of school. For years, I had perfect attendance.

We never had to walk to school because by the time I came along we had public school buses, and since I had S's or E's (for satisfactory and excellent) in all my subjects, I got to be in the school safety patrol. This meant that I sat on the front seat by the bus driver and would help to operate the school bus door and step outside to hold the safety patrol flag in front of the bus while traffic came to a complete stop. Not that there was much traffic on the rural back roads where we lived and traveled. Nevertheless, I was happy to hold that coveted position.

Our elementary school was about five miles from where we lived, and it was not much bigger than a large house. But it was still the biggest building I had ever entered. We could not attend the white children's school, which was less than one mile from our house—within walking distance. Every day, we passed the pretty red brick school with concrete sidewalks in front of it and large hedges and a manicured yard. The white school was two or three stories high with a stone facade and a parapet

2. Gosse, *Father and Son*, 47.

wall spiraling above the slate roof. Balustrades. It had large Greek Revival columns. Oh, and lots and lots of floor-to-ceiling windows. It made education seem important and serious, because the building spoke for itself. It was Jeffersonian. It looked like the ideal school, if there is such a thing. But for me and all the other Black children, it was not for us—off limits.

In stark contrast, just four miles away, was the Black school—Union Grove Elementary School. Window panes were broken. Bricks were missing from the steps. It sat off the main road on the edge of a soybean field and directly across from a cemetery. It was one level, brick exterior, paint peeling off the window frames and the entire structure struggling to resemble a place where learning takes place—much less where it is a top priority. The contrast was glaring. Something was always wrong: leaking faucets, broken light fixtures, window panes missing, ceiling peeling, and roof leaking. I remember some cold days in the middle of January and February when there was no heat anywhere in the school. Was this Siberia or somewhere in the frigid mountains of Eastern Europe? Sometimes, it was so cold that we had to keep our coats on all day long. Those who had coats, that is. A coat in winter was a prized commodity because when you were one of ten poor children, as I was, simple economics taught that not everybody could get a coat. (At least not one that fits perfectly or with buttons or a zipper that worked.) And yet, we learned in spite of the dilapidated building. We learned cultural anthropology and sociology. We learned the meaning of racial difference and the politics of segregation.

During one report card or grading period, the teacher wrote that I complained of headaches and stomach aches almost daily. "James is a good student, but he seems to suffer from constant headaches and stomach aches," she wrote. For the most part, I think I was simply congested and hungry. During those days it was hard for me to get enough to eat. I even looked malnourished. I was skinny as a bean pole. I never could get enough food at home or at school.

My favorite teacher during this childhood period was an elegant, soft-spoken, and prim lady named Mrs. Gladys Oswald. She was so poised, so articulate, so polished. There was not a priggish bone in her body. I thought that the sun rose and set according to the will of Mrs. Oswald. She could write so elegantly on the chalkboard. Every letter was perfectly placed within the lines and her cursive writing was flawless. I wanted, one day, to write like Mrs. Oswald. It was my dream. The Black teachers of that day apparently practiced writing every night when they went home. I certainly thought they did because penmanship was a craft—an art. It was like the poetry of Langston Hughes and Emily Dickinson. Or that of Zora Neale Hurston, Richard Wright, or Adrienne Rich. It was photography, like the captivating shots of Marilyn Monroe's curvaceous, naked body by Milton H. Greene. It had its own narrative to it. It had a language that spoke of precision and respect. Penmanship. It said to the eyes, *Look at me. I have style and class; I am beautiful to behold.* It said to the hands, *I am curvaceous and slender and tall. Keep me within the lines. I am cursive.* Teachers were architects of the word. They were alphabet stylists. Callig-raphers. And we were graded on how well we formed the letters to the alphabet. Style and substance are still one and the same for Black people. Writing well is not a bad thing; although any boy who did so was said to "write like a girl." This was reverse sexism. It's equivalent to saying that a Black student who studies hard and makes straight A's is "acting white." We've heard that craziness before. It is a foolish misinterpretation of Black culture, Black pride, Black achievement, and the love of learning for the sake of knowing; learning as a sign of intellectual curiosity; learning as a sense and symbol of pride. That's what learning means to me. It means possessing good self-esteem. Life-long learning is a virtue like prudence or honesty or truth or justice. It is freedom.

The school building we were housed in—as rickety and ragged as it was—was not as bad as the textbooks. They were the discarded, the dis-continued, the old editions of every subject. They were ragged and worn, marked up and vandalized on purpose. Some of the books had pages miss-ing and backs torn off. White children from years past had used these books until they were deemed discards; then they would be carted off to the Black schools for us to use. Not that there was anything salvific about freedom and justice in the books either. Another example of the blatant inequality of segregation. The books were always splattered with bad words. Profanity. Ugly words: *niggers, spooks, coons, monkeys.* Pictures of Blacks would be embellished: teeth blackened, ears and lips enlarged like they'd been injected with botox. The books looked like they had been edited by Mark Twain's illustrator, E. W. Kemble, who was a master of the caricature of Blacks.

Darker-skinned children (like me) were treated with less favor than light-skinned Blacks by teachers, school administrators, and other chil-dren. It was hard for dark-complexioned children to do well in school. There was a color caste and class system within the all-Black classroom. Educated Blacks, or as Carter G. Woodson said, "mis-educated Negroes," had begun to hate themselves to the point that "white was right, Black get back, brown stick around" was the *modus operandi*. Black teachers had internalized the ways of their colonizers. The darker you were, the less favor you received. Lighter-skinned children were presumed to be smarter by Black teachers. This was a fallacy that my dark-skinned body proved every day I sat in the classroom. I was always in the top group for reading, spelling, and math. Ability grouping or tracking meant nothing to me. I was always in group One A—because there was no word that I couldn't pronounce and no word I couldn't spell. Like Frederick Douglass and Vernon Jordan, James Henry could read. Big words, too!

I looked up to the school principal. He had authority and power. Maybe because he wore a necktie and a starched white shirt every day. He looked like Twain's *nigger* professor. One day he came to our classroom and asked the teacher to allow me to ride with him to the school board office, since I was a model student. I was excited. I got to ride in the principal's shiny new Chevrolet. I was riding with "Mr. Big-shot." The man. Our principal was a cigar-and-cigarette smoking, fast-driving, slick-headed man who ruled the school with an iron fist. To me, he acted very much like a *slave master* or an overseer who kept all the female teachers standing in subjection and fear. He was the only male in the school's leadership and faculty. Black patriarchy was mimicking white authority. The janitor, however, was a Black man, too, but he was voiceless and powerless. A peon. He was of a lower socio-economic and educational class. There was no respect shown him by the principal or most of the teachers. He did all the dirty work: cleaned toilets, mopped floors, collected trash, washed the blackboards, cut the grass. You name it, and he did it.

Black leaders are often chosen because of their ability to keep other Blacks under control and in subjection. Black educators have always been status quo oriented, perpetuating an ideology that is more conformist than anything else. Education for freedom and liberation has not been uppermost in their lesson plans. Education for placation is the norm. Education for becoming a part of the system or education for consolation seems to be more like it. "Don't rock the boat that you are riding on" is the prevailing philosophy for those teaching in the public schools of urban America. It was the case then and seems to still be the case today. Education and the mis-education of the Negro. This is something to think about as we ponder public policies regarding the SOLs and No Child Left Behind. Children are being left behind by the thousands and everybody knows it. Everybody is sworn to secrecy and pretending all is well.

FREDERICK DOUGLASS, AN AMERICAN SLAVE: ON READING AND FREEDOM

The life of the slave is chronicled with vivid detail by Frederick Douglass. The detail is such that the reader feels the pain and agony of the violence, hate, and evil of the slave system. Maybe this is my dilemma and accounts for the tears I shed every time I read certain scenes in the book. The story of his slave grandmother's death has had that affect on me. Like many passages in the book it is almost unutterable and unreadable for me:

> She had served my old master faithfully from youth to old age. She had been the source of all his wealth; she had peopled his plantation with slaves; she had become a great grandmother in his service. She had rocked him in infancy, attended him in childhood, served him through life, and at death wiped from his brow the cold death-sweat, and closed his eyes forever. She was nevertheless left a slave—a slave for life—a slave in the hands of strangers; and in their hands she saw her children, her grand-children, and her great grandchildren, divided, like so many sheep, without being gratified with the small privilege of a single *word*, as to their own destiny.[3]

After spending her entire life in service to the slave master—nurturing him, the plantation, his children, and the system itself—she is left to die alone and in despair. This system fostered a "sickness unto death" greater than even Søren Kierkegaard could imagine. Douglass feels that this "base ingratitude and fiendish barbarity" exhibited toward his grandmother, calls for the intervention of a righteous God to visit the earth and correct these dreadful and horrid atrocities.

For Frederick Douglass reading and writing was the pathway to freedom. The slaves who could read—persons such as Nat Turner, Gabriel Prosser, and Denmark Vesey—were considered the most dangerous and useless to the system as an institution. Douglass recounts his experience of learning to read:

> Very soon after I went to live with Mr. and Mrs. Auld, she very kindly commenced to teach me the A, B, C. After I had learned this, she assisted me in learning to spell words of three or four letters. Just at this point of my progress, Mr. Auld found out what was going on, and at once forbade Mrs. Auld to instruct me further, telling her, among other things, that it was *unlawful*, as well

3. Douglass, *Narrative of the Life of Frederick Douglass*, 51.

17

as *unsafe to teach a slave to read*. To use his own words further, he said, "If you give a *nigger* an inch, he will take an ell. A *nigger* should know nothing but to obey his master—to do as he is told to do." Learning would spoil the best *nigger* in the world. Now, he said, if you teach that nigger (speaking of myself) how to read, there would be no keeping him. It would forever unfit him to be a slave . . . From that moment, I understood the pathway from slavery to freedom . . . I set out with high hope, and fixed purpose, at whatever cost of trouble, to learn how to read.[4]

Reading is freedom, and freedom is reading. And, like Frederick Douglass, the slave preacher was one of the few people who early on learned to read. It was the ability to read that separated the slave from the free man, and for Douglass, his slave master had inadvertently taught him a lesson that would make freedom possible. Douglass felt that he could read and write his way to freedom, because learning was the key to liberation. Douglass continues his interpretation of the slave master's words, which convinced his wife to abandon all efforts to teach him.

The very decided manner with which he spoke, and strove to impress his wife with the evil consequences of giving me instruction, served to convince me that he was deeply sensible of the truths he was uttering. It gave me the best assurance that I might rely with the utmost confidence on the results which, he said, would flow from teaching me to read. What he most dreaded, that I most desired. What he most loved, that I most hated. That which to him was a great evil, to be carefully shunned, was to me a great good, to be diligently sought; and the argument which he so warmly urged, against my learning to read, only served to inspire me with a desire to and determination to learn. In learning to read, I owe almost as much to the bitter opposition of my master, as to the kindly aid of my mistress. I acknowledge the benefit to both.[5]

Douglass soon learned that his slave mistress could be as tyrannical and evil as her husband. He learned that kindness could turn to stone, and she became more violent than her husband toward the idea of him becoming a reader. Clearly, "education and slavery were incompatible with each other."[6] Education was the pathway to freedom, and while today it is not a panacea, it still leads to that sacred and reverent goal—freedom.

4. Ibid., 40–41.
5. Ibid., 41.
6. Ibid., 44.

The knowledge of this history motivates me to demand that my seminary students focus on reading and writing in all of my preaching and homiletics classes. We read both fiction and nonfiction, because I believe the lessons on writing with clarity in the fields of ethics and theology are found in both genres. I pair novels, poetry, and creative nonfiction with philosophy, theology, history, and social science to broaden the students' horizons in a way that will prepare them to go directly into the practice of ministry or continue their graduate studies. Every year some of our most serious students are accepted into excellent graduate programs. And oftentimes they will tell me that my homiletics courses were essential to their ability to navigate the difficulty and quantity of their required readings in doctoral programs. Students learn early on that preaching is first and foremost about reading, writing, and interpretation of texts. After getting that understanding straight, then they are allowed to stand before the class and deliver a sermon based on the method I call "dialectic textuality." This means that the launching pad for the sermon is the scripture text, not something heard on the radio or television, or something seen on a billboard or in the street. In other words, the text gives rise to thought, and that thought may lead to the sermon's introduction. However the sermon begins, its grounding should be scripture text based. That is one half of the dialectic: the thesis.

This is complicated by the fact that the other half of the dialectic (the antithesis) is designed to explicate the real life situation that the scripture text engages. The antithesis deals with the particularity of the real. This inevitably leads the preacher to deal with the struggles Black people have with the ineluctable reality of oppression and injustice that permeates the culture. Often this is a natural outgrowth of understanding the scripture text from a negative or antithetical perspective. The sermon's engagement with the everyday provides the best way for the preacher to confront issues such as racism, homophobia, patriarchy, sexism, injustice, white supremacy, Black on Black crime, self-hatred, egoism, and a host of other realities.

While context deals with the reality of the everyday, scripture often presents an ideal, something to aspire to. For the Christian, it represents the Good News of faith, salvation, forgiveness, love, peace, justice, grace, and freedom as seen and reflected in the scriptural text. One or more of these ideals is then contrasted with the reality, by creating and exacerbating the tension between the two (real vs. ideal or antithesis vs. thesis).

THE PHENOMENOLOGY OF READING
AND WRITING

Reading provides the opportunity to experience the presence of the world presented in the text in a way that correlates that world with the correlatives within the text as well as those outside the given text, that is, correlatives in the experiential life of the reader. Because the writer and the reader are both "conscious of" something, this consciousness of the intentionality of the text may again find correlatives in the consciousness of the reader—a consciousness that may inevitably be different from that of the text or literary work.[7]

In writing, something critical has to be left to the reader's imagination. The reader is encouraged to fill in the blank spaces as a testament to the writer's lack of presumption and understanding. I want to leave room for the reader's imagination to continue the writing process in the way that benefits the reader and the writer. Also, because I don't presume to know the whole story or to interpret the text completely, the reader is given the freedom and latitude to construct and reconstruct the areas of the story that lack explanation or completion. The writer has to leave room for the text and the reader to dialogue or at least to react by adding words and sentences to the existing text. Even after this the text will still have gaps in it because there is no complete and absolute text. Wolfgang Iser adds clarity to this assertion when he states:

> These gaps have a different effect on the process of anticipation and retrospection, and thus on the "gestalt" of the virtual dimension, for they may be filled in different ways. For this reason, one text is potentially capable of several different realizations, and no reading can ever exhaust the full potential, for each individual reader will fill in the gaps in his own way. . . As he reads, he will make his own decision as to how the gap will be filled.[8]

This gives the reader the power to be creative and imagine a new twist and turn in the story by inserting her own words and images into the text. Each reader recognizes gaps in different places of the story depending on their own level of understanding and experience. This means that my story can become your story depending on the number of gaps being filled by the reader. In effect the new story is not completely new because it is

---

7. Husserl, *Analyses Concerning Passive and Active Synthesis*.
8. Iser, "The Reading Process," 131.

grounded in the existing text. It is how we read and reread the story/text that determines how we find meaning in the story.

Illusion is important in reading because it allows the reader to create and make familiar the unfamiliar world of the written text. It allows the unfamiliar to become familiar. While this is very necessary in reading novels or fiction, it is helpful in nonfiction and scriptural texts as well. However, illusion must not be a sacral element of reading to the extent that it cannot be shattered. The shattering of illusion is also important to the reader because otherwise the reader may allow illusion to become too dominant, thus leading to delusion which is a type of evasion of the mind's capacity to create reasonable meaning.

READING THE TEXT

Reading the text involves three elements of Charles Peirce's semiotics: abduction, deduction, and induction. All three are processes of logical reasoning. Induction is an inference of a generalized conclusion drawn from particular instances. Deduction is an inference from a general principle, i.e., conclusions about particulars follow necessarily from the general. Deduction means to subtract from or to deduce.

Abduction is to take away. It has to do with plausibility rather than probability. Is this a plausible explanation of the text? Can this analysis or conclusion be abducted from a critical reading of this text? In other words, the text enables the reader to think new thoughts and to develop a plan of action that seeks to embody the Word of God. In reading the scriptural text, one is obligated to allow the text to speak its own language and sing its own song. This means that there is a creative element in reading the text such that it shapes and reshapes the reader in her understanding of both the text and the self.

TEACHING AND PREACHING

I am very systematic, yet emotional, about teaching preaching because I think it is a serious life and death enterprise. This means that I insist that students be well read and well-spoken. Their clarity of speech and reading is emphasized such that the classroom is a laboratory for reading texts, scriptural and otherwise. Sometimes students will misrepresent words in the text, and I will encourage them by saying "read that again," or "read what you see on the page." Sometimes, they will become defensive and accuse their eyes, glasses, or contact lens of deceiving them; however, at other times, they will simply conform to the plea to "read the text again" understanding that this repeat reading is to repair an error in the previous reading. The text itself has become a site for correction in oral discourse. I want the modern and postmodern preacher to become at least as *eloquent* as W. E. B. Du Bois claims the slave preacher was, whose "words crowded to his lips and flew at us in singular eloquence."[9] It is the eloquence of the preacher that I am committed to developing and my commitment to this cause is driven by love. I want the preacher, regardless of race or religious persuasion, to be an eloquent speaker and interpreter of the word.

In my classes, I offer a reading list which includes texts that may not necessarily have an immediate and direct relationship to preaching. I have to show that reading broadly is necessary. It eradicates the perception of the Black preacher as an anti-intellectual engaged in buffoonery and his-trionics to mask his or her incompetence as an interpreter of texts. I say over and over to my students that preaching is hard work. "It is like going every day to meet the man." It is a job that requires time to think, read, reflect, research, and write. I am reminded of the foreword to Lyotard's *Phenomenology* by Gayle L. Ormiston. She quotes from the preface of *Phenomenology of Perception* by Maurice Merleau-Ponty: "we find in texts only what we put in them."[10] This language suggests to me that textual analysis and understanding require hard work on the part of the preacher/interpreter. Putting a lot into what we do before writing and preaching the sermon is a prerequisite to standing before the people to preach what "Thus saith the Lord."

My first models for this gift or talent of eloquence were pastors (Rev. George Polk and Rev. Harold Braxton) and my preaching teacher, Miles J. Jones. When I registered for his homiletics class, I was convinced that his voice was the embodiment of the voice of God, and if that premise were correct, then God was experienced through the words of the Black preacher. It was not only the baritone nature of his voice, because God's voice could undoubtedly be soprano or alto, but it was the way that he put words and sentences together: subjects, verbs, objects, adverbs, adjectives, perfect participles, etc., combined with a cadence and rhythm that were captivating and luring to the hearer. This was music to my ears. This man of God was the embodiment of the eloquence of the Black preacher. So, before I read Du Bois's description of the preacher, I had encountered what

9. Du Bois, *The Souls of Black Folk* , 135.
10. Lyotard, *Phenomenology*, 10.

he meant in the person of Miles Jerome Jones, eloquent Black preacher *extraordinaire*. His teaching and preaching were a combination of the philosophical and practical. He used his entire body to preach—especially his voice, hands, and feet. You had to watch the synchrony between his voice and his hands in order to clearly and fully understand and appreciate his sermonic message. And he often tip-toed, thus increasing his height in an effort to highlight the impact of what he was saying. His body rocked and bounced back and forth in his excitement and play with the word and the sentence. He preached "in demonstration of the Spirit and power" (1 Cor 2:4). And yet I never fully embraced all the elements of his method or sought to comprehend the nuances and details of it, though I sought to practice it for over a decade. I did what so many of my own students do in eagerness to preach. I took the little that I had learned and tried to make something meaningful of it. I could not get the scripture text and my understanding of it to cohere fully into a structure that was clear and discernible *to me*. But God took my meager sermonic offerings and transformed them into something else. My naïve and faithful efforts were enough for God to work with. I kept on reading and studying as if my very life depended on it. And, quite frankly, it did. When I taught preaching during my early years, I focused on preaching and imagination, theology, and scripture interpretation; however, I really didn't have a good grasp of homiletic method. While I continue to struggle with the necessity and importance of method, I tell my students that method apart from scriptural textuality is hollow and shallow. And, explication and meaning are more critical than method.

Miles Jones' adaptation of the correlation method (Tillich) utilizes a dialogical relationship between scriptural text and the existential situation of the preacher and hearer. This constant conversation and dance between text and context harbors the essence of the preaching method. I was always challenged by the effort to find a point of entry in the scripture text that would yield a coherent sermon with correlatives in my life-world. While Miles Jones used this method and its hybrids in the most discernible and effective way, I could never fully fashion the intricacies and nuances of the process that would lead to a mastery of the methodology.

Method in preaching is ultimately designed to help determine the meaning of the text which is the goal of every sermon. However, I used this correlation method of sermon preparation until I was accepted into a doctoral program in preaching led by the distinguished pastor and Professor Samuel DeWitt Proctor, who introduced us to the dialectic method of sermon construction. He was a New Testament scholar, theologian, and ethicist, and I was convinced that I had met the most acclaimed homileti-cian and preacher in the world. This was *déjà vu*. I had heard him preach at conferences and in churches and was always mesmerized by his inter-pretive and narrative genius. He was a master storyteller and consummate public intellectual and theologian who could simplify the complex and complexify the simple. He was a biblical scholar who broke texts and meaning down in a way that a child could understand. This was a gift and a display of genius that I was completely enamored by. He could get to the essence of an historical or philosophical issue, a scripture text, or a congre-gational concern with an ease and clarity that was a gift from God. A spiri-tual gift. This man was the combination of consummate intellectual, folk preacher, storyteller, orator, and politician all rolled up into one. He pos-sessed the "singular eloquence" that would have made W. E. B. Du Bois sit up and listen with pride. He believed in writing every word of his sermon. And, he could make those words come alive without "over the top" antics and histrionics—though he too, like most Black preachers, was often quite animated in his style of delivery. Black preachers believe that the sermon, written or unwritten, is the Word of God. The form and content are bound together by the grace of God. It is because of those who were forbidden to read and write for three hundred years, that I take issue with those homi-letic theorists and practitioners who insist that the preacher should preach without a written script. To them, I say that Black preachers have paid a high price for learning to read and write. Some were lynched, and others beaten and flogged. Many have died at the hands of a slave system that for-bade such an accomplishment. For me, to use a written manuscript in the pulpit is a subversive act of freedom. It is a protest against oppression and slavocracy, and it is to tip my hat to my ancestors like Frederick Douglass, Nat Turner, and Gabriel Prosser, who knew firsthand the value of reading. To read the sermon is an act of freedom and liberation and to insist that a Black preacher preach without a manuscript is a taunting and terroristic act by the descendants of the slave master. Now, it is important for the preacher who preaches with/without a manuscript to write the sermon out verbatim in order to develop his or her writing skills and to establish a historical record for future research. This is especially important for the preacher and the Black church because there remains a paucity of written materials on Black Preaching and because the sermon was in fact an oral and unwritten presentation. So, I insist that our preaching students write the sermon as if it is to be published. This means that the sermon must be written, edited, rewritten, and written again before it is preached.

All of this constitutes a spirituality and emotion that surrounds the preacher and the sermon. Black preaching is an emotional enterprise balanced with a moderate dose of research and reason. In Black preaching reason and emotion come together in a way that creates excitement in both the preacher and the hearer. Passionate expression makes the sermon more palatable and understandable to the people in the congregation. There is no place for boredom, so intellect and emotion have to form a marriage where each is equally dependent upon the other. Head and heart are necessary for preaching to the masses of Black folk who expect to be informed, inspired, and encouraged after a week of being beaten and bruised by the simple act of living as a Black person in America. After teaching preaching since the tender age of twenty-four, I can say that I am driven by a love that seeks to free folk from themselves and from the forces of oppression that engulf the church and community. Black preaching is first and foremost an act of love augmented by the grace of God.

THE SERMON IS PHILOSOPHICAL THEOLOGY AND ETHICS

The sermon is the practical manifestation of philosophical theology in every church, black or otherwise. The ethical, political sermon is at the center of a philosophical theology. This is contrary to the way that homiletics is thought of and often taught, and contrary to the way that religious studies as a discipline excludes homiletics as ancillary to theology and ethics. My claim is that homiletics is ethics and theology rolled together into one discourse: the sermonic. And, both Miles Jones and Samuel DeWitt Proctor were examples of this claim, which has been both revealed and confirmed to me through continuous study and reading of almost everything under the sun. While Jones found correlatives to the scriptural text in Black existentialism or everyday existence of struggle and hope, Proctor saw how the Word of God could synthesize the dialectical nature of humanity and the material world. By this, I mean that the people of God are both good and evil, loving and hateful, right and wrong, righteous and unrighteous, etc. I also mean that the material world is itself a dialectic of plenty and hunger, night and day, sunshine and cloudiness, winter and summer, etc. This likewise applies to the social world of rich and poor. The language of scripture witnesses to this understanding of dialectic in the parables of

Jesus (wheat and chaff, first and last) and in other scriptures such as Psalm 1 (godly and ungodly). Proctor could do this through telling stories that found their perfect correlates in scripture, experience, or both.

This means that the sermon is the new vehicle that gives meaning to the biblical story and contemporary understanding of God and the world. Homiletics is the major theological discipline that answers the questions that Paul Ricoeur and other philosophical theologians raise. I am offering in my homiletics classes and throughout this book, however nuanced and muted, the thesis that Black preaching is the unrecognized practice or paradigm of philosophic theology. More precisely, the study of preaching ought to be at the center of the curriculum in theology and ethics, i.e., especially philosophical theology (systematic theology) if philosophical theology has anything to do with wisdom, which is the way I'm using the term. This is not just about African American preaching and theology, but about the broader field of religious studies, because Black preaching deals with life and death issues in a way that no other preaching dares to confront. This is why the real life situation or antithesis of the sermon is so masterfully developed by my Black students and so difficult to develop for my white students. Blacks know intuitively the experience of injustice, suffering, and pain because it is something they live almost every day, so they can passionately develop that part of the sermon's introduction. Conversely, my white students always claim to have difficulty with the real life situation or sermon's antithesis because they do not seem to want to face the role their ancestors or they have played in oppressing Blacks and the poor through slavery, lynchings, segregation, and other acts of personal and social evil. They run from the real, claiming that they don't understand the method. And yet I believe that they understand it all too well. It is often much less complicated than the ideal because it is grounded in lived experience or the condition of existence. The condition of existence or situation in life is to the correlation method as the real (as seen in life and in scripture) is to the dialectic method. They both deal with the issues facing people as they negotiate the real world. It is by nature confrontational and correcting unlike some white preaching which is co-opted by the politics of the white church and theology. It is emotional because it speaks of suffering and pain. It is cognitive because it speaks of freedom and justice in the midst of pain and suffering. It is the new [American] hermeneutic of suspicion that does not need the Germans to explain the meaning of word and event. This is something that Blacks have known and practiced since the days of slavery. Call and response is conversation between the preacher as slave and oppressed and the people as slaves and oppressed. The slaves always preferred hearing a Black preacher rather than the master's preacher because the slave preacher's experience and the experience of the slave were one and the same. So, they could identify with one another on a deep experiential and unconscious level to the point of believing that the grace of God is not an abstract concept, but a real experiential event in their lives. In the language of the Black church, it was God's grace that woke us up this morning and kept us from the "chilly hands of death." In the spirit of Mark Twain and Huck Finn; it was not something we done did, but something God "done done for us," by God's grace and mercy.

The Black preacher has believed historically that the sermon is a sanctified word event. The sermon is not the sole property of the preacher, but it comes from God and belongs to God. The preacher preaches the sermon, but God takes that human word uttered by the frail, weak preacher and sanctifies it to the point of transforming it into the Word of God through the spiritually transforming event of preaching. The Black sermon is the gospel, i.e., the good news for a people who need and want to hear a word from the Lord. This word is not from the preacher, but from the Lord. The Black preacher uses the same formula that the prophet Nathan used in conveying God's message to his servant David: *Thus saith the Lord.* This means that the sermon is only the penultimate word; God has the last word. The ultimate word is the Lord's word, which interrupts the human word of the preacher and infuses it with the Holy Spirit. This point of interruption is the point where the sermon becomes the Word of God.

READING, WRITING, AND STUDYING AS HOLY ACTS FOR THE PREACHER

The preacher must begin his/her day by reading something meaningful. It could be a novel or the newspaper or magazine. It could be scripture, biography, theology, history, or philosophy—but the important thing is to read broadly, carefully, and discriminatingly. What one reads initially is less important than the act of reading because the latter establishes the habitual practice necessary to good preaching. The preacher who doesn't read and study should be taken behind the church and beaten, pebbled, and paddled by the members, deacons, and the elders of the church and declared a heretic and profligate and disallowed to speak from the church's pulpit. Only those preachers who understand the critical seriousness of preaching and those who yearn to expand their minds will develop into powerful preachers and homileticians. Preaching is a calling that demands continuous serious study, constant prayer and meditation, and a disciplined imagination fueled by reading and more reading before writing and rewriting the sermon.

Preaching is a life-long calling that requires life-long learning. Those who finish seminary and graduate school believing that their study is complete will seldom, if ever, become great preachers,[11] because if preaching is a life-long calling, then it demands a life of study and learning—both formal and informal, especially given the fact that a large number and percentage of students entering the seminary today are already finishing up another career to begin anew in ministry. The likelihood that they already possess what it takes to become a powerful preacher and pastor is very slim because many have no training in history, literature, or philosophy—not to mention writing. I say this because investment of time and discipline for the development of the mind, heart, and soul are necessary to achieve eloquence of speech and understanding of scripture, theology, and culture. Unfortunately, there are those who have a great following without being accused of being great preachers. This should be attributed totally to the grace of God, not the effort or wisdom of man or woman. If congregations were more demanding of decent sermons, preaching would improve almost overnight.

Many of my students who approach ministry and preaching as an appendage or auxiliary to their day job seem to have no clue as to the meaning of being a pastor, preacher, or homiletician. As a teacher, I ask that students seek to make connections and appropriate various readings to the discipline of preaching. They have to first understand that this is a theological, practical, and spiritual discipline that requires a certain knowledge base grounded in philosophy, history, and theology—both historical and contemporary. This means that not everybody who has a big church or a doctor of ministry degree is qualified to teach preaching. Homiletics is minimally about stylistics and voice quality as some folk in the church believe. A great voice, deep and loud, does not a preacher or teacher make. Homiletics and hermeneutics are first and foremost about reading and understanding as a prelude to preaching. This means that one

---

11. I use the superlative "great preachers" with a level of trepidation and caution because the terminology is very subjective and plastic. In today's culture, "great" is synonymous with "popular" and antithetical to Jesus' admonition to his disciples "that the first will be last and whoever wants to be great must humble themselves" (Mark 9:35).

cannot teach that which one does not understand. It is about interpretation of texts (written and unwritten), contexts, and people. Some of my most difficult preaching students have sweet voices and histrionic actions that they depend on to whip people into a frenzy—but they often have no sermon. So, in the first class on sermon preparation, I explain that reading widely and asking questions is the essence of my Socratic teaching method. The motto is "Read, Read, Read and then Read some more!" Students have to learn a new language that is not Greek or Hebrew, but reading that is philosophical and theological as well as literary. A language that is hermeneutical and communicative. My focus is on philosophical hermeneutics and textual analysis, utilizing interpretation theory and literary criticism to foster understanding. Students are encouraged to approach scriptural texts with a hermeneutics of faith and suspicion such that every word and sentence are subject to analysis and interrogation. This process also allows the text to interrogate the preacher in a way that challenges and confronts the writer, the reader and the hearer. Most scriptural texts need clarification, as Peter Ochs says about rabbinic homiletics: "if a text is clear, there is nothing to be said about it."[12] Most texts are not clear to me because I am separated from them by time, culture, political, and social teachings, language, and race. So there is a lot to be said and understood about them. In short, my context is very different from the one that surrounds the scripture text, and I have to work hard to interpret that text for myself and for my people. This interpretation is facilitated by a wide *and* varied process of reading, studying, and meditating. These are all acts of holiness that are pleasing to the heart of God.

In my preaching classes the assignment of two to three novels by Zora Neal Hurston, Ernest Gaines, Leo Tolstoy, Albert Camus, J. D. Salinger, Nella Larsen, James Baldwin, or James Joyce serve as a point of entry into the complexity of interpretation for sermonic discourse. This is followed by reading W. E. B. Du Bois, Paul Ricoeur, Mikhail Bakhtin and Roland Barthes. Then, we read selectively from several of my own texts and those of persons such as Cleophus LaRue, Samuel Proctor, Marvin McMickle, Ronald Allen, Paul Scott Wilson, Jana Childers, Clayton Schmidt, Tom Long, or Nora Tisdale that deal with preaching from a particular perspective and/or other perspectives.[13] The aforesaid names are

---

12. Notes from a seminar taught by Larry Bouchard and Peter Ochs. Peter Ochs is Professor of Modern Judaic Studies and Philosophical theology at the University of Virginia. He made this observation in a graduate seminar: "Charles Peirce and Paul Ricoeur on Script, Text, and Scripture."

13. See Harris, *Preaching Liberation* and *The Word Made Plain.*

examples and not intended to suggest that this list is exhaustive because the readings are tweaked each semester. The course is interspersed with lectures on stylistics, multimedia, performative hermeneutics and literary criticism. It is a lot to focus on, and there are some complaints about the number and complexity of the readings. These are all understandable, but not compelling enough to merit an easing of the readings, because my deep and abiding love for students demands that I require them to read an array of materials. They may eventually become pertinent in the students' quest to become the best preachers that they can be, given that many of them have gotten a late start in this preaching enterprise. It often takes years for many of them to thank me for insisting that the preacher be one of the most well-read persons in the congregation and community. I must note that many of our students know a lot about the practice of preaching before setting foot in the seminary because they have been preaching a long time before coming to us. This is mainly an asset to them especially if they recognize that they are in school to learn and not simply to receive a diploma. It is also a liability to those who want us to simply reinforce what they already know and practice without expanding their horizons. And for those who pastor large churches, it takes a lot of humility for them to expose themselves to the ego-busting critique of a homiletics course. My responsibility is to help them develop a "thick skin" while simultane-ously encouraging them to strive toward excellence. As a teacher, I walk a tight rope of "helping" students learn how to become a better preacher by pressing toward the mark of the high calling from God (Phil 3:14) while correcting their sermons to the best of my ability, so help me God. And, my teaching method is *maieutic* therefore Socratic in both style and substance.

TEXTUAL TITLES FOR SERMONS

The sermon title is critical because it provides the thread that connects with the scripture text in a way that is discernible to the hearer. Sometimes this is not immediately obvious, but unfolds as the sermon gets under-way. I have a certain disdain for popular culture, sensational, meaningless titles, taken from songs and movies, and yet the title of the sermon should not be too revealing or obscure. The title should lend itself to explanation and development of the scripture text from which it has been drawn. This means that the sermon title should be lured from the text, teased from the text, after much reading, prayer, and study. Study is critical because most preachers don't have a problem with praying and divining God's will. It is *study* that needs to be emphasized. Serious continuous study is a prelude to all preaching. Studying, like preaching, is a Godly act. The preacher who studies faithfully demonstrates his or her love for the people and the Word of God in the most humble way possible.

There should be no semblance of apparent inadequacy in the sermon title. It should reflect the spirit and the semantics of the scripture text if it is to claim grounding in textuality rather than topicality. Topicality is the most popular medium for preaching: satiating, non-confrontational, palliative, and sometimes meaningless sermons about harmless "feel good" topics and personal spiritual development at the exclusion of the other. These sermons are not concerned about societal issues of freedom, oppression, injustice, and racism. All the focus is on inspiration and adjusting to the environment rather than transforming it. These sermons are full of "fluff." This type of preaching should be banned from the church's pulpit and relegated to the theater's stage or to the community's carnival. It should be placed where it belongs—on a non-church stage as a form of entertainment. The gospel is too serious, too much of a life or death mandate to be approached with a nonchalant attitude. This is a struggle because every preacher is a human vessel who harbors elements of the theatrical in his or her own body. These elements are always seeking ways to manifest themselves via the sermon. It may be through singing, gestures of the body or some other spectral act devoid of textual integrity and analysis.

There should be clear commensurability between the sermon title and scriptural text. The consequences of the lack of commensurability between the sermon text and sermon title are such that the death of the sermon is a real possibility. This means that the life of a textual sermon is contingent upon the connection and comparability that exist between the scripture, the sermon title, and the sermon itself.

The sermon is more like a song than a newspaper article, and the title is like a reprise that keeps the preacher and hearer focused on the subject and the meaning of the text at the same time. Titling the sermon based on textual analysis and understanding is itself an art, but the preacher needs more than a catchy, beautiful, and sweet title. Taken alone, the sermon title is no more than an appetizer. The title must reflect what the scripture and the sermon are about.

STARTING WITH THE SELF

My life is a tensive reality burdened by stability and instability, weakness and strength, hope and nihilism, meaning and meaninglessness. This tension that runs through the human mind, body, and soul also runs through every aspect of the material world and can come apart at any point where one meaning intersects with another and one's sense of self intersects with the Other. New meanings are created at these intersections of discourse. The tension is fundamental to self-understanding, because one is constantly negotiating his/her overlap with elements of the self and other. Narrative or one's inner history is the structure by which understanding of the self is made possible. We are situated beings, and our existence, physical and spiritual, is grounded in the tension between the cognitive and the emotive, the actions of others as well as the self. We are tentatively stable, but our stability—of the physical body, the mind, and our mental state—is precarious, always teetering on the brink of instability because there are so many forces that constantly impinge upon us. And these tensive forces need constant mediation.

This is why the preacher's message and understanding of self are so critical. The preacher is a mediator, and the Word is the sanctified event that soothes the torment of the self. To be human is to live in tension and ambiguity. This is the nature of the fallible self. We don't have before us the pure presence of what is, because what *is* is always unfolding, i.e., revealing itself or masking itself in absence. Thus we are compelled to interpret what seems to be. And, what seems to be is always only a fragment of what is. It is never a complete whole, though it may think itself to be. Therefore, our relationship to what *is* is indirect. And, we are distant from the self as well as the Other inasmuch as the self is always constitutive of Otherness and the Other is constituted by elements of the self.

SERMONIC DISCOURSE: "NO LONGER BOUND"

"On a Sabbath Jesus was teaching in one of the synagogues, and a woman was there who had been crippled by a spirit for eighteen years. She was bent over and could not straighten up at all. When Jesus saw her, he called her forward and said to her, 'Woman, you are set free from your infirmity (weakness).' Then he put his hands on her, and immediately she straightened up and praised God. . . . [Later Jesus spoke,] Then should not this woman, a daughter of Abraham, whom Satan has kept bound for eighteen years, be

*set free on the Sabbath day from what bound her (enslaved her). —Luke 13:
10–17 NRSV*

In the Book of Deuteronomy we find these words: "Remember that you
were slaves in Egypt and the Lord your God brought you out of there with
a mighty hand and an out-stretched arm" (5:15). This too may have been
on the Sabbath. The Sabbath is a freedom day—a day of liberation.

Too often we seem to be restrained and restricted by the power of
some force that seeks to determine our destiny. It could be illness or age-
related deterioration; it could be physical or social; it could be something
like American chattel slavery, which victimized Black people for over three
hundred years. This bondage kept our backs bent over picking cotton or
baling hay from sunup to sundown. Today, this is hard to imagine, much
less experience. It's hard to imagine because we seem to have forgotten our
history—a history of captivity and bondage—bound by chains and fetters
that enslaved both the body and mind, both the heart and spirit. Many
of us are still in bondage today, held captive by some social stigma, some
demonic force, some power of Satan that has inflicted us with dejection
and denial, indifference to the plight of our Black brothers and sisters—
an indifference seen in the sale of drugs to Black children and teenagers,
reinforcing the cycle of poverty and pain, creating the illusion of success
while caught in the crossfire of Black on Black violence. Our acts of self-
destruction do not subvert the system, but play into a vicious cycle of
destruction that does not benefit our communities nor our families. We
are bound. We are still in bondage to the power of a crippling Satan. This
text is really about the power of Satan vs. the power of God. It is about not
staying bent over or being bound by our condition. It is about being in
bondage or about straightening up. It is about looking down vs. looking
up. It is about walking slow, half walking or walking tall.

In the text, Jesus is again teaching in the synagogue on the Sabbath,
and a woman who was crippled by a spirit for eighteen years was there.
She was bent over and could not straighten up at all, says the text. When
Jesus saw her, he interrupted his teaching, called her forward and said to
her, "Woman, you are set free from your infirmity. Then he put his hands
on her, and immediately she straightened up and praised God."

This text teaches us that Jesus means freedom. In the theological language of the German theologian Ernst Käsemann, Jesus means freedom,
but also in the broken language of our slave foreparents, Jesus means freedom. Jesus speaks freedom to the poor and the oppressed. When people

come into the house of God, when folk enter the church, it ushers in something liberating, something transformative, something healing, such that a renewal of the mind and body will take place. This woman in our text simply came into the synagogue. She didn't ask for anything. There was no prayer request, no plea for healing, no begging—but her condition, her need caught Jesus's attention and caused Jesus to call her forward and to speak her transformation into existence: "Woman, you are set free from your infirmity." You are set free from the power of Satan; you are no longer bound by your debilitating condition. You are set free from your infirmity! You are set free from scoliosis; you are set free from the curvature of the spine. You are set free from your disease i.e., set free from this condition you have been in for eighteen years. You are set free from whatever has been holding you down, holding you back, keeping you in the grips of a burdensome bondage. Jesus Christ has the power to set us free.

I don't know what binds you today. I don't know what holds you in bondage. I don't know what restrains and restricts our minds and bodies on this holy day, but I believe you can be freed of it by the power of the word of the Lord. Jesus speaks freedom. The speech itself is an act of liberation. "Woman, you are free from your infirmity." You are free from the fearful and failed state of not being able to stand straight. Jesus spoke straightness into her bent back, her bad back, her diseased back. You can change your quasi-horizontal state into a state of verticality where you can now look into the face of your friend or foe. The horizontal has been transformed into a vertical state of ontological transformation.

Jesus counteracts and counter-balances our condition by placing his hands on us as he did this woman. The text says, "Then he put his hands on her, and immediately she straightened up and praised God." This is a daring and subversive act. He touched a woman, no! He didn't do that. Yes, he touched a woman with his own hands, a diseased woman, in the synagogue. The synagogue ruler was mad. Upset. Furious. Instead of testifying, instead of allowing the law and the Sabbath to testify to the power of God through Jesus, he was mad; distracted in this case by his desire to maintain the status quo. In other words, this text translated contextually means to us that the deacons were disturbed because this was out of order—this was against their tradition. It was against the law. Jesus did it anyhow because he is not restrained or restricted by law or custom. "And immediately she straightened up and praised God." Jesus can and does straighten us up. If your back is bent, burdened by the strain and stress of disease or fear and doubt, there is power in the compassionate and caring hands of Jesus.

This woman was not just suffering from an illness or a deteriorating disease in her back, but she was thought to be Satan—bound, possessed by a crippling spirit, a spirit of weakness. But when Jesus straightens her up, when he straightens her out, and when he straightens us up, she can praise him and we can praise him; we can glorify his name without fear, without shame, without worrying about what others will say, without restraint because only you know what he has done for you. Like the synagogue ruler, everybody is not going to praise God; everybody is not going to be excited and happy for what the Lord has done for you on the Sabbath. Eighteen years. Bent over; eighteen years being ostracized; eighteen years being sneered at, eighteen years of stares, glances, and whispers, eighteen years of feeling sorry for yourself, eighteen years of hopeful anticipation, eighteen years. That's a long time. It's a generation, almost two decades, bent over, crippled for eighteen years and Jesus comes along and speaks and touches this woman and she is healed and begins to praise God. To God be the Glory, Great things God has done.

When we encounter Jesus, we are one thing, we have one name or no name, but afterwards we are totally transformed into a new creation. We encounter Jesus as this person or that individual—but Jesus transforms us from one person into another and even gives us a new name. This woman in the text was bent over and unable to stand up straight. "Jesus invites her to stand up straight, and then lays his hands on her. In verse 16, Jesus calls her a "daughter of Abraham." Daughter of Abraham, like Isaac and Ishmael, she is somebody. In this text, she started out as a nameless woman. "A woman was there with a crippled spirit," says the text. Her social context was suspect. She was of low estate—in the language of the writer; she was a woman, a generic genderized character. A woman. But wait. She was not just a woman, but a crippled woman. She was flawed socially and physically. She was deprived of wholeness and strength according to the cultural norms. She was weakened by her condition. Crippled. She was dysfunctional and in society's eyes she was also worthless. And this worthlessness, this shame, this low self-esteem had been accepted as a way of life. She was destined to be bent over, crippled, and dysfunctional. This was her life. This was her bio, her lifelong fate, her destiny, her lot; this was her condition of existence. It was the nature of her being—bent over and broken by the weakness of her body and by the indifference of everybody around her except Jesus.

But notice now how Jesus offers a counter-verdict. He changes her name. He renames her. She started out in this short text as a "crippled woman" socially isolated and ostracized. She started out in this short story crippled, bent over for eighteen years. She had no name, just a woman, and now Jesus has completely countered her condition. She is now standing up straight. She is now praising God, and now she has a brand new name—a name connected with the founding father of the faith. She is now "daughter of Abraham." From woman to daughter. From woman of no known heritage or social status to Abraham's seed. From crippled woman to somebody with a name. Beloved, her name may not be John or Paul, it may not be Matthew or Mark, it may not be Mary or Martha. It may not be Hannah, or Rebecca; it may not be Esther or Phoebe—but she has a new name, Daughter.

I don't know what your nameless name used to be, I don't know what your condition was; I don't know what crippling disease held you in bondage; I don't know what social condition held you down; I don't know what folk used to call you—whether it was a drunk, a drug addict, an unfit mother or father, crazy in the head, a no good skank or scamp who would never amount to anything; I don't know what your name used to be, but today you have a brand new name. It's not woman, not cripple, not Satanbound, not deformed, not dejected, not any derogatory descriptive, but "daughter"—a child of the King; daughter, a member of Abraham's family; daughter, a part of the household of God. Today, like this woman in our text, you too are somebody connected to a name which is above every name, that at the name of Jesus, every knee shall bow, every tongue confess, that Jesus Christ is Lord. *"I am free, praise the Lord, I'm free. No longer bound, no more chains holding me . . ."*

Chapter 2

Black Preaching as an Act of Love

". . . When nothing else could help, love lifted me."
—Hymn

*"Love a man (sic) even in his sin, for that is the semblance of Divine
Love . . . Love is a teacher; but one must know how to acquire it,
it is dearly thought, it is won slowly by long labor."*
—Fyodor Dostoevsky—*The Brothers Karamazov*

IN THIS CHAPTER I will make the constructive claim that Black preaching is ultimately an act of freedom and love. Preaching as an act of freedom and love destroys that which is against both freedom and love in an effort to bring about love in the community of faith, the church and the world. This destructive nature of preaching is grounded in love as an effort to overcome separation between God as creator and the created. To preach is to love God as the ground of life and to extend that love to the Other in service to the power of the preached word.[1] Preaching as an act of love transcends the antithesis of pettiness and evil of church life (politics) and

---

1. Tillich, *Love, Power, and Justice.*

transcends the deficiency of the preacher.[2] Miles J. Jones had a working definition of preaching that speaks to my theological claim. While he implored his students to learn and memorize a definition of preaching advanced by G. Ray Jordan in his book *The Art of Preaching*, Jones had also advanced beyond his earlier dependence on other better known scholars and literary theorists such as Paul Tillich and I. A. Richards by the time of his death in 2002. He based the correlation method of preaching on his understanding of Tillich's method of correlation as explained in *Systematic Theology, Volumes One and Two*. James M. Wall, in an editorial in *The Christian Century*, "The Sermon: A Work of Art," suggests that in preparing a sermon, the preacher can be guided by the following quote from the famous literary critic I. A. Richards: "The degree to which (the artist's work) accords with his relevant experience is a measure of the degree to which it will arouse similar experiences in others."[3] The best way for the preacher to communicate with the congregation is to figure out how to correlate his experiences with their experiences. This means that the preacher is called to live among the people symbolically and actually. The preacher's experience and the people's experience become more meaningful at the point of intersection. This was true during slavery.

The witness of the preacher is critical to communication. This means, in my constructive approach, that the inner history of the preacher helps to form the sermonic narrative and the theological perspective of the preacher and the people. When this witness or testimony is motivated by love, the understanding of the hearer and the meaning of the preacher are evidenced by "Aha!" This brings me back to the more advanced definition that Miles Jones wrote before he died. In a handout to his students he wrote the following definition of preaching: "Preaching is the action that creates the avenue for love's entrance into human affairs."[4] In this definition, Jones began to distance himself from the decades-old definition he had been using to define preaching. He was no longer satisfied with the mechanical, detached, and sterile definition of preaching that he had advocated for so long. The sermon as "statement of faith" was now inadequate—unable

---

2. Miles Jones's working definition of preaching in an unpublished handout to his class on the preparation and delivery of sermons, Virginia Union University, School of Theology, 2001.

3. Richards, *The Principles of Literary Criticism*, 94.

4. Miles Jones's working definition of preaching in an unpublished handout to his class on the preparation and delivery of sermons, Virginia Union University, School of Theology, 2001.

to express the deep meaning that preaching held for him. He expounded upon his new definition by saying:

> As "action" the sermon becomes more than statement; it is statement with a dimension of depth that includes the recognition of deed in order to participate in the next level of proclamation. The sermon as statement only begs for an expression of performance that validates the exhortation and affirms the imperative that is implied in the proclamation itself.[5]

The sermon is an action or deed that is expressed through the act of preaching. Preaching is a performative act that creates something new—something that heretofore did not even exist. The sermon unleashes the procreative power resident in the act of preaching. This language of sexuality signifies creation and newness. Jones states: "The stimulus for the arousal is attributed to the procreative relationship inherent in the matter of sermonizing. Preaching implies an engagement between two entities of what is (the situation) and that which works on the situation, namely, the creative potential of the word."[6] Preaching is engagement between situation and scripture. This is classic Miles Jones because the structure of his argument remains correlative and thus dyadic. Action is correlated with consequence.

The specific modes of love that I believe need to be advanced in the Black community in service to agapeic love are: self-love, ecclesial love, and liberative love. I want to begin with an explication of the language of love.

After discussing these love modes, I will end the chapter with a sermonic discourse that seeks to embody materially this love ethic. Love is in fact a revolution in the sense that a people or community can show via their actions that love is the antidote to violence and self-destruction. Love is also revolutionary because it develops a new understanding of community similar to what Martin Luther King, Jr. called the beloved community.

5. Ibid.

6. Miles Jones, unpublished handout to students in his preaching class at Virginia Union University, Fall 2002.

THE ETHICS OF LOVE: KIERKEGAARD, BRUNNER, AND TILLICH

Christianity and poetry are dissonant entities such that the poet embraces the rash notion "to love a human being more than God,"[7] which applies to erotic love and friendship; however, this favoritism is out of synchrony with the tenets of Christian teaching. Kierkegaard says that "Christian teaching is to love one's neighbor, to love all of mankind, all men, even enemies, and not to make exceptions, neither in favoritism nor in aversion."[8] This thinking certainly obviates many Protestant marriage vows which clearly state that the betrothed should be favored "above all others." And Kierkegaard says no, this favoritism is a type of untruth, a lie that is in effect antichristian. He states "there is only one whom a man can with the truth of the eternal love above himself—that is God."[9]

Søren Kierkegaard has written a commentary on love that presents itself in sermonic form and elevates "neighbor love"[10] as Godly love while indicating the *lack* inherent in erotic love and friendship. True love is the love of God (love in God) and one's neighbor. Moreover, unlike Kierkegaard, I believe that the preacher, certainly the Black preacher, is a poet whose language, words, and gestures are a vivid expression of agapeic love. The scripture asserts that "We know by this, that he laid down his life for us—and we ought to lay down our lives for one another. How does God's love abide in anyone who has the world's goods and sees a brother or a sister in need and yet refuses help? Little children let us love, not in word or speech, but in truth and action." (1 John 3: 16–18.) This is the meaning of agapeic love.

Everybody wants to be loved. There is a desire on the part of every human being to be loved. No matter how boastful we may speak, no matter how macho, muscular, or manly—we need love, we want love, we desire love. This is a distinct difference between human beings and other animals. Humans are animals too of a higher order. But other animals are ruled and controlled by instinct and a season of desire. Dogs, cats, squirrels, deer, birds, bees—these animals and insects are sexual, but not emotional—sex is for procreation, not for pleasure. So it's not a year-round

---

7. Kierkegaard, *Works of Love*, 36.
8. Ibid.
9. Ibid.
10. Ibid., 59.

thing and there is no money involved; no roses or flowers, no plans, no dates, no promises, no weddings, nor divorces.

There is no pretense, no rapping, no lies, no expectations. It's not about beauty or bounty. It's not about looks and possessions. The only thing the squirrel can share is an acorn, a nut—and I watch them play every day. They are just as happy running and jabbering from limb to limb. No fussing and cussing, no fighting and complaining, no threats and counter-threats. And, a dog, for example, only has a bone to share. No diamonds, no pearls, no silver, no gold.

Now the relationship between these animals cannot be called love— it's instinct. It's the rawness of nature. It's the pure pleasure of life devoid of consciousness and reflection, and yet, it's more godly than the way we as human beings, we as Christians believers can often claim.

In many ways we are lower than the animals. We are more base, more evil, more corrupt, more selfish, more subjective, more hateful, and more harmful.

The question in the preceding scripture text from 1 John 3 is a question for us: How does God's love abide in anyone who has the world's goods and sees a brother or a sister in need and yet refuses to help? Is this true love? No!

Subjective self-love is to be greedy and godless—indeed without God's love. The world's goods whether possessed by us or some multinational corporation like BP Amoco, or Walmart, or Citigroup, or a teacher, a factory worker, a businessman, a bus driver, a cook, or custodian. We who have the world's goods—rich food, high fashion clothes; you who have the world's goods—Nike, Polo, and Guess, and Hugo Boss, and Gucci, and Ralph Lauren, Jones of New York, and Cartier, and Rolex and Mercedes and BMW and Infiniti, and Ford, Cadillac, Porsche—and sees a brother or sister in need and yet refuses to help. There is *no* abiding of God's love in any of that behavior.

"Little children, let us love, not in word or speech, but in truth and action." The scripture text assumes that word or speech is lacking in substance and truth and devoid of doing. Let us love *not* in word or speech. So *not* talking is a godly act. Not talking is an act of love. It shows what love is and what love is not. Speech or talk is not love. It's only talk that evaporates as soon as it is said.

True love is action. It is doing, not saying. It is act. Action, action, action is the essence of true love. The scripture says, "Little children let us love, not in speech and word, but in truth and action" (1 John 3:18).

41

EMIL BRUNNER'S *DIVINE IMPERATIVE*

"If a man say, I love God, and hateth his brother, he is a liar" (1 John 4:20). The decisive point of view for ethics is conduct. Indeed, Emil Brunner defines Christian ethics as "the science of human conduct as it is determined by Divine conduct."[11] All human conduct falls within the purview of ethics; however, Christian ethics, in particular, and philosophical ethics in general, recognize that human conduct can be good or bad. Conduct driven by love for the other is ethical, i.e., agapeic love (cf. Kierkegaard). More specifically, actions motivated by the love of Christ can properly be called Christian ethics. Brunner makes a distinction between the *what* and the *why* of actions. "What is to be done results from the given situation; why something is to be done results from the love of Christ."[12]

Ethics ultimately is driven by the central question: What *ought* we to do in a given situation. This makes ethics a very practical discipline that confronts the person and society head-on. The question of *ought* should also lead to justice, but often doesn't. I'm thinking of the fact that knowing what one ought to do does not necessarily lead to right action. We are caught in the same dilemma that the Apostle Paul reflects on—acknowledging the desire to do good (right action) is often trumped by that which he does not want to do (evil): "For I know that nothing good dwells within me, that is, in my flesh. I can will what is right, but I cannot do it. For I do not do the good I want, but the evil I do not want is what I do" (Rom 7:18–19).

Paul's words to the church at Rome complicate the practice of Christian ethics as conduct (Brunner) and neighbor love or love in action (Kierkegaard). This conflict of the heart, mind, and soul is where the "rubber meets the road" and where *is* and *ought*, i.e., reality and ideality represent the dialectic of human existence. Maybe this chasm can only be bridged by divine reconciliation between creation and redemption or anthropology and divinity. We are indeed caught in a metaxalogical relationship between good action and evil action as the state of being in the world.

Scholars and exegetes continue to parse words on the issue of slavery in Pauline writings (e.g., 1 Cor 7:17–24). I find most of these explications unacceptable and offensive to the African American. Slavery is a violation of the humanity of the other and is antithetical to the ethics and theology of God and Jesus as the incarnate Lord. So, I don't have any tolerance

11. Brunner, *Divine Imperative*, 86.

12. Kegley, ed., *The Theology of Emil Brunner*, 1962, 349.

with the myriad explanations for scripture texts that are laden with the language of slavery. My project and life's work involves freedom, justice, and liberation of the oppressed, not contentment with one's condition, or the imposed condition of the Other.

Accordingly, action or conduct of the individual or community is particularly of concern to anyone whose ancestors were subjected to chattel slavery in America. The white church (Christians) was complicit in the propagation of injustice rather than justice. This is why I am suspicious of Christian ethics as practiced by those who espoused love and justice as Christian ideals but not as personal or community practices. There has been no love of the Other in American history if the Native Americans (Indians) and Blacks (African Americans) are embodiments of otherness. While Kierkegaard's and Brunner's conception of Christian ethics are commendable theoretical constructs, the lack of any engagement with the greatest modern manifestation of oppression and injustice toward human otherness is seen in nearly three hundred years of chattel slavery, not to mention the "Middle Passage."

We are called to move from scripture texts to action and from theory to practice (Habermas). And, the sermon itself is an action—a type of prelude to the real action of the preacher and the people. And, ultimately we are called to act as Jesus tells us in his conclusion to the Sermon on the Mount in Matthew 7:24: "Everyone then who hears these words of mine and *acts* on them will be like a wise man who built his house upon a rock." Hearing the word should lead ultimately to action. By action, I mean practice. So, the life of Jesus Christ and His teachings should move us to a type of liberative and transformative action that broadens our understanding of the self and other via the love and grace of God.

PAUL TILLICH, *LOVE, POWER, AND JUSTICE*

In Paul Tillich's ethics "love transcends justice"[13] and neutralizes the effect of power. This is seen vividly as Black people confronted America's power grid evidenced by her laws maintaining segregation in all walks of life: education, commerce, social institutions, marriage, burials, and everything else imaginable. In order for love to transcend justice, it has to be more powerful than the elements of justice, i.e., distribution and redistribution which are thought to be fair. But justice and fairness have never been actions that Black people could count on neither in law nor in

13. Tillich, *Love, Power, and Justice*, 13.

custom because where and when one was embedded in law, the other ob-viated it in practice. What I mean is where justice prevailed legally, custom often stepped in to obviate or mediate it to the point of nullification. For example, the Voting Rights Act was often obviated by poll taxes and other local customs designed to terrorize Blacks and keep them from voting. Justice has always been suspect in American jurisprudence particularly as it relates to Blacks.

The power inherent in the law has historically been a barrier to racial justice. Prior to this, American chattel slavery was the most blatant insti-tutionalization of injustice in the modern era. Modernity is bookended by the transatlantic slave trade on the front end and the Holocaust on the back end. Black people have given America hundreds of years of free labor while the Constitution and the architects of democracy sought to make injustice an ontological reality by diminishing Black Being to the concept of property, thus seeking to obviate Being itself. If love is ontological as Tillich claims, then its antithesis, hate of the other, is also ontological. Black people are indeed the hated other. And yet, Blacks continue to love whites in a way that can only be attributed to agapeic love at work in the lives of those who are powerless in every aspect of life—except in showing love of self and others.

Black love is a concrete example of Tillich's theoretical claim that love transcends justice. Moreover, love is dialectical; it is described as "extreme happiness and the end of happiness"[14] Either way, this makes love an emo-tional phenomenon which contradicts Tillich's earlier notion that love is not emotional. But, love is emotional through and through. This does not obviate its ontological nature. Emotionality is being. It is life in spite of and because of its ontology. The sublation of emotion and feeling is death.

Love is infused with emotion though it is not constituted completely by emotion, but even in its emotionalism, it harbors the possibility of rea-son and rationality. There is no emotionless love, whether eros, philia, or agape. Emotion is a constitutive element of being human and if love is a human trait, then love is grounded in emotion. And God is an emotional Being. God is love.

Tillich maintains that the qualities of love, that the *libido,* the *phil-ia,* the *eros,* and the *agape* qualities "are present in every act of love."[15] This means that every act of love harbors sexual desire, friendship, and

14. Ibid., 2
15. Ibid., 3

neighborly or Godly love. Tillich says that "love is a passion."[16] And passion like preaching is emotive. Black preaching is also a passion. This means then that preaching is also sexual, friendly, and Godly. It is driven by love. This interrelationship of the qualities of love makes love a powerful element of the human body and mind. The Apostle Paul is right in saying that love is greater than faith and hope. Love is an act of being and preaching, particularly in the Black church, is an act of love.

ON BEING A PREACHER IN THE CHURCH: SELFHOOD AND SOCIAL ONTOLOGY AS AN ACT OF LOVE

Inasmuch as self-love is a necessary concomitant to any form of love, it cannot extricate itself from the love of God. Self-love is grounded not in the ego, but in the God of creation, the God of love. Blacks have not always internalized the meaning of self-love. On the contrary, self-hatred seems to have been more operative, as manifested in Black on Black crime and other negative behaviors. This is complicated by the social and economic reality that Black folk face: high poverty rates, joblessness, poor housing, etc. Nevertheless, Blacks are called to reexamine the meaning of love as it relates to the self and others with the understanding that all Black people are manifestations and reflections of the self. There is no Black Other— only the Black self as reflected in another.

The reader needs to understand that my use of Bonhoeffer's work is indicative of my abiding respect and love for his writing and his commitment to freedom and justice. It is my understanding that during his post-doctoral work at Union Theological Seminary in New York, he was impressed with the Black church and often visited the Abyssinian Baptist Church in Harlem, where Adam Clayton Powell, Sr. was the preacher. Out of all the worship centers in New York, he was most comfortable and inspired by the freedom of religious expression he found in the Black church. Gerhard Ebeling said: "Only in the Negro churches in the United States did he see seeds of promise."[17]

My critique of his early work should not be misinterpreted. He is one of my favorite theologians of the twentieth century. Likewise, I have the same love and respect for Charles Marsh, whose lectures and writings have helped to transform my own appreciation of Dietrich Bonhoeffer and Martin Luther King, Jr. While Bonhoeffer, King, and Marsh are towering

16. Ibid., 27

17. Ebeling, *Word and Faith*, 284

figures in my constructive theological perspective, I still offer a critique of their work to the best of my ability. Bonhoeffer's later works such as *The Cost of Discipleship*, *Letters and Papers from Prison* and *Christ the Center* are much more reflective of his distance from the Enlightenment Philosophers such as Kant and Hegel. My focus is on his earlier writings which are more theoretical and less popular.

In Dietrich Bonhoeffer's *Act and Being: Transcendental Philosophy and Ontology in Systematic Theology*, there is a sustained discourse on Being but little or no clear philosophy of action or consideration of the acting self in the community. The self in action seems peripheral to the thick theological discourse. The emphasis is on self and being to the exclusion of the social or the action of the self. Bonhoeffer states:

> Act should be thought of as pure intentionality alien to being. Given that the act takes place in consciousness, we must distinguish between direct consciousness (actus directus) and consciousness of reflection (actus reflexus). In the former, consciousness is purely "outwardly directed," whereas in the latter, consciousness has the power to become its own object of attention, conscious of its own self in reflection.[18]

This distance between act and being is lengthened by the dialectic Bonhoeffer creates between the two concepts. He writes that "all of theology crucially depends on whether it begins with the concept of act or of being."[19] That this either/or choice permeates the piece is not implied in the title, which suggests a nexus rather than a bifurcation of the concepts. Bonhoeffer seems to vacillate on this point because he also says, "truth is only in the pure act. Thus, the concept of being is resolved into the concept of act. Being is only in reference to knowing."[20] This, to me, seems like a non sequitur. The statement should conclude by saying that being "is" only in reference to *acting*. He merges epistemology and ontology at the partial exclusion of the self as a social or acting being. For Bonhoeffer social ontology seems to translate into epistemology—knowledge and being appears to be his real focus. He states: "Epistemology is the attempt of the I to understand itself. I reflect on myself. I and myself move apart and come together again. This is the basic posture of transcendental philosophers."[21] Additionally, he states, ". . . for the question of knowledge is the question

18. Bonhoeffer, *Act and Being*, 28.
19. Ibid., 30.
20. Ibid., 37.
21. Ibid., 33.

of the I about the I, about itself . . . The meaning of epistemology is anthropology."[22] Bonhoeffer's autonomous I is problematic because it is not only autonomous but also fictive, i.e., self-creating and confounding to the other. This I or self is a temporal, transitory entity, an inconstant, fictitious entity constantly being created and recreated by the subjective nature of its ontological essence. Whatever constancy or continuity this self possesses is found in its ability to adjust to both internal and external phenomena. Bonhoeffer substantiates my assertion regarding the fictive self or "I" when he writes:

> The I is creative; it alone is efficacious, going out of and return-ing to itself . . . yet if the I is the creator of its world, what is there outside itself from which it might derive knowledge of itself? Spirit understands spirit (*Geist*). Therefore, I can understand myself from myself—one may even say "from God," to the ex-tent to which God is in me, and to the extent that God is in the unconditional personality, which I am.[23]

This idea of the oneness of God and I seems to elevate the self to a deis-tic level, going beyond the concept of *imago Dei*. Quite frankly, the au-tonomous self is as problematic as Descartes's *cogito ergo sum* because it seems to supercede other concepts of self, such as social selves. Moreover, Bonhoeffer reiterates his high hermeneutic, in which the "I" is just a step below the diety—an almost godly self:

> It remains to be said that in Kantian transcendentalism as in idealism, reason gets entangled in itself. "To understand one-self" consequently can mean only "To understand oneself from or out of oneself." "I am" therefore means: I think (cogito sum). Similarly "God is" means: Spirit comes to itself, it knows in the unity of consciousness . . . It is clear now that on its own, the I cannot move beyond itself.[24]

Why should it have to if the I is as self-contained and self-sufficient as Bonhoeffer seems to postulate? Self-understanding may in fact be no understanding at all if one is determined to take seriously the "creative efficacious" (Bonhoeffer) nature of the self. I am more interested in the sacrosanct self, the I that may develop as a response to the environment

22. Ibid.,30.

23. Ibid., 41.

24. Ibid., 45–46.

and culture. This political self is as possible as Bonhoeffer's authentic self.

Finally, Kant's influence on Bonhoeffer is evident in his elevation of reason to a higher status than faith and word. It puts anthropology (man) and theology (God) on the same plane. He says, "Man is like God especially if man comprehends God." Moreover, he states:

> What reason can perceive from itself (as Hegel puts it) is revelation, and so God is completely locked into consciousness. In the living reflection on itself, the I understands itself from itself. I relates itself to itself, and consequently to God, in unmediated reflection. That is why religion equals revelation; there is no room for faith and word, if they are seen as entities contrary to reason.[25]

Bonhoeffer's self seems to suffer from a lack of sociality, finding refuge and sanctity in its autonomy rather than in relation to others or community. In *Reclaiming Dietrich Bonhoeffer: The Promise of His Theology*, Charles Marsh offers a compelling and refreshing explication of Bonhoeffer's understanding of Hegel and Barth, particularly Hegel's dialectic and his notion of Spirit in community. Marsh states:

> According to Hegel, the content of the Christian faith is presented in the life of the single individual Jesus of Nazareth. As the God-man, Jesus was not only concretely real as a living historical person, but through the torment of his death he becomes present in community. The life of Jesus is an essential moment in the life of Spirit's self-discovery.[26]

It is precisely the "torment" of the cross that allows oppressed peoples to identify their "self" with the Jesus of history. The cross as a visible symbol of suffering grounds the humanity of Jesus in concrete experience rather than in the thick, theory-laden postulates of Hegel and Kant. Marsh further states,

> Of course, in the community there is the awareness that God's reconciliation of the world to himself is a reconciliation for humanity; the celebration of this event is the veritable heart of the church's worship and compassion . . . In the community, the conceptual truth of the idea of God continues to be suppressed

---

25. Ibid., 53.

26. Marsh, "Christ as the Mediation of the Other," 83–84.

in a thinking shaped by difference and alienation; Spirit has not
become self-conscious subject.[27]

The problem that seems to be integral to Hegel's conception of community and reconciliation is that it presumes reconciliation without its precondition, which for me is liberation. There can be no true, i.e., real reconciliation without freedom and liberation. Marsh quotes Hegel, "As Hegel writes, 'The Christian religion is the religion of reconciliation.'"[28] Moreover, Marsh states: "Hegel's idea of reconciliation includes the stark presentation of the God who takes into himself the negativity and sorrow of the world, and the narration of this moment in light of the suffering Jesus."[29]

Contrary to both Hegel and Marsh, I submit that the Christian religion as embodied in the life of Jesus and the church is ultimately about reconciliation *and* freedom, and I would point out that freedom is not implied, and usually not inferred, from the term reconciliation. Reconciliation without liberation is too easy and too unchristian, too theoretical and idealistic, i.e., too Hegelian. The mandate of Jesus as metaphor and symbol of freedom and as *primary* and reconciliation as secondary to *communitas* is found in the Lukan text, "The Spirit of the Lord is upon me because He has chosen me to bring good news to the poor. He has sent me to proclaim *liberty* to the captives and recovery of sight to the blind, to set free the oppressed and announce that the time has come when the Lord will save his people" (Luke 4:18–19).

DISILLUSIONMENT AS THE PRELUDE TO COMMUNITY

Bonhoeffer suggests that genuine community happens not in joy, but in pain and sorrow, not in happiness, but in disillusionment. Disillusionment means the overcoming of illusion i.e., the coming to grips with reality and truth. He states in *Life Together* that:

> Only that fellowship which faces such disillusionment with all
> its unhappy and ugly aspects, begins to be what it should be in
> God's sight, begins to grasp in faith the promise that is given to it.
> The sooner this shock of disillusionment comes to an individual
> and to a community, the better for both. A community which

27. Ibid., 87.
28. Ibid., 91.
29. Ibid.

cannot bear and cannot survive such a crisis, which insists upon
keeping its illusion when it should be shattered, permanently
loses in that moment the promise of Christian community.[30]

Disillusionment is a *sine qua non* to genuine Christian community because it is grounded in reality. The ideal community is seldom if ever
genuine community because the ideal excludes the ugly and unhappy
aspects of life representing illusionment. A life that African Americans
know all too well. There is indeed no living genuine community whether
church, home, school, etc. that escapes disillusionment. Bonhoeffer says
that "Every human wish-dream that is injected into the Christian community is a hindrance to genuine community and must be banished if
genuine community is to survive."[31] Well, maybe, or maybe not. However,
I do agree that wish-dreaming must be accompanied by a plan of action if
the dream is to have any hope of becoming a reality.

Genuine community seldom if ever exists in the family or the church
without a crisis, because we live in illusion even when disillusion is all
around us. Whenever disillusionment is so thick and blatant that it can
no longer be ignored, covered up or denied, then the church, for example,
refuses to move toward the embracing of genuine community. Instead it
seethes and pines and brews and stirs up an internal implosive anger that
threatens to destroy community. Bonhoeffer suggests that a community
that survives a crisis of disillusionment is in the process of becoming a
genuine Christian community, whereas a community "which insists on
keeping its illusion" never reaches the point of genuine community. This is
equally true for the individual.

THE PREACHER: LIVING IN THE MIDST OF ENEMIES

One of the most moving and profound statements Bonhoeffer makes in
Life Together is this: "Jesus Christ lived in the midst of his enemies. At the
end all his disciples deserted him. On the cross he was utterly alone, surrounded by evil doers and mockers."[32] It is true that the life of Jesus tends
to place all of life in perspective. This theme of living among enemies is
in fact a reality that exists inside and outside the church and community.
At first glance it seems a rather ominous and preposterous postulate; yet,

30. Bonhoeffer, *Life Together*, 27.
31. Ibid.
32. Ibid.

preachers and pastors readily recognize its inherent truth. I often feel alone and sometimes despised by the church and society, an outcast, a stranger or, as Langston Hughes says, "a refugee." However, living among enemies enables the preacher, church leader, and theologian to move beyond illusion, moving closer to disillusionment.

In many ways, the preacher within the church, like Jesus's disciples, lives among enemies and prayerfully, a few friends. The church is a microcosm of the world inasmuch as it is not an ideal community, as so many insiders and outsiders tend to think. Moreover, many prophetic preachers often feel isolated and alienated—out of synchrony with the hegemony of the church and community. The prophetic preacher, given the homeostatic nature of the church, will always be living among enemies. This is not to be thought of as a totally negative assessment. It is just a reality that must be recognized because it is unlikely to change given the political nature of the church.

Knowledge of God has been replaced with self-absorption. There is a yearning in the heart and soul of man to "know thyself," a dictum passed down from Socrates and reconfigured in Descartes's *"Cogito ergo sum."* The quest to come to grips with the self through knowledge and understanding is a life-long journey. But when the obsession of the I, the subject, becomes the goal of knowledge, problems and complications arise. Bonhoeffer states:

> Knowing of good and evil in disunion with the origin, man begins to reflect upon himself. His life is now his understanding of himself, whereas at the origin it was his knowledge of God. Self knowledge is now the measure and goal of life. This holds true even when man presses out beyond the bounds of his own self. Self knowledge is man's interminable striving to overcome his disunion with himself by thought; by unceasingly distinguishing himself from himself he endeavors to achieve unity with himself.[33]

Bonhoeffer in this language elevates the knowledge of self to the height of Kant's moral law. This high and mighty epistemology seems to become the ground of ontology and when taken alone suggests a wholly self-centered ontology and epistemology. Yet Bonhoeffer also has a low epistemology, suggesting that the self is nothing without God. In his *Ethics,* he says,

> For without God what meaning could there be in a goodness
> of man and a goodness of the world? But God as the ultimate

33. Bonhoeffer, *Ethics*, 29.

reality is none other than He shows forth, manifests and reveals Himself, that is to say, God in Jesus Christ, and from this it follows that the question of good can find its answer only in Christ.[34]

The perception of self shapes one's ontological connections to the social and political realities of racism, injustice, love, the church, etc. White theologians have been preoccupied with the "disappearing self" (Marsh) beginning with Descartes' *cogito ergo sum*, where the self is grounded in thinking to the exclusion of other actions. Why not "I feel, therefore I am" or "I love, therefore I am" or "I protest, therefore I am" or "I do, therefore I am?" Kierkegaard's self as a synthesis of finitude and infinity and Paul Ricoeur's "oneself as another" vis-à-vis Emmanuel Levinas's self in transcendence and Martin Luther King's self in action seeking justice—all of these concepts have contributed to my understanding of preaching as an ultimate act of love.

Martin Luther King shows his familiarity with Paul Tillich, who for him is representative of existentialist philosophers. King adeptly shows the nexus between love, power, and justice after first defining power as the achievement of purpose. It is evident that Black Power is connected with the African American's love of self, which seems to be a prerequisite in Jesus' mandate to "love thy neighbor as thyself." Self-love, i.e., self-respect and self-esteem were inherent in the notion of Black Power and King understood, advocated, and respected that. However, King also realized that Black Power should never mistakenly conclude that it could survive a violent confrontation with the government. Any such notion was nihilistic and a negation of self-love. Likewise, Howard Thurman in his book *Deep Is The Hunger* concurs when he writes: "Self-love is the kind of activity having as its purpose the maintenance and furtherance of one's own life at its highest level. All love grows basically out of a qualitative self-regard and is in essence the exercise of that which is spiritual."[35]

THE CHURCH AS SYMBOL OF GOOD AND EVIL

I want to be carefully understood here; I am reflecting upon a practical theological problem that I have faced as a pastor for over thirty years. I used to think, through the mythic and idealistically clouded lens of St.

---

34. Ibid., 187.
35. Thurman, *Deep Is the Hunger*, 109.

Augustine, the North African Bishop of Hippo, that the church was God's kingdom on earth. And, to some extent, I still believe that, though much less than before. Augustine identified the "City of God" with the church! Unfortunately, the church is grounded in fallibility and weakness. Historically, the white church sanctioned and propagated a slave culture such that its theology was more evil than godly. Dwight Hopkins asserts that the white plantation master replaced Jesus Christ with himself as the intermediary between the slave and God. Hopkins states that "The final purpose of slavery faith institutions encompassed the *replacement of the intermediary being of Jesus Christ* with white authority functioning as the only door to God."[36] This evil and blasphemous practice of displacing Christ with the slave master is arguably the most callous and twisted theological manipulation of scripture ever practiced by the protestant church. Hopkins further explains that:

> According to traditional Protestant doctrine and practice the primary go-between facilitating union of the supplicant and God was the "Son of God." No one can come to the "Father" except through the "Son." But when such ecclesial affirmations were applied to black chattel, the rules of faith were altered. "When a slave wanted to 'jine the church,'" in the memory of Shade Richard, "the preacher asked his master if he was a 'good nigger,' if the master 'spoke up for you'; you were taken in; but if he didn't, you weren't." The word of the master on earth replaced the authority of the Master in heaven. Slavery churches imbued black servants with the notion that their old divinity, before their Christian conversions, had been replaced by a new, more powerful one; the plantation owner with his God complex.[37]

Indeed, the slave master was a god. He was autonomous and infallible such that law and custom bowed to his every will. He was the architect of the law. He was judge and jury. He was ruler and king of the plantation and the government. He had absolute power over his chattel slaves, who were subject to his interpretation of God and the world. This history is incontestable and the effects of it spread into the twentieth century. But, the main focus here is not the white church of any era, for we have documented their crimes against humanity before. My focus is on my experience in the Black church—an institution that I love and respect, but one that I refuse

---

36. Hopkins, *Down, Up, and Over*, 86.
37. Ibid., 86–87.

to have any illusions about, because I have been sufficiently disillusioned by her time after time. She too is in need of a corrective. A redemption.

When I was twenty-three years old, in my third and final year of seminary, I was called to serve as pastor of Mt. Pleasant Baptist Church in Norfolk, Virginia. This church was filled with a host of beautiful, God fearing people who came from all parts of the United States. Norfolk is a navy town with the largest naval base in the world. People came and went by the hundreds, but the church's membership remained the same because there was a "revolving door practice" that the members knew how to enforce. Over the fourteen years that I was there, nearly 2,500 persons joined the church, but the membership never exceeded 600 because the people who ran the church made sure that its growth was controlled. It was a neighborhood church, and the women and men of the Titustown neighborhood controlled all the positions of leadership. And, as a young inexperienced pastor, they also sought to control me. And, they did!

Two of the biggest controversies in the church had to do with women in ministry and the iconicity related to a mural of Jesus in the Garden of Gethsemane. One day, several years after I arrived, the painters came to paint the sanctuary and they asked me,

"Do you want us to paint everything?"

"Yes, paint everything," I said.

"Do you mean we should paint everything neutral?"

"Yes, paint the entire sanctuary," I said.

Well, the sanctuary included a mural of a white Jesus kneeling in prayer in the Garden of Gethsemane. It was directly behind the pulpit or the stage area and was central to the asymmetrical architecture of the large worship space.

When I first arrived at the church, some ten years earlier, the mural was covered by custom made velvet curtains from floor to ceiling, and each Sunday as the clock struck 11 a.m., a deacon would step forward and slowly open the curtain to expose the mural as a sign that the worship service was about to begin. This ritualistic act was very important to the congregation's conservative understanding of worship and their Christological view that Jesus was white. His image in the sanctuary was of a white man with blue eyes and long flowing hair. This picture painted on the wall of the Black church was not unusual in the 1980s, fifteen or more years after the Black theology of James Cone, Gayraud Wilmore, Albert Cleage, and J. Deotis Roberts. For me, the mural symbolized a myth propagated by hundreds of years of theological discourse grounded in an

Enlightenment philosophy that correlated Eurocentricity with universalism. God and Jesus were white, and theology itself was a product of this racial hegemony. It seemed to me that this was exactly what Bonhoeffer had been talking about: an illusion in the community. J. Deotis Roberts was dean of Virginia Union's School of Theology during my first year there. And, he was a scholarly gentleman who spent his only year there teaching Black liberation theology, as his book *A Black Political Theology* was being released. As a part of a year-long course in systematic theology, I had to read James Cone's *Black Theology and Black Power* and *God of the Oppressed*. Cone had also come to lecture at our school during my middler year, and my interest in Black theology was growing exponentially. This new Black theology was a freedom theology, and as a young pastor, I felt free to critique liberal and conservative theological perspectives in service to my love for the Black church. Well, the Black church was not so eager to talk or hear about this new radical theological perspective. Some folk in my congregation said that I was being racist. "Why is it that you don't like white people?" they said to me. One day during noon-day Bible study, I was raising questions about conservative evangelical theology, particularly as represented by the Tidewater based Christian Broadcast Network and Pat Robertson, when one of the leaders of the congregation yelled out: "Pastor, why are you so hard on white people, God loves everybody."

"Yes, ma'am. This is true. God is a God of love, and I love people too. But love demands that we critique human behavior. And, white people have done some awful things to Blacks from slavery to the present time. As pastor it is my responsibility to address these issues, wouldn't you agree?"

"Well, this is a Christian church and God wants us to love everybody," she said again.

Blacks often speak in defense of whites thinking that this is the Christian thing to do. And, because the Black church is so warm and kind, it is difficult to teach persons that to be critical and skeptical of the behavior and actions of the oppressor is not an act of hatred, but an act of love. I agree that Blacks are a very loving and forgiving people toward whites—moreso than they are toward each other. I claim that this is the affect of colonialism and postcolonialism upon the Black psyche, and thus the Black church and community.

The painters came and painted everything—including the mural of Jesus which had graced the sanctuary for over fifty years. It was the most prominent icon in the building and it had been painted over at my direction. While I did not specifically ask the painters to paint over the mural, I did not correct them when they asked if they were to paint everything. So, I took responsibility for my own iconoclastic action.

On the Sunday morning following the "transformation" of the sanctuary, people gathered in somber silence and awe. Others were mumbling and wiping back tears of sadness, anger, and disgust. The air was thick that day, and I was at the center of a storm with hurricane force winds forming all around me. At the end of this particular worship service, I was ushered to my office by the Chairman of Deacons and several persons followed. One lady burst into the office in anger. More like obnoxious mendacity personified and embodied her behavior.

"Reverend Harris, who gave you permission to paint over our mural? This mural have been in our church for fifty years," she said with tears in her eyes.

"Sister Velma, don't get any closer to the pastor. You are in his private space," the deacon said.

"You don't tell me what to do. I can get in his face if I want to," she yelled.

"Please, step back a little so the pastor can get out of his robe," the deacon said.

At that moment, Sister Velma launched forward and hit Deacon Sam in the chest as he was shielding me from her venomous attack. When she assaulted the deacon, I asked someone to call security, and as the person was dialing the number, Sister Velma yanked the telephone cord from the wall and scuttled out the door mumbling and cursing. This particular action was indicative of her behavior. She had earlier gotten into a fight with another church member in the lobby of the local hospital. They both worked in the hospital laundry. In addition to this behavior, Sister Velma would come to church late, walk down the aisle immaculately dressed in hat and white gloves, sit two seats from the front and shout on every song, scripture reading, and testimony. But, as soon as I stood up to preach the sermon she would do everything possible to turn her back to the pulpit in protest of my leadership, a visible sign of her distaste for the preacher.

Evil is a structural reality in America, seen vividly in almost every institution and social practice perpetrated against Blacks from the Middle Passage through chattel slavery, Reconstruction, the civil rights era to the current day. It is deeply embedded in history and memory with history being as subjective as our memories.[38] But, it is not just Blacks as a race, it has been women, Native Americans, homosexuals, the poor, the uneducated,

38. Townes, *Womanist Ethics and the Cultural Production of Evil*, 7ff.

etc. who have been victims of the ugliness of evil. Yet Black folk are not all angels either. I speak what I know from personal experience and from self-understanding. I write not as a saint, but as one who has also fought against evil while being accused of evil. Though not meant to be an excuse, my so called "acts of evil" have not been intentionally harmful nor as heinous as, say for example, King David in his murder of Uriah, the Hittite in order to have sex with his wife Bathsheba (2 Sam 11:1–27). David's behavior is described by the Lord as "evil": "Thus says the Lord, the God of Israel: I anointed you King over Israel, and I rescued you from the hand of Saul; I gave you your master's house, and your master's wives into your bosom, and gave you the house of Israel . . . Why have you despised the word of the Lord, to do what is *evil* in his sight?" (1 Samuel 12:7–9).

It was the blatant violation of God's Word, motivated by desire and lust that compelled David to murder for personal satisfaction. This act is different from my earlier discussion of evil as a systematic and ubiquitous presence as Emilie Townes explains it as a "cultural production" that must be dismantled. She writes:

> Through a sometimes subtle, at other times not so subtle, interplay between such images of Black women as Aunt Jemina, (the Black Mammy), Sapphire . . . there is a productive entrée into the different manifestations of systematic and structural evil I consider . . . I turn to, now history, memory, the fantastic hegemonic imagination, and counter-memory to ground the discussion and to introduce strategies that can aid in dismantling the cultural production of evil.[39]

Evil is also an inherent element in the individual psyche and a constitutive element of the individual regardless of goodness, piety, and spirituality. Both good and evil emanate from the same human source or subject. The book of James, in classic sermonic tone, makes this clear in asserting that from the same mouth comes good and evil—even the mouth of the preacher (cf. Jas 3:10). It is also important to reiterate the claim that good and evil often exist in the same space and at the same time. That's why I can assert with a healthy dose of trepidation, that the Black church like the white church is both good and evil, exemplifying the same dialectic as the individual human being.

Sister Velma, who I spoke of earlier, was not simply a force of evil in the church and community, but she was also one who exemplified attributes of love and goodness. She would prepare scrumptious and delectable

---

39. Townes, *Womanist Ethics and The Cultural Production of Evil* 12–13.

meals complete with linen tablecloths and napkins served on exquisite chinaware with silver utensils. I would get invited regularly to these events as a display of hospitality and spirituality. Sometimes these dinners and fellowship meals were the result of competition for the pastor's attention, or to impress other families in the church and neighborhood; but more often than not they were symbols of good Christian hospitality.

The other serious issue in this church concerned the licensing of a woman, Sister Corine Brooks, to the preaching ministry. The leaders of the church and the local pastors were all against it and I had been forewarned and physically threatened if I dared to follow through on such an "ungodly, biblically unsound action." But, I saw it as an opportunity to correct some longstanding wrongs and to recognize that the proclamation of the Word of God is not limited to the male gender. And I don't take too well to threats because my self understanding is that the preacher is compelled to speak out against any and all forms of injustice. Well, defying the officers of the church, I invoked a classic element of Baptist polity by appealing to the congregation to decide if this sister should be licensed to preach by the church. On the night of the vote, the fellowship hall was filled to capacity. There was not a vacant seat to be found, and some folk were standing around the wall. This issue had already split families and friends. And this was a community church where everybody was related to somebody either by blood, marriage, rumor, or speculation. The church was very patriarchal. There were no women deacons and maybe one woman trustee. I called the meeting to order and indicated the purpose of our gathering. As I was speaking, a woman interrupted me:

"Brother Pastor, I just want to say that you should have never called this meeting. Didn't our officers already vote not to license Sister Brooks?" she said.

"Yes, that's right, but we are a church that operates under congregational polity. And, that means . . ."

"I know what that means," she interrupted with alacrity and attitude.

"Ma'am, if you will let me finish. It means that the people, i.e., the congregation can make the decision regardless of what the deacons and trustees said. The church body is autonomous; not the officers."

"You using all them big words like we don't understand," said one man.

"What does the Bible say?" another person chimed.

"Don't the Bible say that women should not be allowed to preach?" said another.

This debate went on and on for nearly an hour before I finally framed the issue as one of justice and fairness. I don't know everything I said, but I made the claim that no one in the room was godly enough or qualified enough to act as if he or she were God. I said that preachers are called by God and I believed that God was God enough to call whomever God decided. Finally, I said, "This lady has been trying to get the church, a church where she has served for fifty years, to sanction her calling and allow her to become a licensed minister. I know I am young and inexperienced, but I don't want to stand in the way of anyone, male or female, who claims that God has called her to preach God's Word." Then I called for a motion. There was a deaf silence. So I again said, "May I get a motion that Sister Corine Brooks be given an opportunity to preach an initial sermon and granted a license to preach?" Someone in the back of the room stood and said, "Brother Pastor, I move that Sister Brooks be allowed to preach her sermon and we should license her as a preacher."

Then several persons stood at once and there was a chorus of voices who seconded the motion. I asked for any unreadiness and there was none, so I repeated the motion and called for the vote. There was an overwhelming majority to grant her an opportunity to preach in order that she would be licensed to the gospel ministry. With that vote my "honeymoon" as pastor ended that very night because I had forced families, neighbors, and friends to take a public stand for justice and to do the right thing toward their own sister. But, don't be mistaken, I lost a lot of love and support from the members of that church by pressing the issue and encouraging them to make an ethical choice between good and evil in the name of love and justice.

SCRIPTURAL DISCOURSE ON LOVE

> If I speak in the tongues of men and of angels, but do not have love, I am a noisy gong or a clanging cymbal. And if I have prophetic powers, and understand all mysteries and all knowledge, and if I have all faith, so as to remove mountains, but do not have love, I am nothing. If I give away all my possessions, and if I hand over my body so that I may boast, but do not have love, I gain nothing. (1 Cor 13:1–3)

This is one of the few texts attributed to Paul that Blacks have been historically comfortable with. It is often read during weddings and other special occasions. Paul's letters are approached by Blacks with a hermeneutic of suspicion because they were so beloved by the slave master and his preachers. And one hundred fifty years later, that fact still does not bode well for Blacks. One of the most beloved Black preachers and scholars of the twentieth century was Howard Thurman, who served as dean of the chapel at Howard University and later at Boston University. In his book *Deep River*, he tells a story about his grandmother that captures the spirit of my focus on the importance of love and reading in Black folk's quest for freedom and justice. I quote the story in its entirety because it is so poignant. Thurman writes:

> When I was a boy it was my responsibility to read the Bible to my grandmother, who had been a slave. She would never permit me to read the letters of Paul, except on occasion the 13th chapter of First Corinthians. When I was older, this fact interested me profoundly. When at length I asked the reason, she told me that during the days of slavery, the minister (white) on the plantation was always preaching from the Pauline letters—"slaves, be obedient to your masters," etc. "I vowed to myself," she said "that if freedom ever came and I learned to read, I would never read that part of the Bible!"[40]

While there are parts of the Bible that can be justifiably avoided by Black people because of an apparent bias against certain races, classes, and types of persons, I agree with Thurman's grandmother, that this particular Pauline text on love just might be useful to Black preachers and theologians. Thurman's language that "except on occasion" he could read 1 Corinthians 13:1–16 encourages this discourse on Black love.

There seems to be a debilitating disease that is very much like a demon that has gotten into the moral and social fabric of the Black community. We see it in movies, on television, and in the real everyday world. We see the lack of love by Black folk who betray each other. We see it in all of the "Soul Food" movies. For example, in the movie *Madeas Family Reunion* and many of Tyler Perry's movies, we see Black folk fighting each other, making fun of each other and deceiving each other on a grand scale. Recently, in the movie *Welcome Home Roscoe Jenkins*, starring Martin Lawrence and Cedric the Entertainer, we saw the same rivalry between brothers, cousins, spouses. As bell hooks says "Black folk may suffer together, joke, and have fun, but love will leave us . . . what Black characters do best on television and movie screen is slaughter one another. Blackness

40. Thurman, *Deep River,* 16–17.

represents violence and hate."[41] What a tragic and breathtaking observation. A searing and keen indictment. What a challenging thesis that runs throughout bell hooks's work. Black people don't seem to know how to love each other. If we don't see it in movies, television or in books, that means that we cannot even imagine it. Love has been erased from our imagination by greed, hopelessness, violence, hate, distrust, dejection, poor self-esteem, doubt, and everything else. We have to love our youth, our boys and girls—we have to love those in our neighborhood, in our schools, in our classrooms, in our churches, in our families. We cannot glorify the violence, the du-raging, pants-sagging, foot-dragging mentality and actions of those who are locked up and locked down. Yes, we know there is still injustice and white supremacy that rules the system—but that cannot be allowed to keep us down. We must shake off the chains of self-hatred and loose ourselves from the bondage of doubt and destruction and learn to love again. I'm not talking about sexual love but a love that is driven by what is right, driven by what is fair, driven by what is just, driven by what is kind, driven by what is uplifting, driven by what is helpful and hopeful.

Paul's treatise in praise of love is more poetic than Plato's *Symposium* in praise of eros. This love Paul writes about is not desire or sexuality—but that which is spiritual. Love is indeed a spiritual trait. It is making a connection with God. It is drawing from the power of God. It is being driven by the lure of God. In the Church at Corinth, Paul shows forth his own rhetorical skills—his own poetic flair saying, "If I speak in the tongues of men and of angels, but do not have love, I am a noisy gong or a clanging cymbal. And if I have prophetic powers, and understand all mysteries and all knowledge, and if I have all faith so as to remove mountains, but do not have love, I am nothing. If I give away all my possessions, and if I hand over my body so that I may boast, but do not have love, I am nothing." (1 Cor 13:1ff)

Love is more than talk. One can talk pretty and be as eloquent as Churchill or Kennedy, as poetic as Martin Luther King, Jr., or as challenging as Malcolm X, or one can even sound like an angel—but if there is no love, you are essentially making noise. What we say and do *have* to be grounded in love. Some folk in the church can talk pretty. Those who can speak coherently and concisely—can even be calm and collected, cool and objective—but the love is often lacking. Some folk can run their mouths a mile a minute, jabbering and pontificating, speculating and saying all the

---

41. hooks, *Salvation: Black People and Love*, 53.

right things—but if the love is lacking, then one is simply making noise. There are a lot of noise-makers in the church, including preachers. Blacks and whites must stop making so much noise and learn how to practice love towards one another. A love which manifests itself in helping one another and in doing "the things that make for peace" within the community.

Love is more than "All." It is more than understanding all mysteries; it is more than having all knowledge and having all faith. In other words, prophetic powers and "All" ain't all that after All. Without love, all of the knowledge, faith, and understanding end up being essentially nothing.

One can be the most intellectually astute person in the family, or the smartest person in the church and in the community. One can be a prophet who has a great understanding of global climate change or knows everything in written books—math, science, psychology, physics, history, economics, law, business, medicine—all knowledge. One's faith can be bigger than Mt. Everest and wider than the Grand Canyon, and yet, without love, one is reduced to nothing—no isness, nothing. Not a thought, not a sound, not a word, not a deed, nothing. Love is the driving force of life's power to transform itself.

Malcolm X once said, "We ourselves have to lift the level of our community, take the standards of our community to a higher level . . . We've got to change our minds about each other. We have to see each other with new eyes."[42] To paraphrase Martin Luther King, Jr., we have got to get on the right road; the road to love and respect, the road to wholeness. Likewise, James Baldwin in *The Fire Next Time* says that love is a state of being, a state of grace "not in the infantile American sense of being made happy but in the tough . . . sense of quest and daring and growth."[43]

If we are to grow as individuals and as a community, there has to be a powerful love ethic that engulfs us—males and females. Black, white, brown, and yellow. Everybody needs love—especially Black males who are often the most hated—the most neglected, the most scorned, the most talked about of the human species. We use the language of criminality, the language of punishment, the language of discipline, behavior problems to describe Black boys. It is said that Black boys are too aggressive, too playful, too lax in their academic pursuits—too violent, too uninterested, too this and too that—all negative. Well, that perspective, that philosophy, that description is over, dead, past. Today is a new day. A new day to love Black boys and Black girls. Boys, I have a warning to you: there is no place

42. "The Ballot or the Bullet" (speech) delivered April 3, 1964, in Cleveland.

43. Baldwin, *The Fire Next Time*, 95.

for you to treat girls like commodities. They are no longer B's and ho's. No longer a possession to be pissed on and treated like dirt. This is the time for love.

Reverend Martin Luther King was the love prophet preaching love to the souls of Black folks, and white folks alike. Not sex. Not greed. Not physical hormonal release. Not jealousy. Not physical lust—but brotherly and Godly love. Love is the fundamental key that unlocks the door to the soul, i.e., the heart, the spirit. "Let us love one another, for love is God and everyone that loves is both of God and knoweth God" (1 John 4:7). God is love. We can't claim to be religious or spiritual without love. We can't claim to be members of the Christian church, the synagogue or the mosque without love. We can close these religious institutions down if all we are going to do is hate one another or tear one another down. To be human is to be loving. "Love never ends. But as for prophecies, they will come to an end; as for tongues, they will cease; as for knowledge it will come to an end. For we know only in part, and we prophesy only in part; but *when the perfect comes* [when the complete comes] the partial will come to an end." (1 Cor 13:8–10)

Love is infinite. Love never ends. This means that love is a transcendent reality. Love is a God equal quality. Love exceeds desire. It is more complete than human desire. It embraces the other with complete acceptance. Love is infinite and total—beyond the preservation of the self. Love is more powerful than speaking in tongues—more powerful than knowledge—which will cease. Science, physics, mathematics, psychology, philosophy—these things will all come to an end. And, when they all end, love will be standing there like a tree planted by the rivers of water. Love will be sitting there with crossed legs and outstretched arms. Love will be lying there with supine complete composure. Love never ends. Love is close to perfect. It is the meaning of completeness. When the perfect comes, that which is partial shall be done away with.

Paul writes that "Love is patient; love is kind, love is not envious or boastful or arrogant or rude. It does not insist on its own way; it is not irritable or resentful; it does not rejoice in wrong doing, but rejoices in the truth. It bears all things, believes all things, hopes all things, endures all things." (1 Cor 13:4–7)

The word *patient* means to be able to bear pain and trials calmly and without complaint when provoked or when things are hard. To control yourself and not allow yourself to be pulled into a brawl, an argument, a fight or an attitude that is mean and ugly is the practice of the virtue of patience. Patience means that you do not allow yourself to be hasty and act before you think or speak before you think or say something ugly in response to something ugly said to you.

Kindness means acting or showing affectionate or loving behavior. Kindness is to be helpful and gentle. It is to try to put yourself in the other person's place. Kindness is an attitude and practice of hospitality that reflects the spirit of Abraham and Jesus Christ. It costs us nothing to be kind to one another, but it gains us a seat in the kingdom of God.

Paul also writes about the positive qualities of love because these qualities are the opposite of the Corinthians' behavior. There was apparently little self-control in that church, no ability to work together, no real love for one another. Instead, there were revilers full of greed, drunkards, folks boasting about themselves. Some were envious, begrudging one another. That's what envy is. It is to resent what someone else has achieved because you don't have it, but you want it. No, "Love is patient; love is kind, love is not envious, not boastful and not rude." It is not discourteous, not offensive in attitude or action.

Black and white people are being called to love one another in the church, in the family, in the schools, on the job, in public and in private. Love is patient—love is kind.

Paul's hymn in praise of love continues: "And now faith, hope and love abide, these three, and the greatest of these is love" (1 Cor 13:13). These three virtues are tied together in a way that means that they cannot be disentangled or disengaged. Faith, hope, and love are inextricably linked. They are bonded together like the birds and the bees, like three peas in a pod, like the three Stooges, Larry, Curley and Moe—like the English numbers 1, 2 and 3 or the Spanish uno, dos, tres or the German eins, zwei, und vreá—faith, hope and love. And, yet as we look around today, as we read the local newspapers and watch the national news, we see what can only be described as a faithless generation, a hopeless tribe of individuals who seem to have given themselves over to the wiles of the devil—whether that devil is racism, elitism, consumerism, egoism, greed or the destruction of the other while exalting and glorying the self. Isn't this hopelessness exactly what Friedrich Nietzsche, the German philosopher, and Cornel West, the Black philosopher, called "nihilism"? I hear of crimes committed by one person against another person—a person of the same complexion, the same slave heritage whose ancestors were Harriet Tubman, Sojourner Truth, and Frederick Douglass, a person whose great grandfathers and mothers were freedom fighters and educators and teachers and preachers—folk like W. E. B. Du Bois and Booker T. Washington, Mary McCloud Bethune and Fannie Lou Hamer—folk who worked from sunup to sundown—those who labored long and hard under duress, under the searing heat of the sun and the scorching sizzle of summer's long and endless days. Yet, they did not lose faith and they did not lose hope. I can hear them in their southern dialect saying "we done done all that us can do, now we must put our fate in the hands of God"—that's faith. That's hope. That's love.

Like the Corinthian church, we too feel that spirituality is manifested more in style than in substance. Those who can sing the loudest and the prettiest must be more spiritual than others. Like the Corinthians we have those who feel that their knowledge is a sign of superiority. And yet, knowledge of science and of art is still not enough to make us love each other: "If I speak in the tongues of men and of angels, but do not have love, I am a noisy gong or a clanging cymbal. And if I have prophetic powers, and understand all mysteries and all knowledge, and if I have faith, so as to remove mountains, but do not have love, I am nothing . . ." (1 Cor 13:1ff).

There is a nexus—a necessary connection between faith, hope and love. There is a powerful permanence to these three practices. It seems to me that faith and hope need love in order to do what needs to be done. Faith can move mountains if it is girded by love—"If I have all faith, so as to remove mountains, but do not have love, I am nothing." Love hopes all things, endures all things.

These three (faith, hope, and love) march in lockstep together. These three hold hands in perfect harmony like brothers and sisters. These three—faith, hope, and love—are the stalwarts of Christian practice. These three are what hold churches and families together, enabling parents and children to work toward unity and peace. These three are what will turn the tide of violence and hatred in our communities and transform us from a battlefield of destruction and despair to an oasis of brotherhood. These three—faith, hope, and love—can conquer the apathy and indifference that run rampant in our communities where too many drop out of high school, too many fall prey to the lure of the fast lane that is really an illusion that leads to nowhere.

Paul is saying to the church at Corinth that certain things will not last: speaking in tongues, prophecy, possessions will cease—they will come to an end. Knowledge will come to an end—all of this stuff that we cherish so dearly will come to an end. But faith, hope, and love abide. Faith, hope, and love remain steady. "And the greatest of these is love."

Love is tied to faith and hope, but ultimately love has no equal. Love is the greatest. It exceeds faith and it surpasses hope. Paul has already said that love is patient. Love is kind. Love is not envious or boastful or arrogant or rude. Love seeks not her own. Love is not resentful. It bears all, believes all and hopes all. Now, he says "the greatest of these is love." This love ethic will redeem the community and the church and enable the spirit of our ancestors to rest in peace.

The sermon is a chance for the separated to come close together—the world, the scripture text, and the people. The sermon performs this such that it creates the space for both freedom and unity for the preacher and the listener. The sermon is an act of love that overcomes selfishness and its attendant egoistic behaviors.

SERMONIC DISCOURSE: "[UNFIT] TO FOLLOW"

As they were going along the road, someone said to him, "I will follow you wherever you go." And Jesus said to him, "Foxes have holes, and birds of the air have nests; but the Son of Man has nowhere to lay his head." To another he said, "Follow me." But he said, "Lord, let me first go and bury my father." But Jesus said to him, "Let the dead bury their own dead; but as for you, go and proclaim the kingdom of God." Another said, "I will follow you, Lord; but let me first say farewell to those at my home." Jesus said to him, "no one who puts a hand to the plow and looks back is fit for the kingdom of God."
–Luke 9:57–62

Sometimes each one of us might be too eager to say what we can or will do. I know I'm guilty of jumping into things too soon. Thoughtlessly. Too often there is a disconnect, a gap between our eagerness and our willingness to say what we can do and our ability to actually do it. And, the issue is not that we don't mean what we say. We simply don't have everything it takes to fully understand exactly what we are saying. Our desire is driven by a naiveté that ends up derailing our plans. Desire can easily be derailed if it is not grounded in a deep commitment, rather than a shallow notion of need and notoriety. Following Jesus apparently was the hip, the sheik, the current, the *en vogue* action. A lot of folk were doing it, and it seemed easy enough; it appeared like the thing to do, so this particular man who felt a certain level of comfort spoke out of an eager naiveté gone wild. They are walking along the road. I can imagine it was a beautiful day with the sun peeping through the clouds and freckled upon the ground. The breeze of the wind was whisking ever so slightly across the road. This road trip is so revealing. There is something about a road trip, whether by foot or by car, that facilitates an incipient revelation heretofore unknown. The mode of transportation doesn't seem to matter that much. It's the road. Long, winding, or sloped with hills and curves. It's the going along the road that creates familiarity and comfort and causes folk to say simple and sometimes downright silly, even thoughtless things. Absurd like Grant in *A Lesson Before Dying*, "I was not there, yet I was there" or absurd like Mersault in Albert Camus' novel *The Stranger*, "Mama died today, or yesterday maybe, I don't know." Absurd like this person walking along the road with Jesus: "I will follow you wherever you go." Thoughtless. Weird. Absurd. Crazy. Extreme naiveté masquerading as commitment unmediated by experience and troubled times.

Now after the first guy volunteers, Jesus drafts the second fella saying "Follow Me;" but this man says "Lord, let me go and bury my father." I got some things I need to take care of. In other words, after I do what I need to do, then I can follow you. And, it seems so reasonable; it seems so basic to the nature of family, to the clan, to the culture. Common sense coupled with tradition teaches us that we have to bury our loved ones and we ourselves will have to be buried by someone. So the reasonableness of the request is apparent. It is humane. It is caring. It is customary. It is ethical. It is the moral and right thing to do. It is the meaning of love and responsibility. And yet Jesus is unfazed and uninterested in this cultural and moral responsibility. He is unfeeling towards this man's plight. Jesus doesn't ponder this request; he doesn't push back with any semblance of sorrow or any tepid torpor or any inkling of interest in this man's personal dilemma. Without hesitation, without flinching, without skipping a beat, Jesus says "Let the dead bury their own dead, but you go and proclaim the kingdom of God."

The third man wanted to again do something first, and Jesus makes it clear that the focus must be on the kingdom of God, not on our own desires, wishes, and wants—ourselves or our desires have no privilege in this pericope. Firstness is redefined. This is not the easiest thing to hear, to listen to, because Jesus doesn't go along with or support the reasoning of anyone in this text. He causes a stir by suggesting that we have it all wrong. Our priorities are not his priorities and our priorities are all tied up with our ego and ourselves—not as disciples embodying the meaning of the kingdom of God in our actions—but as folk still trying to tell Jesus how to act and what to do, as if the created and the creator are somehow equal. Friends. Cohorts. In each of these vignettes, the story is the same; however, the situation is different. And, so it is for us. All of our situations are different. Some of us are young, others are old. Some are concerned and caring, others are vicious, mean, and destructive. Some are naïve, while others are romanticist and living in their dreams—in their *Inception,* in their own *Matrix*—trying to escape the real world of sorrow and pain—the real world of death and destruction. We too are trying to escape the real world of deep commitment and followership necessary for the kingdom of God. Don't get this confused with our own desire to impress and to follow Christ on our own terms. If we learn anything from this text, we must know by now that there is no easy way to follow. We seem to be unfit to follow whether we volunteer to follow Jesus or whether we are drafted by Jesus himself. Either way doesn't seem to satisfy Jesus—nor us for that matter. "I'll follow you wherever you go," said this first man. Jesus warns him without calling him a dunce or an egomaniac, saying, "Foxes have holes, birds of the air have nests, but the Son of Man has nowhere to lay his head." And, the second man doesn't volunteer, but is drafted by Jesus. He has to bury his father first and basically asks Jesus's permission—Lord, let me go . . . but Jesus said No! You don't have time for that. There is too much trouble in the world. People are killing themselves and each other. There is injustice, and indifference. There are power hungry dictators pummeling the people and depriving them of their dignity and their humanity. Death is all around us. You go and proclaim; you go and preach; you go and declare; you go and sing from the rooftops—proclaim the kingdom of God. Proclaim that the first will be last and the last will be first; proclaim the kingdom of God where the widows and orphans will be taken care of and the sick will be healed and the rough places will be made plain and the glory of the Lord shall be revealed to all flesh. You go and proclaim the kingdom of God. Proclaim that Jesus is Messiah. Proclaim that Jesus is Lord of Lords and King of Kings. Proclaim that in the kingdom of God there will be no more bickering and backbiting; no more social stratification; no more racism; no more hatred. The third man said, "I'll follow you Lord, *but* let me first say goodbye to those at my house." Jesus says, "No one who puts his hand to the plow and looks back is fit for the kingdom."

We can't even claim to do what we claim we want to do because we don't fully understand the meaning and consequences of our own self-constructed claims. Jesus scratches everybody's itch and makes the gospel message plain. If we don't want to be unfit followers, we have to recognize what it takes to make ourselves fit. Anytime we want to follow Christ on our own terms, we are in fact unfit; following Jesus Christ without understanding the high costs makes us unfit; following him after we do everything else we want to do makes us unfit. Fitness is a forward-looking faith and action. Fitness is keeping your hands on the plow and not looking back. Don't look back because there is a lot of regret back there. Don't look back because there is a lot of pain and suffering back there. Don't look back because there are a lot of aches, anger, and agony back there. Don't look back because there is abuse and abjection back there. Don't look back because there are all kinds of skeletons and scars back there. Don't look back because there is no redemption and hope back there. Hope is the vision of the future. Hope is a proleptic phenomenon. Hope is a forward moving engine that drives us toward freedom. Hope is a determinant of the kingdom of God. My hope is not built on a looking-back practice, but on a faith that the Lord will make a way somehow. My hope is not grounded in the failures of the "looking back" past, but in the unfolding grace of the future. Hope is a proleptic vision of redemption. It is the future bearing down upon us now and telling us that the impossible has now been made possible by the grace of God.

The truth is that it is through unfitness that we are made fit. It is through all of our mess—through the wretched wranglings of our behavior, our attitudes, our wilting, weak minds and bodies that we come to claim through the miracle of the Cross that Jesus has paid the price for us. These three characters in our text are symbols and metaphors for each of us today. I confess to you and to Christ Jesus that I am that man who spoke up too soon. I am that man who said "I'll follow you Lord wherever you go." I am that man you called to follow, but I had to do something else first. And, I'm still doing something else first. I am that man who is still saying even today, "I'll follow you but let me tell my friends and family—those at my house, bye." I am that man who continues to put his hands to the plow and look back. I am that man who is unfit to follow. And yet I follow. I follow in my unfitness. I follow because of my unfitness. I follow in spite of my unfitness.

Yes, we are unfit, but I am so glad that God can take what is unfit and make it fit. God can take the unfit man, the unfit woman, the unfit deacon, the unfit choir member, the unfit preacher and teacher, and make us fit by the love and by the blood of his Son Jesus, whose trip to Calvary miraculously makes us fit by atoning for our sins. Come here Simon Peter. Unfit. Come here Paul of Tarsus. Unfit. Come here James and John. Unfit. Come here James Harris. Unfit. We are all unfit to follow and yet God makes us fit . . . God is a "making us fit" God.

Chapter 3

The Preacher Struggles with Life, Suffering, and Death

"I'm Free, Praise the Lord, I'm Free
No Longer bound, No more chains holding me
My soul is resting, It's such a blessing
Praise the Lord, Hallelujah, I'm Free."

— GOSPEL SONG

"I am never more haunted by the necessity of
dying than in moments of happiness and joy."

—JACQUES DERRIDA

W. E. B. Du Bois's description of the Black church revival experience begins with an admission of distance between him and the action of the event. He says, "I was a country school-teacher then, fresh from the East, and had never seen a Southern Negro revival."[1] This is an admission of his ignorance of the Black church and its particularity. He proceeds to explicate and expand on the difference between his own bourgeois church

1. Du Bois, *The Souls of Black Folk*, 134.

experience and what he is currently witnessing. For him, this particular Black church experience is beyond belief, and he describes it in hyperbolic terms indicative of the "awe" he felt. His language is a bit condescending, to wit, "a little plain church," and "a sort of suppressed terror hung in the air and seemed to seize us."[2] He was terrified by their Black religious behavior. The language clearly differentiates between "us" (he and his friend) and "them" (the people at the revival). He had never seen anything like that before, and because it was a new experience for him, his interpretation teeters on the edge of the negative. He had no inner history of this type of religious expression, and it scarred him to the point of terror. He perceives the actions of "that mass of Black folk" in complex dialectical terms. He hears both eloquence and inarticulateness. He describes the event with graphic sociological and literary precision:

> —a pythian madness, a demoniac possession, that lent terrible reality to song and word. The black and massive form of the preacher swayed and quivered as the words crowded to his lips and flew at us in singular *eloquence*. The people moaned and fluttered, and then the gaunt-cheeked brown woman beside me suddenly leaped straight into the air and shrieked like a lost soul, while round about came wail and groan and outcry, and a scene of human passion such as I had never conceived before.[3]

Du Bois's own language indicates that this experience of the Black church was something beyond his grasp of understanding and imagination. It was a display, "scene of human passion such as I had never conceived,"[4] he writes. These scenes, he says "appear grotesque and funny, but as seen they are awful."[5] Du Bois seems to use language that describes a carnivalistic and spectacular atmosphere, much like Mikhail Bakhtin or Jean Baudrillard. We still see his images in some churches, conventions, and conferences. The meaning of his language is slippery, phantomic, and hard to interpret because all of the words have multiple meanings, both positive and negative. For example, "awful" could mean reverence inspired by the sacred or it could mean extremely objectionable emotion. I think Du Bois's language suggests his own struggle with balancing reason and emotion, his intellectual elitism mediated by his love for the mass of Black people.

2. Ibid, 135.

3. Ibid.

4. Ibid.

5. Ibid.

This struggle is my own struggle, because there is a love and hate for the preacher who considers reading and studying, questioning and interrogating the text as an act of holiness, as I do. From my perspective, studying is indeed a godly act, a reverent display of the meaning of grace and agapeic love. It is like prayer and meditation because it contributes to understanding the self and Other—broadening the preacher's horizons. So, I have spent much of my life studying with teachers who are like coaches to me. My own study is both interdisciplinary and intersubjective because my mind vectors in so many directions. I seek to be a generalist scholar, a philosopher, theologian, and preacher. I get bored easily, so I study and read to ameliorate the boredom I see and experience daily. My intellectual interests have been wide and expansive: philosophical hermeneutics, homiletics, phenomenology, critical theory, scripture interpretation, linguistics, literature, pragmatism, semiotics, history, logic, narrative fiction and nonfiction writing, social science research, psychology, theology, ethics, cultural studies—and all of this in service to the church and preaching. I do this because I believe that the sermon is the living manifestation of the Word of God—the embodiment of the gospel and the event of transformation and freedom. And, the preacher is called to bridge the gap between theory and practice in a way that makes the Word of God come alive. I am first and foremost a preacher of the Word of God and all my work proceeds from that basic self-understanding. For me, all roads, i.e., all disciplines formal and informal, lead to preaching. The non-studying preacher is anathema, an oxymoron. And, I dare say not simply an oxymoron, but moronic. Interpretation of any text requires study and more study. Preaching requires reading and rereading such that the sermon is written and rewritten before it is preached.

The religion of the slave was characterized by the preacher, the music, and the frenzy, with the preacher ranking first in Du Bois's powerful triad. Du Bois privileges the preacher as the leader of this Black religion. The preacher's personality and eloquent speech constitute the glue that holds the church together. It gives credence to his or her preeminent position, from the days of slavery to the contemporary black church. The typological preacher is not homogenous, but varies according to geographic and cultural location. In this regard, however, I think the message includes both positive and negative connotations. The hyperbole used to describe the Black preacher contains an implied antithesis. He is the "most unique personality developed on American soil," "politician," "boss," "intriguer," and "idealist." All this speaks of a dimensionality that makes me suspect Du Bois's double-sided linguistic characterization. He writes:

> The preacher is the most unique personality developed by the Negro on American soil. A leader, a politician, an orator, a boss; an intriguer, an idealist—all these he is, and ever too, the center of a group of men, now twenty, now a thousand in number. The combination of a certain adroitness with deep-seated earnestness, of tact with consummate ability, give him his preeminence, and helps him maintain it. The type, of course, varies according to time and place.[6]

The terms "politician," "orator," "intriguer," and "idealist" are inherently rhetorical and Aristotelian and to me suggest a subtle and coded message that begs to be interpreted. Du Bois seems to be saying: the preacher should be trusted, but not too much. Du Bois is decidedly ambivalent. Likewise, the language "adroitness with deep-seated earnestness" and "tact with consummate ability" describes the complexity of the Black preacher as archetype and leader. His description of the Black preacher is both negative and positive. The preacher is a complex person often torn between balancing a love of this world with the hope of the Kingdom of God as a proleptic eschatological event. How can he describe the slave preacher as an "idealist" and a "politician" at the same time except to convey the dialectic struggle that the preacher faces as leader and teacher among the people in the church and the community. An idealist is a utopian, while a politician is a pragmatist who on occasion will bargain with the devil.

DEATH AND SORROW IN THE BLACK CHURCH

In my experience, the Black preacher usually acts very different and yet similar to the "boss" man at Du Bois's revival. For the most part Du Bois had it right because he was able to capture in a few short sentences the Black preacher as archetype. It takes a strange and confident individual to claim to be a preacher. This is why the call to preach is so serious and important. The preacher can be elevated from obscurity and anonymity to prominence in a matter of days—"becoming the center of a group." This can be a very dangerous elevation to "preeminence" because it is personality driven as Du Bois describes. The Black preacher is a "unique personality." No, the "most unique personality developed by the Negro on American

6. Ibid.

soil." That's saying a lot by one of America's most acclaimed academics and activists. It is the Black preacher not the doctor, lawyer, teacher, or businesswoman who is unique. Du Bois' connection of the preacher with personality makes this a psychological characterization almost or potentially devoid of theological depth. As a matter of fact, Du Bois's preacher embodies the best and the worst of traits. He makes no reference to truth, justice, righteousness, godliness, etc.—only to the preacher as orator, politician, boss, intriguer, and idealist. Du Bois' description of the preacher seems more and more negative as I read and reread *The Souls of Black Folk*.

It was prayer meeting night just as it is every Wednesday in the Black church, and several persons who are normally present were absent. It was the Wednesday after Christmas, and there was a slight sense of joy still lingering in the air. I had to visit Mr. Lemon at home because his dear wife was noticeably absent from our prayer meeting and Bible study. She was always there. A woman of strong faith and classic poise. She spoke softly with a determined air of confidence and care. She was a faithful member of one of our mission circles. She loved people and smiled often. I could tell when I first met her that she was not a Richmonder; at least she was not from the old Black Richmond *faux* aristocracy. Quite a number of our people were real down to earth, everyday people. Unpretentious, without a scintilla of snobbery in their blood. These people were not the Black First Families of Virginia (BFFVs) who had been in Richmond as free Blacks during slavery. Don't misunderstand, some of them were nice folk too, but I tended to migrate toward the presence of the poor working class folk in the church and community—those from the underside of culture. These were the doubly poor and oppressed.

After prayer meeting and Bible study I went to the home of Earl and Geraldine Lemon. At first, I missed my turn and wound up in the heart of a notorious housing project. I recognized where I had gone wrong so I made a quick U-turn to avoid the distant sound of gunfire I had either heard or imagined I heard. It was now after 9 p.m. when I rang the doorbell, and Sister Lemon came to let me in. She was cheerful and gracious.

"Please, let me take your coat, Reverend," she said.

"Thank you, ma'am, but I'm ok."

"Would you like something to drink? Water, juice, soda?"

"No thanks. I'm perfectly fine."

"Well, have a seat for a minute. Rest your feet."

"Thanks."

As Sister Lemon went to the back room to clear the way for my visit, the living room was sparkling with Christmas lights in the front picture window and across the mantle. A feeling of merriment mixed with sadness and tiredness filled the room. She and her nine-year-old grandson were the only ones in the house with her sick husband. Her son was expected to come over later to spend the night with them.

When I entered the tiny room where Mr. Lemon was lying on a rented hospital bed, it took every ounce of energy and stoic restraint I had to show courage and strength as my eyes fell upon the man. He was dying. Every breath was a challenge to his lungs and to my weak spirit. I have not been able to reconcile my constant need to deal with the sick and the dying and my own faith. During these times, I am almost speechless because anything that I say seems platitudinous and weak. I don't want to sound like Job's three friends Eliphaz, Bildad, and Zophar who each had a deep and disturbing theological discourse to explain their friend's sickness (Job 3:1ff). They had misinterpreted his life and actions in service to their own narrow and misguided theology. I didn't want to be like them, so I said very little as we all formed a circle around the bed as I prayed. This was brother Lemon's last night alive. By daybreak, I received a phone call saying that he had passed away during the early morning hours.

THE PREACHER SPEAKS OF DEATH

I don't know what to make of it, how to explain it to myself. For as long as I can remember when someone died, I became sick to my stomach, overcome by nausea. Lethargy sets in, and often I get depressed and sad—though I tell others not to be sad and not to languish in the stream of melancholy and sadness that engulfs my own mind and body. These are not just words, because more and more I struggle with them. I question what I'm saying. I am saying it to comfort others while I am myself a wreck inside—torn apart by anguish and my lack of understanding. These things are so deeply painful and universal to the human experience.

I was doing OK until recently. Including Mr. Lemon, I had three funerals in one week. Death was surrounding me. For two of the people, I had been at their bedside for months and weeks and days. I had participated in discussions about "Do not resuscitate," no tubes or "excessive efforts to revive." I had been told by Mr. Jones's daughter that his heart was weak, operating at thirty percent and that he wanted to be baptized by me because he thought I was a "good pastor." He was too weak to leave the hospital and too obstinate and cantankerous to cooperate with the doctors and nurses.

I got the call at 8:30 p.m. on a Wednesday. He wanted to see me. It was urgent. Whenever people want to see the pastor, it is always urgent. I got up from the chair and dressed in my turtleneck sweater and long overcoat to make the drive to the hospital. It was blizzard cold, 18 degrees Fahrenheit outside. When I walked into the dimly lit room Mr. Jones was waiting. I spoke to him and said that his daughter had called indicating that he wanted to see me right away.

"Yes, Reverend Harris. You know me, don't you?"

"Brother Jones, I know who you are."

"Remember, you preached my first wife's funeral and I want you to preach my funeral in a few days."

"I see," I said softly.

"You don't do a lot of this screaming and hacking that I hear so much of today. That's why I want you to do it. I don't like so much of what I hear, but you know what to do," he said.

"I understand," I said, keeping to my commitment of a minimalist approach to this type of hospital visit.

"You know, I want you to baptize me before I die," he said gruffly. "People say I need to be baptized, but you know every time it rains, I feel that God baptizes me."

"I see. I understand," I said.

"So, I have been baptized a thousand times. I know it's not exactly the same. I'm ninety years old and its time now because I'm on my way out of this world," he concluded.

"I can baptize you tomorrow at 1 o'clock right here in your room," I said.

"I'll call my daughter and my brother and let them know."

The next day at the appointed hour, I went to the hospital and baptized Brother Jones by sprinkling him with warm water taken from the bathroom faucet. This is not the Baptist way of doing things, but I had to be more practical than doctrinal. Immersing him in a baptistery would be equivalent to waterboarding. Death by baptism. So much for symbolism.

"Do you believe in Jesus Christ as your personal Lord and Savior?" I asked.

"Yes, sir, I believe."

"Do you believe that Jesus Christ died for your sins and was raised from death in order that you may have eternal life?"

"Yes, sir, I believe."

"Brother Jones, upon the profession of your faith in Jesus Christ as your Lord and Savior, by the authority vested in me, I baptize you in the name of the Father, and the Son, and the Holy Spirit."

I sprinkled him with a few drops of water from a bowl that his daughter had brought to the room especially for this ritual occasion. I prayed and then served him and his family communion. We sang a short verse of a hymn led by his brother. Then, I gave him the right hand of fellowship and welcomed him into the church and the *communio sanctorum*. This was Wednesday, a week before he died. On Friday, February 5, I eulogized him in a graveside funeral at Riverview Cemetery. "Earth to earth, ashes to ashes, dust to dust," I said, as the bronze coffin was lowered into the grave.

THE DIALECTIC OF SPECTACLE AND IMITATION TO THE SPECTACULAR

A few months after I eulogized Mr. Lemon and Mr. Jones, I attended the funeral of a person I had known all of my life, and I came to the realization that every participant in the funeral service was engaged in a dramatic spectacle. I have always maintained that the character Reverend Ambrose in the novel *A Lesson Before Dying* (by Ernest Gaines) is correct in saying that there is a lot of lying going on in the church by everybody who has a performative role in its ministry—from the preacher to the parishioners. But, the spectacular, performative nature of that particular service was distractive and distortive. It was a distraction because each reader, singer, and speaker was in a performative mode such that I began to laugh quietly at how funny the whole service had become. I thought it was as tragic as it was comedic. The corpse itself was the epitome of the imitative—all dressed up and decorated with powder and blush to imitate life and not death. Everyone who sat on the pulpit was a dialectic of the stoic and the grief-stricken vs. the happy and celebrative. And, every act was preceded by and peppered with "praise the Lord, everybody." I felt like I was a patron in a theater or an actor in a play. Or even worse, a clown in a circus act. The only thing that I could not determine was whether I was a character or spectator in a comedy or a tragedy. I thought to myself that Aristotle was right in characterizing tragedy as an imitation, a "representation." Apart from the death of the individual, the worship service was a tragic display of grief and praise.

The imitatively simulated service was indicative of the predictability of much of what transpires in contemporary Black church worship—from the period of simulated "praise and worship" to the delivery of the simulated sermon where the preacher imitates another more established, well-known, media-savvy preacher whose antics are broadcast weekly across the airways. There are gestures and set sayings that are repeated *ad nauseam* by a host of preachers imitating a model that has been rewarded by popular culture support—financial and otherwise. This imitation nevertheless harbors elements of freedom and inhibitionless boldness, and yet it is only displayed by the Black preacher who believes that it is easier to imitate than to develop one's own interpretative style. In truth, no style is completely one's own because of the intertextual and intersubjective nature of the sermonic discourse that culminates in the actual delivery of the sermon. Sermon delivery is privileged in the Black church such that it potentially obviates all other pre-understandings and understandings of the scripture text and its development. Various sermonic codes are built into the delivery: "Come on now," "Watch this," "Don't leave me, now," "Follow me closely," "Can I get a witness," "Say yea," "Do you love Him this morning," and my favorite "Ain't He Alright." I am guilty of this, so I speak from experience. The Black church worshipers know this language and identify with it as a testimony to faith and the power of God. The inherent code built into the rhetoric is identifiable by everyone in the congregation, i.e., from Aunt Jane as symbol of illiteracy to Doctor so and so as symbol of the educated elite and the economically successful. Now, basically no one in the church knows or cares anything about the new hermeneutic of Heidegger, Bultmann, Fuchs, and Ebeling, and yet everyone understands the symbolic language of sermonic discourse when it is dressed in the elegant rhetorical style of the Black preacher. This is often not the case of the theologian whose style is less rhetorical but equally textual. Textuality as *ecriture* is not enough to transform the Black community. It has to have an element of rhetorical flair, grounded in the poetics not so much of Aristotle, but of Black preachers like Harry Hooshier, John Jasper, Sojourner Truth, Fannie Lou Hamer, and the unnamed poets of the Black pulpit.

ESCHATOLOGY AND ATONEMENT: SISTER WILLIE MAE AND THE CHURCH

The truth is often found in narrative fiction. The following short story is indicative of the complication and ethical dilemmas often seen in the church.

Willie Mae's youngest daughter was only sixteen when she was raped by Joe Williams, Willie Mae's sister's son. He was supposed to be cleaning the gutters and cutting the grass for his aunt Willie Mae while she went to the market to buy groceries. It was scorching hot that Saturday before Labor Day, and Joe had almost finished mowing the front yard when he had an insatiable thirst for something to cool his hot, languid body.

The door was always kept unlocked and shut during the daylight so he walked into the kitchen not knowing that Sarah was there sipping lemonade from one of the jars that Willie Mae used for canning string beans and beets. Instead of getting water, he walked over to Sarah and began to put his body against her breasts. She was fearful and shocked and tried to run out of the front door, but he caught her by the arms and pulled her into his grasp saying, "Just let me hold you. I won't hurt you. This is not wrong. The Bible is my witness."

She tried to resist, but he was too strong as he pulled down her tight shorts and began to caress the place where life and love merge, what he once overheard the preacher call "the gates of heaven."

There were no screams, just grunts and moans as she lost her virginity to the incestuous appetite of her own cousin, Joe Williams. Joe died that same day at the hands of his aunt, Willie Mae, who bashed him with a hammer and dumped his mangled body into the Chesapeake Bay to be swept off into the Atlantic Ocean, and devoured by the hungry sharks that longed to feast on human flesh and blood. For Willie Mae, incest was worse than slavery and more heinous than murder.

She vowed, "No child of mine will forever be tortured by seeing the face of her rapist at family reunions and Thanksgiving dinner. No, as God is my witness, he deserves to die."

This was a secret that Willie Mae Williams thought she would take to her grave, having believed that justice was served—life for life. His life for the new life that was growing in the too young womb of her daughter, Sarah. Yes, she had taken the life of her sister's child, and not even her own sister would ever know it.

There were some things that the law could not solve, and only "an eye for an eye" could bring peace to the soul, reasoned Willie Mae. And although she had avenged the rape with a murder, she never fretted about attending church. She had sat there for years listening to the rants and ravings of the preacher about sin and evil, love and hate, and family solidarity. Yes Willie Mae often thought to herself that she could have castrated Joe with one of those steel blade straight razors she kept in her room. It was like the Word of God, "sharper than a two-edged sword" and could have sheared his penis from the base of the scrotum in one sweeping whack. This would have been more cruel and caused an eternal suffering, a body in perpetual pain. She felt, upon retrospective reflection, that she had done the more just and humane thing by hammering him upside the head—two hard blows to the temple of his head had killed him almost instantly. The memory of this tragedy would never leave her. That's why she always prayed for forgiveness and wisdom and over the span of years she had become a mentor for many young people who actively participated in church. She would cook chicken and pork chop dinners to raise money to help send some of the youth off to college. She saved all her own money and some not her own to send her daughter Sarah's child, her grandchild, and grandnephew to Norfolk College of the Arts, where he joined the Navy ROTC and studied to become a science teacher. All this was done to help atone for her sins.

So after the two-year search for a new pastor ended with the church calling Reverend Joseph Jeremiah Brooks as the third pastor of the one hundred year old Mt. Zion congregation, everybody was sitting back whispering and wondering what was going to happen. One man said, "I came to church today to see this young, fast talking preacher man. I heard he was arrogant and stuck on hisself. Uses a lot of big words that us regular folk ain't too familiar with." Another church member of twenty years grumbled, "I hope to God he don't come in here trying to change the way we do things. You know how we do."

"Yes," said Sister Willie Mae, "I've been the clerk around here for thirty years, since I got out of college and ain't no new minister going to change me. God himself would have to take me out of my position."

On the Sunday that Reverend Brooks drove up to the church's parking lot in his shiny, silver Mercedes Wagon with his wife and three small children, Alexis, Courtney, and Joseph Jr., all under ten years old, there was excitement in the air; but hovering over the excitement was a cloud of fear and trembling. He was new, and people did not know what to expect from this new minister who had only five years earlier graduated with a Phi Beta Kappa Key and *Magna Cum Laude* honors from Virginia Union College. And, just three years after serving as pastor in a small rural church in Montpelier, a suburb thirty-five miles west of Atlanta, he was now the pastor of Mt. Zion with its thirteen hundred members.

The sermon went well that first day and a plethora of young people poured down the center aisle of the church to confess Christ Jesus and become candidates for baptism. When this phalanx of bodies had been counted, there were forty-six people who had joined the church on this, the pastor's first Sunday preaching. They were attracted to his smooth talking voice and his tall, dark frame. He was six feet-four inches tall and slightly over two hundred pounds.

"The bigger the better," said the sisters in the church. "No one wants to listen to a small, scrawny preacher. He looks too tepid. People need to stand in fear and trembling of the man of God, and only a big, burly, Black man can command the respect of some of these daring and doubtful saints."

His body exuded authority and his use of language was skillful and poetic. No big words. Well, some, but the folks could understand them in context. He was indeed a powerful pulpiteer with a touch of flamboyance in his public persona. And yet, he was a humble spirit who kissed babies, shook hands with every parishioner after service, and set out from the beginning to visit the sick and advocate on behalf of the poor.

Willie Mae was livid seeing all the attention and love the new minister was receiving. She felt powerless as she grumbled, "I'll be damned if he thinks he's going to come in here and take over my church."

"My church! Where did you get that from?" asked the head deacon. "This is the Lord's church, and we got us a real pastor now."

After that first highly successful Sunday, Pastor Brooks called a meeting with the church members to lay out his plans for Mt. Zion, and to share his new vision with the leaders and the people. He told them that the church's existing officers needed to be on a rotating schedule, what that meant, and why.

They were so enamored by his presence that one of the deacons stood and said, "Brother Pastor, I motion that we adopt each one of your recommendations, effective immediately."

The motion was seconded, carried, and almost passed until Willie May raised her hand to express her objection. "I don't see no reason for all these changes."

"I assumed this was as good a time as any to . . ." the news pastor said before he was interrupted by Willie Mae.

"Your problem, Mr. Brooks," said Willie Mae, refusing to call him Reverend, "is that you come in here to our church making wild assumptions. You don't assume nothing up in here."

"Well, Sister Willie Mae, I been praying about this for a week now, and I thought this was the right time to bring it to the congregation."

"You thought wrong!"

"Now Sister Willie Mae, there is no reason for you to be disrespectful. We can work this out."

"Well you thought wrong. We been doing fine all these years without your thoughts and recommendations."

You could hear several Amens and folks saying, "You're right Sister Willie; speak the truth."

This discussion of the motion went on for over an hour and what initially seemed like a home run for Reverend Brooks was now almost a strikeout. After much discussion back and forth, the pastor called for the vote on the motion. Everybody seated on Willie Mae's side of the aisle kept their eyes on her as the pastor said, "All in favor, raise your hand." Eighty-eight hands went up and the clerk meticulously counted each one of them. "Eighty-eight in favor," he said as he called for "all those opposed." And everybody on the left side stood up to emphasize their objection. The clerk counted out loud, "85, 86, 87." That was it, 88 in favor and 87 against. The motion passed by only one vote. Willie Mae and her followers were mad as they refused to shake hands with those on the opposite side. One of Willie Mae's sorority sisters went to shake her hand and Willie Mae cursed her out.

"You are a sly bitch, always smiling in the Pastor's face. I know what you are after. Don't you ever speak to me again, you heifer."

"You are just mad because you lost. Your power grabbing days are coming to an end."

Sister Willie Mae mumbled as she left the sanctuary boiling in anger with the church and the new pastor.

See, Pastor Brooks had asked Sister Willie Mae Williams to step down from serving as church clerk after thirty-two years. She didn't like it at all, and a lot of church folks felt it was wrong for him to do so. But the vote had been cast. The majority, however slim, had spoken. They felt it was callous and cowardly of the Reverend to cower to the demands of Deacon Ernest Willie Hanes. He was really the one who wanted Willie Mae out of the position because she had refused to give him pleasure after repeated attempts at seduction over the past twenty years.

The reason Sister Willie Mae Williams couldn't entertain Deacon Jones was both opaque and clear at the same time. Everybody with eyes to see knew how she catered to the former pastor's every whim—bringing him water and juice to the pulpit when he was preaching the word, wiping the sweat from his brow with Egyptian cotton handkerchiefs, and taking his perspiration-soaked undergarments to her house to wash every week. For years, she did this for the Reverend Doctor John Herbert Hill, just to spend an occasional moment in the grip of his strong arms. Oh, she was in love, but he wasn't.

Not a soul could speak disparagingly of Reverend Hill in her presence without being whiplashed by her searing looks of revenge and wrath. Now he was dead. It was her duty, she felt, to protect the church from anybody new. During the two years that the pulpit remained vacant, Willie Mae was in her glory—calling meetings, writing letters to guest ministers, directing the choir, and counting the Sunday collection as she had done for years.

She had taken over the church. Matriarchy had replaced any false sense of patriarchy. The pastor was now dead! The power struggle between the deacons, the trustees, and the church clerk was a battle royale. And because Sister Willie Mae Williams was in contact with each and every member, the deacons and trustees didn't have a chance at getting control of the church. Willie Mae was at the helm, the *ex officio* leader, the *de facto* pastor of the congregation. She was in her glory during those days, but not anymore.

Word spread like wildfire that the church clerk, the chair of deacons, the chair of the trustees, and the president of the Missionary Society, who all had been in positions for more than twenty years, would be relieved of their duties by the year's end. Everybody took this news in stride except the ubiquitous Sister Willie Mae Williams. Then came Sunday.

Everybody in the church was worried because Willie Mae Williams was not there in her seat of twenty years. She sat in the third pew, just one seat behind the deacons and mothers of the church. And come rain, sleet, or snow, she was always there because she lived only two blocks over from the church. She had stopped attending church—except on the first Sunday of the month. And, on those Sundays when she did attend, she would turn her back to the preacher whenever he began to speak. The deacons pleaded with her to no avail. She ceased her sophisticated shout and started a gossip campaign against Reverend Brooks, spreading rumors and lies. People were saying that he was having trouble in his marriage.

Janice Collins, the head usher said, "That's why he is always smiling at the new girl who works in the office. I know something is going on between them."

Peter Jones, a choir member, said, "I heard him cussing on the telephone one day."

Even a new member, Pearl Johns, swore on a stack of Bibles, "I smelled alcohol on his breath when he was counseling me about my divorce." And she continued flauntingly, "He looked at me with lust in his eyes. I could feel it as he gazed down at my breasts. I was wearing that low-cut blouse just to test his sincerity as a man of God, you know."

The rumor mill became a feeding frenzy and within a month Sister Willie Mae Williams had gotten over one hundred people to secretly sign a petition to oust the new preacher. The names were to be certified by a notary just one day before Willie Mae was found dead in her own bed by two of the choir members and the leader of the Church's Prayer Band. They visited persons who were visibly absent from church on the previous Sunday, so they had recently been frequenting Willie Mae's house.

When the fire trucks and the police arrived, the paramedics could not find a pulse anywhere on her body, so they shook their heads as an indication that she had expired, and there was nothing else they could do to revive her.

"She is as dead as a doorknob," the young white EMT said to the two prayer leaders. But, she left a letter she had written to her daughter. It was taped to the mirror on the dresser in her room. "To Sarah," it said. "To be opened only when I'm gone." When her daughter arrived at the house, she opened the letter to find that it was a confession of sorts that explained the secret murder and told of two other people who knew about it but kept quiet because she knew some secrets on them. It turned out that Willie Mae was having an affair not only with the former pastor, but also with the head deacon all of those years. And after the previous pastor died, the deacon learned that he and Willie Mae had bought a house in Williamsburg with the church's money. They had embezzled $100,000 over the past ten years and the deacon could not speak against it because he was in love with Willie Mae.

She wrote, "To my church members. Please forgive me for my sins. Love, Willie Mae."

Deacon Jeremiah Lewis, unbeknownst to Willie Mae, had been so overwhelmed and mesmerized by the power of the new pastor's preaching that one Sunday after church he had confessed everything he knew to the Reverend Brooks.

"For a long time now we been doing wrong. We been stealing money bit by bit. Skimming from the offering plates. And, I done been unfaithful for many years now. I love that there woman, Willie Mae. And I believe a few folks in here might suspect something, but they don't have no proof. I blackmailed her into sleeping with me at first cause I saw what she did to her nephew. She didn't see me. But, I saw her with these here eyes of my own."

"Tell me what happened. What did you see her do?"

"Well, I was trout fishing that day on the banks of the Bay. She drove up along the path where the land meets the water. I knew I heard somebody. I had stepped back in the bushes to take a leak. The bushes were thick. I could see out, but nobody could see me. I saw Willie Mae go into her trunk and struggle to get Joe's limp body to a waiting boat. The skipper was a tall white man with a beard. She handed him the thick, large, manila envelope filled with some of the church's money as he helped her hoist the body onto the boat to be taken out to where the current of the Atlantic and the roving sharks would completely devour it. I kept the secret for a while until I worked up enough nerve to tell Willie Mae what I seen."

"You didn't see nothing," she said.

"Then I told her the day, time, and place where I saw her. I told her I had pictures, but I didn't. When she asked me what I wanted, my lustful body almost exploded with satisfaction. For all this time I been sleeping with her once or twice a week—most of the time since Reverend John Hill died, in the house in Williamsburg."

Sister Willie Mae Williams's funeral was held on the Jewish Sabbath at the eleven o'clock hour, the same time as the regular morning worship for Baptist churches. At Mt. Zion, they used to have funerals for their prominent members on Sundays right after the regular worship, but the new pastor, Reverend Brooks, changed all that.

On the day of Willie Mae's funeral, every seat in the church, including the balcony, which could hold three hundred and fifty people, was filled. People continued to meander into the sanctuary, squeezing themselves into tightly filled pews, even fifteen minutes after the choral introit had been sung by the choir and the invocation given by Elder Brent Woods of the neighboring Pentecostal church, Bethany Church of God in Christ. Chairs were placed in the narthex and in every nook and cranny of the sanctuary as more than fifteen hundred people were packed into a building built to hold only thirteen hundred. It was more crowded with Black folk than many of the local jails. People were crying; some were jovial—smiling and frowning at the same time. Others were there to witness the homegoing of this pillar of the church and some, out of curiosity, waited with pregnant expectancy to hear what the preacher, Reverend Joseph Jeremiah Brooks, would say about his main nemesis, his most determined antagonist. While she had planned for his demise, she met her own end as a battered, broken spirit—a symbol of evil to those who witnessed the chaos and confusion she orchestrated against the Lord's anointed. After two and a half hours of greetings, condolences, church hymns, reading church papers, and other hyperbolic utterances, even more lies would be told before the final words would be pronounced—"ashes to ashes, dust to dust."

The preacher stood up and spoke in a characteristically clear and eloquent voice—embodying the essence of the meaning of the word "eulogy." First, he read his scriptural text in a dramatic voice, characteristic of the depth of the words of Goethe's *Faust,* James Weldon Johnson's *God's Trombones,* or Langston Hughes' poem *Landlord.* He began to read from the Holy Bible. The second book of Timothy, fourth chapter, verses six through eight:

> As for me, the hour has come for me to be sacrificed: the time is here for me to leave this life. I have done my best in the race, I have run the full distance and I have kept the faith. And now there is waiting for me the victory prize of being put right with God, which the Lord, the righteousness Judge, will give me on that day.

After he read the scripture, he looked searingly into the eyes of the surviving family members. Concentrating on the youngest one who shed innocent tears, he boldly, yet compassionately spoke his first words. In an eloquent, booming and performative voice, he slowly said,

"*Willie Mae Williams was a renaissance woman, a woman of myriad gifts and talents. She was complicated not just with language and words and sentences and paragraphs—not just with nouns and pronouns, adjectives and adverbs, prepositions and participles—but her life was one filled with the dialectic of the human predicament. Like all of us, she too was prone to sin, lured by desire and resistance, the acceptable and the forbidden. Come on now. Ya'll know what I mean."*

Amens could be heard throughout the church, while some frowned and looked puzzled. The preacher ended his eulogy without telling any secrets because he knew that some things should not and cannot be spoken about the living or the dead. He cleared his throat and said, "*This sister is dead and gone and a lot of history will be buried with her. Peace be with her soul! Amen."*

Uncharacteristically, the people applauded and rose to their feet as a visible ovation to the eloquence of the sermon by Reverend Brooks. The organist began to play "When We All Get to Heaven" as the preacher made his final remarks. The choir sang to the glory of God, and harmonious melodies rang throughout the bodies of the people processing out of the church.

One lady started to scream and another one fainted as they walked past the open bier with Willie Mae powdered up, looking almost as white as the flower petals that graced the pale blue lining of the casket.

In the short procession from the sanctuary to the burial grounds, some of the people whose names were on the petition commandeered the deacons and almost started a fist fight. Mabel Wilson's hat came off when she punched Deacon Lewis on his right shoulder. Caught off guard, he yelled, "God damn it woman, what's your problem? God don't like ugly."

She just cussed and fussed as she picked up her wide-brim hat. Mary Ellen Watson tried to calm her by whispering, "Not here . . ." but then she was verbally attacked with a cascade of curse words . . . They accused each other of acts of deceit and lies perpetrated against the new pastor and Willie Mae. As they neared the burial site, the drama lessened, but the tension was still thick and heavy among certain factions of the church. Like always most folk had no idea of what was going on. But, those in the church knew that the factious discontent would eventually tear the church apart.

As the casket was dramatically and ritualistically lowered into the shallow grave, the pastor uttered the final words over the body of Willie Mae Williams, "Ashes to ashes, dust to dust. . ." The interment of Willie Mae Williams was done.

That same night, in the early morning hours, just before the breaking of daylight, the sky was filled with a blazing light. A landmark in Titusville, Mt. Zion Baptist Church, was ablaze. The fire, a towering inferno, which began in the pastor's study, burned the church to a smoldering heap of ashes. There was no explanation for this except one deacon said, "Willie Mae's ghost is still haunting us. From the grave, she has shared the fires of hell with us all."

"God has spoken against the evil that harbored itself within our church. Maybe we can start over now," said one of the children, thirteen-year-old Jennifer Jones.

A crowd gathered. Shocked and weary by the sight of flames and smoke, some folk began to sing and cry as they watched the tall strong structure, to some, the symbol of the community's faith and love, the embodiment of the blood, sweat and tears of the faithful, with the quickness of a twinkle of the eye, turn to a heap of sanguine, smoldering dust and ashes. To others, it was exactly what they thought would be just punishment for a church that was a symbol of evil. A godless sanctuary of faithless people whose religion was no more than self defense and the idolizing of Mt. Zion Church.

Reverend Brooks, standing in the shadows of the flickering flames could be heard mumbling the words of Saint Paul of Tarsus, "Oh death, where is thy sting? Oh grave, where is thy victory? The sting of death is sin" (1 Cor 15:51ff.) . . . and the wages of sin is death" (Rom 6: 23).

EULOGISTIC DISCOURSE—"A CONFESSION OF FAITH"

"I know, O Lord, that your judgments are right, and that in faithfulness you have humbled me." –Psalm 119:75

In many ways, today is a day of infamy and dread. This is a day that I'd rather not face—a day I wish had never come to be and yet here it is thrust upon us like thunder and rain pelting against my head and my heart, and the heads and hearts of this wife and these children and grandchildren and this church.

Deacon Lucas, Stanley, Stan the man, was one of the first persons I met when I came here twenty years ago. He was down to earth, an everyday guy who had been endowed with "mother-wit" and the wisdom of God and the wisdom of the world. I don't know whether it was the navy or the Post Office or driving the city bus that taught him how to read and understand people, how to get along with the high and mighty and the lowly. Deacon Lucas knew what it meant to be oppressed and treated with indignity and injustice, but he also knew how to stand up and be a man, a leader and a friend. He was a preacher's friend, my friend, my unofficial pastor, my deacon who could listen and discern. He had a lot of common sense and book sense too. He had a natural feel for this city—its landscape and monuments. I used to call Deacon Lucas whenever I needed to find a place or a street—I used to ask him the quickest way to get somewhere. Whenever I got lost, I would call him and he would get me back on the right path. I remember one time I asked him how to get to a certain church and I said "Deacon, I'm on the street you told me, but where is the place?" He would say "go to the next block and look to your left. The church should be right there." And sure enough there it was. Deacon Lucas was our GPS before we could afford the portable, electronic ones.

He loved the church and knew every corner and crevice of the building. But, it wasn't ultimately the building that he loved, but the people of God. He took pride in Second Baptist as the custodian, the ambassador of hospitality up until his health failed. And, he loved it. He was the chief greeter when you walked through the door and he made people feel comfortable and welcome here. But, he also got to do a lot of hugging and hand shaking and a fair amount of kissing by being at the door. He was more than a custodian because not only did he sweep, mop, and scrub floors, clean bathrooms and toilets, but he would answer the phone, take in the mail, open and read my mail, pick up food for the poor; and he took great pride in doing all of these things.

So, is this a lament? Yes. We are anguished, grieved by the loss of this man of faith and love and justice. Deacon Lucas worked hard, never made a lot of money, never received a lot of acrimony and praise—but he knew that his family, his wife loved him and this demonstration of affection was evident anywhere Gloria and "her sugar," as she called him, went.

This Psalm 119 is a purely literary enterprise with a mosaic of themes grounded in a type of poetic brilliance. And yet the Word of God and the law of God are integral and critical to every element of our lives. And, this is the same for Brother Lucas and the way we feel today. For he loved the Word of God and he studied the word and sought to practice it.

Deacon Lucas loved the Lord, loved his family and the church, and he loved others. He was treated as the Other for so many years. Some folk treated him as Other and yet he sought to be a friend to all. I have had no greater friend in the church. He was like a father, like an older brother. You could tell him anything. Nothing shocked him to the point of judgment because he saw himself in others. He knew what it meant to be Otherized—to be dejected, mistreated and oppressed. Deacon Lucas became chairman of the Diaconate during some of the most turbulent years of my administration. And some people thought that he could be intimidated and ignored—but there was a great awakening. Deacon Lucas was compassionate and kind, but he was strong and bold and willing to stand up to forces of tradition and social stratification that permeate the Black church—especially those like this one, which was organized in the 1840s.

The words of this Psalm have impelled me to stand here today. And, they have kept me through many tears and much sorrow and sadness. "I know, O Lord, that your judgments are right, and that in faithfulness, you have humbled me." Very seldom does a pastor, a preacher have the opportunity to be as close to someone as I was to Deacon Lucas.

When he first got sick and began to forget—to lose his short-term memory—we would talk about it. I would ask how he was doing and what the doctors were saying. And he'd be defensive and say, "Reverend, I can remember when you couldn't find your keys yesterday—well, who found them for you? Who found your cap when you misplaced it?" "You know the answer to that question," I said.

And then almost like a flash, this disease—Alzheimer's—hit him so hard and fast that he was unable to remember how to walk on his own. This strong, very alert, talkative, happy, and jubilant servant of the Lord was unable to tie his words together to make a complete sentence. It started slowly and gathered speed like a freight train–driving his life toward the dark path of suffering and death. And yet, just a few weeks before he died, I visited him at home, and when I walked in the room and called his name, he opened his eyes and acknowledged my presence.

Today, in spite of our entire lament, our grief, our misery, our sorrow and pain, the Psalmist helps us to know without a doubt that God is righteous and just in dealing with us. "I know, O Lord, that your judgments are right." This is a direct statement of belief in God. This is a confession of faith. This is an unfettered, an undaunted, and an unfaltering statement of faith in the grace and mercy of God. No matter what the situation is; no matter how difficult it was to see Deacon Lucas, a strong, robust, delightful man succumb to the ravages of disease, to see this wonderful, kind, praying man plummet to the deep dark dungeons of disease and despair. This inexplicable event humbles us all. We seek understanding, like Anselm of Canterbury our faith seeks understanding, healing, and hope from God. This humility that the experience of seeing Deacon Lucas lose his posture, his demeanor, his self-assurance, his self-determination, his smiles, his wit, his jokes, his laughter—seeing him, witnessing him lose these beautiful characteristics has awakened a new reality in my own life. We recognize that the Psalmist's confession is our confession of faith in spite of our broken human experiences, in spite of our weaknesses and frailties, in spite of our suffering and pain. We too join the poet, the Psalmist, in saying: "I know, O Lord, that your judgments are right, and that in faithfulness you have humbled me." Yes, we are afflicted in every way, but not crushed; perplexed, but not driven to despair; persecuted, but not forsaken; struck down, but not destroyed" (2 Cor 4:8–9) because we have a building not made with hands, eternal in the heaven (2 Cor 5:1).

No Longer Bound

We can hear the Jesus of the Gospels say, "In my Father's house there are many mansions . . . I go to prepare a place for you (John 14:2–4). And, we can hear Paul speaking to the church at Corinth saying "Death has been swallowed up in victory . . . the sting of death is sin, and the power of sin is the law. But thanks be to God, who gives us the victory through our Lord Jesus Christ" (1 Cor 15:54ff.).

Chapter 4

Sermonic Discourse

Interpretation and Performance

"... For the dialectical method the central problem is to change reality."
—GEORG LUKÁCS

When Israel was in Egypt's land: Let my people go,
Oppress'd so hard they could not stand, Let my People go.
Go down, Moses, Way down in Egypt's land,
Tell old Pharaoh, Let my people go.

—NEGRO SPIRITUAL

PREACHING IS A SPIRITUAL passion—an anointing driven by love and the ability to communicate effectively. It is a deep desire to say and do something verbally and visually that will transform the individual and the community. Preaching is more than exegesis and interpretation: it is an emptying of the self in service to agapeic love. (Miles Jones says that the sermon begs to be performed.) I feel like Paul of Tarsus: "Am I not free ... Woe is me if I preach not the gospel" (1 Cor 9:1b, 16). This means that the Good News of the gospel is central to the preached word. The gospel is about self-examination, self-understanding in relationship to God and Jesus Christ. These relations are seen through the lens of the scriptural text, the experience of the preacher, and the needs of the community. Much of this may not even be recognized by the community, but the responsible preacher wrestles with the need to do justice to the scripture text and the community as text to be interpreted.

Also, preaching is a corrective action motivated by love. Jesus says, "If you love me, then feed my sheep" (John 21:16). The people of God deserve to be cared for by the Word. This Word challenges, encourages, and corrects the wider community, the preacher as text, the preacher's congregation as text, and the scriptural text, all in service to God and the community. As one who loves to read and study the Word of God in written scriptural texts, I am also convinced that textual preaching is the means by which transformation and freedom take place. Preaching then is an act of freedom and love—Godly love, brotherly and sisterly love, community love, and love driven by the desire to understand texts as signs and symbols of hope and redemption.

BLACK CHURCH WORSHIP AS DRAMATIC FREEDOM EVENT

On a recent Sunday during Black History month, a celebration established by the historian Carter G. Woodson in the early twentieth century, the choir in our church sang a Negro spiritual exemplifying and symbolizing the struggle of our fore-parents who lived under the system of chattel slavery. They sang the eschatological spiritual "Deep River, My Home Is Over Jordan" and dramatized the song with a performance of a small but highly significant component of the slave system—the auction block. Inasmuch as Richmond, Virginia was a major point of entry for the transatlantic slave trade and the site of Lumpkins Jail—a holding cell for slaves after their disembarkment from the Port of Richmond—most folk in the congregation were already familiar with the city's history and the role slavery played in its economy and culture. This fact had been emphasized the Sunday before when Dwight N. Hopkins, the liberation theologian, author and University of Chicago professor, had preached a sermon titled "Out of Africa" to the congregation from Psalm 68:31: "Princes shall come out of Egypt. Ethiopia shall soon stretch out her hands unto God."

Throughout the month of February there had been Black history lessons given by congregants competent in historiography and narrativity.

We learned for the nth time that our congregation split from a predominantly white church in the 1840s here in Richmond, nearly twenty years before the Civil War and the Emancipation Proclamation. The myriad reasons for this self-extrication from the bonds of oppression, institutionalized within the white church and American traditional religion, cannot be reduced solely to race and white supremacy. However, racism did play a major role in the people's decision to pull out of that congregation after years of mistreatment. That history is the backdrop for what happened during the choir's rendition of the sorrow song "Deep River, My Home Is Over Jordan." While a narrator spoke about slavery, a ragged and scantily dressed male choir member—shackled and chained, naked from the waist up, barefoot and bent over from scoliosis—struggled into the sanctuary as two tall formally dressed white men in long tuxedo-like coats with top hats followed. This was high drama. Theatrical. It was designed to communicate a sense of history which is often brushed aside in both today's history books and Black churches. The Black man, symbolizing the Negro slave, proceeded to take his place on the raised platform in a corner of the pulpit area. The platform itself was a symbol of the slave auction block. The fact that this performance could be integrated into our worship as a ritualized enactment of an experience was so painful that one hundred fifty years after the actual event, it created a deep sense of memory such that persons were trembling and in tears. Others were angry, and some were ambivalent and baffled by their rediscovered emotions. While I don't really know the essence of their experience in the sanctuary on that particular day during that particular moment (because "the fundamental solitude of each human being"[1] does not allow my experience to be totally transferred to the other), I do know the depth of sorrow that I felt. Paul Ricoeur says "my experience cannot directly become your experience . . . yet something passes from me to you."[2] This "something" is not the direct experience of the event, "but its meaning."[3] The meaning of this event was not bound by time or space because the experience of slavery has a simulacrum in the experience of the descendants of slaves, such that a dialogical impulse was ignited in the present day observers of the drama—an imitation of slavery and the slave auction block. Ricoeur makes this clear when he states: "The instance of discourse is the instance of dialogue. Dialogue is an event

1. Ricoeur, *Interpretation Theory*, 15.
2. Ibid., 16.
3. Ibid., 17.

which connects two events, that of speaking and that of hearing. It is to this dialogical event that understanding as meaning is homogeneous."[4]

Everyone in the room, on that Sunday morning, understood the meaning of American chattel slavery and felt the pain of being sold or auctioned to the highest bidder. The dialogical nature of the experience was evident, although there was a sense of speechlessness on the part of most people in the congregation. This speechlessness was itself a profound form of communication. The message was clear and the meaning of the spoken and unspoken, the gestures of the slave and the two white men depicting the slave masters were also clear. This was high drama and the Black church has an abiding love for that which can be expressed dramatically—which is almost everything spoken.

THE ULTIMATE KERYGMATIC SPEECH EVENT: PREACHING THE WORD

It is a truism that preaching is a speech event, and for the Black Protestant community it is pre-eminent, taking center stage in the church as the ultimate didactic and kerygmatic moment. But what constitutes the gospel is a more compelling and complicated question, because much of what I hear in the church and in the media is more performative than transformative. Moreover, the question of how we understand texts is the hermeneutical concern of most Black people. While the interpretations of the author's intention is privileged by those who glorify the historical-critical method, Paul Ricoeur says that the intention of the author may or may not be the deciding factor in understanding a text. The reader may understand the text in a way that the author never could have intended, especially if the reader and author live in very different times or situations. I like this because the Black preacher could understand the scripture text before he could read the text. The author's intention is not decisive as the ultimate harbinger of meaning. Ricoeur stops short of Roland Barthes's assertion that the author is dead, but he does say that the "text is mute," which is tantamount to saying that the author is dead. Barthes says "writing is that neutral, composite, oblique space where our subject slips away, the negative where all identity is lost, starting with the very identity of the body writing."[5] This Tillich–like "eternal nowness" of the text, according to Barthes, is no more than a

4. Ibid.

5. Barthes, *Image, Music, Text*, 142.

tissue of quotations and the book is a "tissue of signs, an imitation that is lost, infinitely deferred." [6]Again the author has been superceded by the reader, who is the final destination of textual discourse. The reader is the final arbiter and interpreter of the words and sentences on the written page. The way a text is read is more important to understanding and interpretation than knowing who wrote it. Black people read with reason and emotion since learning to read in English was a crime, punishable by fifty lashes or, God forbid, the castration of the tongue. So even when Blacks read scripture they have something to shout about.

Now, the text certainly has an author or many authors, thus it is not authorless even if the author is dead! Roland Barthes confounds the issue a bit more in the last line of his article "The Death of the Author" which seems to contradict what he argues previously. He states, "we know that to give writing its future, it is necessary to overthrow the myth: the birth of the reader must be at the cost of the death of the Author."[7] What is the referent of the myth? What is the signification? Is it the reader, as I surmise that it is, or am I mistaken? No, the reader is in fact more important to interpretation than the author.

THE PREACHER AND THE SERMON AS SIGNIFIERS

Signifying in the Black church is something that the preacher and the parishioners have mastered. I learned this the first day on the job when I asked the custodian if he were the one who cleaned the church, and he said to me that he was the pastor. "I'm waiting on the new guy to come in here and clean these toilets. I thought you was the one." "No, I'm the new pastor." He said, "Then what are you waiting for? Let me show you where the toilets are" . . . mumbling under his breath without cracking a smile.

Ricoeur says in his fourth postulate about Saussurean structural linguistics that semiotic systems are "closed" possessing an internal reality that has no relations "to external, non-semiotic reality." Ricoeur states: "These two aspects are the signifier—for example, a sound, a written pattern, a gesture, or any physical medium—and the signified—the differential value in the lexical system."[8]

However, Ricoeur says that words bear both sense *and* reference. The former is Saussurean meaning: how the word relates to other words in

6. Ibid., 147.

7. Ibid.

8. Ricouer, *Interpretation Theory*, 7.

an ideal form of the language. The latter describes the way a word points out of the ideal system and into the world. In an Saussurean system, you would think that "janitor" was related to "toilets" and "pastor" was related to "preaching," "counseling," or the like. But the janitor let me know that the sense of "pastor" wasn't necessarily the same as the "reference" of pastor. Outside of the ideal language system, the "pastor" was actually the one who cleaned the church's "toilets." In other words, the pastor is the one who deals with all the "shit."

The signifier and the signified are necessary for the concept of the sign. They together constitute the sign and provide the criteria for semiotics. Language then is a world of its own independent of any extra or external linguistic relations. It is a homogeneous enterprise that operates within a system of interplay where opposition and difference are constitutive elements of the same system. Because of this closedness or internality of this system, Ricoeur concludes that "At this extreme point language as discourse has disappeared."[9] But, has it disappeared in any way other than in the extreme? Apparently not, because language as discourse is also a speech event manifested in words and sentences. Speech as an event harbors the message and meaning of discourse. "Discourse is a temporary present event as speech and therein *is* contained the message in time and space."[10]

Speech as an event is key to understanding the dialectic of event and meaning because while the event is temporary and transitory, constrained by and within time, meaning perdures as an unfolding manifestation of understanding. Speech as event is key to understanding the transition from linguistics as code to linguistics as message. Again, no event endures, but the vanishing of the event does not necessarily mean that its meaning has vanished too. Although a particular meaning may change over time, meaning as a mode or system of understanding does not vanish with the vanishing of the event. It is possible that meaning only unfolds as time elapses between the occurrence of the original event and the later interpretation of the event.

This is the nature of historical events. Ricoeur says "only the message gives actuality to language since only the discrete and each time unique acts of discourse actualize the code."[11] True. But does the event vanish or does it take on a new form? The actuality of the event fades from his-

9. Ibid., 6.
10. Ibid., 7.
11. Ibid., 8.

tory, but never really fades from consciousness because of the anamnestic nature of the psyche. Moreover, historiography and orality (as storytelling), though often romanticized, tend to keep events alive, thus giving them a contemporaneous attribute that is grounded in their historicity. I am thinking particularly of the Exodus and the release of the Hebrews from Egyptian slavery, their tendency to vacillate between forgetting and remembering and God's tendency to remind them via the prophetic word. Analogous to this Biblical event is American chattel slavery where Africans were transported via the transatlantic slave trade over a period of 300 years to a land of unfreedom, where slavocracy and the slave auction block constituted the symbols of oppression. These events, coupled with the Holocaust and genocide in Dafur, Sudan are representative of the perseverance of meaning *and* event. Yesterday's events are today's events because they are etched eternally in the community consciousness of the oppressed. This means that event and meaning are time sensitive, but not time restrictive in the sense that the passage of time does not diminish the reality of the narrative. William Faulkner is right in saying that "the past is never dead. It's not even past."[12] And, the narrator in Ernest Gaines's novel *A Lesson Before Dying* is also correct in his opening lines, "I was not there, yet I was there."[13] And yet, we cannot romanticize the past because those conditions are in need of radical corrections. The past, as recent as yesterday, is in need of repair, revision and a radical alterity that only a proleptic vision of hope and love can capture for the community of the faithful. My message for Black people is to study the past with an objective passion, and allow the lessons learned to help shape the future. Don't even try to deny or run away from the pain and suffering of the past.

THE INTERDISCIPLINARITY OF INTERPRETATION AND PREACHING

The preacher is concerned with the meaning or the search for meaning in the scripture text and in the existential context. In other words, a meaning that has meaning and resonance in the context of the hearer's experience. Resonance is what we are looking to achieve; however, dissonance may in fact be discovered as we excavate meaning from an ancient text to a modern and contemporary reader and hearer. Wrestling with the scripture text in a way that results in illuminating the text and one's experience

12. Faulkner, *Requiem for a Nun*, 80.
13. Gaines, *A Lesson Before Dying*, 3.

is what has to be achieved in preaching. Constructing a powerful current-day counterweight to the scripture text is critical to understanding both the text and one's situation in life (*sitz im leben*). Black people understand dialectical thinking without the help of Ricoeur.

Now, a lot of preaching deals with the intent of the author, as the father of modern theology Friedrich Schleiermacher asserts. Yet as a Black person, an oppressed person, a person whose ancestors were colonized and enslaved, I'm not too keen on the intent of the author who is dead or alive and probably privileged. My concern is more with the applicability of the text to the particular needs of the community I serve. Particularity is critical here because it can reflect the experience of the oppressed. This does not obviate the value and meaning of plurality, but it does recognize that plurality and universality are sometimes morphed into a tautology that I cannot accept. Too often universality is a code word for a certain particularity—the particular viewpoint of the dominant cultural interpreter.

The new hermeneutic embraced by Martin Heidegger, Rudolf Bultmann, Gerhard Ebeling, Ernst Fuchs, and others "holds that language itself is an interpretation and cannot be understood in reference to ancient texts as somehow embodying objective truth. Understanding is existential, involving a 'hermeneutical circle' in which selfhood and the text come together in contemporary daily life."[14] There is no absolute, exactness to hermeneutics, but sermonic discourse has to probe the text and context in a way that brings these two horizons together similar to the way that Hans Gadamer talked about the fusion of horizons in his book *Truth and Method*. Gadamer's concept of "play" is more like what the preacher and sermon do as event. Playing with words and gestures is endemic to Black preaching.

There is a blatant theatrical element to preaching and worship in the Black church tradition that appears to be more pandemic today than in the past. The Russian theorist Mikhail Bakhtin refers to this typologically as carnival.[15] And, there is a carnivalistic atmosphere and *geist* that permeates postmodern Black worship. This is not new, nor is it negative. It has its roots in African religious expressions. African religious practices are very expressive and carnivalistic, where dancing, verbal adoration, and acclamation are directed toward God. Dance forms and verbalizations of praise are integral worship. This is not only a Black church phenomenon, but also can be seen in the white church across denominations and religious

---

14. Heidegger, *Being and Time*, 158.
15. Bakhtin, *The Dialogic Imagination*.

persuasions—whether Catholic or Protestant.[16] In the Black church the lines between perceived authentic expressions and caricature are blurred—not simply as an interpretive act of performance, but as representation of the genre. Thus, we have comedians like Arsenio Hall and Steve Harvey mimicking performances of the Black preacher. Their performance of sermonic discourse is devoid of textual analysis and exegesis but sounds as authentic as any real or actual Sunday performance. Indeed, like the film *The Matrix*, it is hard to determine where the real ends and the simulation begins, especially for television preachers. The difference between the fake or pretensive and the real or authentic is thoroughly obfuscated by television media, which demands an extravagant performance. In other words, dialectical differences between the true and the false, the real and the imaginary are almost impossible to discern. Practice makes perfect for disciplines in which copying and imitation help to constitute authentic performance, such as a performance of a Bach fugue for organ/piano or a violin concerto by a young artist; however, in preaching some practices can lead to inauthenticity and imitation in a way that blurs the difference between the "true" and "false." Thus, every black stand-up comic has a routine that includes imitating the Black preacher. And more disturbing is the fact that the preacher is imitating a set of practices that are voice related (oral and aural) and magnified by tonal quality and cadence such that these often natural gifts are thought to constitute authentic sermonic discourse. Certainly, this is a complicated claim and requires more explanation, but suffice it to say that the imitative is not always inauthentic in the preaching process. Sometimes, it is the basis for identity development and the process of becoming oneself. The preacher often starts out like the singer or the pianist—imitating her teacher or some other mentor. However, after a few years, she should begin to develop her own style, reflective of her own learning, experience, and faith. One should not be imitating another after ten or twenty years in the pulpit. This prolonged imitation circumvents the necessity of interpretation. It makes interpretation a fake act, a reductionist enterprise dependent on the past performance of another rather than the present performance of the preacher. Jennifer DeVere Brody in her article "Black Cat Fever: Manifestations of Manet's *Olympia*" says something that not only applies to art history (painting and sculpture) and performance studies (plays and social ritual) but also to the art of sermonic discourse as a performative act. Brody makes it clear that sermonic art requires more than imitation, which I suggest is partially

16. Rice, *The Embodied Word*, and Ward, "Performance Turns In Homiletics."

devoid of interpretation. She states that "the act of interpretation is an interaction that is performative."[17] The performative nature of sermonic discourse should be grounded in interpretation, which is inherently interdisciplinary. It is the interpretation that is necessary to mediate against imitation.

THE MEANING OF "PERFORMATIVE"

The constative utterance "John is preaching a sermon" may in fact be true if John is not masquerading as a preacher and if the preaching is not masquerading as a sermon. The statement is constative because the truth or falsity of the statement remains a possibility. It is capable of being judged true or false depending upon the criteria used to determine what constitutes "preaching a sermon." Preaching and preaching a sermon are not identical because a sermon has to have certain attributes and preaching has to be differentiated from reading, reciting, or singing. Ideally, the preacher is not "just saying something" because "just saying something" would be nonsense especially if what is being said could be described as either true or false. The statement, "John is preaching a sermon" is not the same as preaching a sermon because preaching a sermon is an action. It is doing something that constitutes an action. It is doing love. It is doing grace. It is doing mercy. It is doing forgiveness. To preach a sermon as a performative act is doing that particular sermon. To preach is to love, to forgive, to show mercy. It is equivalent to J. L. Austin's example of to say "I do" under certain circumstances and in a certain place and time is to be married. Saying the words "I do" as uttered in the course of a marriage ceremony is to perform the action of marriage. Austin in his first lecture in *How to Do Things With Words* writes:

> What are we to call a sentence or an utterance of this type? I propose to call it a *performative sentence* or a performative utterance, or for short, "a performative." The term "performative" will be used in a variety of cognate ways and constructions, much as "imperative" is. The name is derived of course, from "perform;" the usual verb with the noun "action:" it indicates that the issuing of the utterance is the performing of an action—it is not normally thought of as just saying something.[18]

17. Brody, "Black Cat Fever," 95–118.
18. Austin, *How to do Things with Words*, 6–7.

Black preaching is an action—a performative action in demonstration of the spirit and of power similar to Paul's description of his own preaching to the church at Corinth. Now, there are certain criteria necessary to call the sermon a performative action. It must be scriptural, that is grounded in a particular text; and, it must interpret that text in a way that critiques, corrects, and encourages the particular congregation or hearers. Conversely, it must not be a senseless obfuscation of the scriptural text nor should it shun or avoid the text in service to histrionics and calisthenics. This is not what I mean by performance or a performative sermon. This is better described as clowning, playing, or masquerading as preaching a sermon. No, preaching a sermon has to be an authentic action—one grounded in faith and commitment to the Word of God. And when this happens, in the pulpit or some place else, on a Sunday morning or at any other time, preaching the sermon is *doing* the sermon. It is not just speaking, talking or conversing—it is *performing* an action in service to God and the church. J. L. Austin's performative action, or *doing by saying* is equivalent to Paul Ricoeur's illocutionary act. Black preaching is more performative than constative, more illocutionary and perlocutionary than locutionary because it involves gesture, intonation, cadence and voice modulations vis-à-vis commitment and faith. Preaching is a marriage to the scriptural text. It says to the text "I do love you," "I commit myself to you," "I promise to interpret you to the best of my ability, so help me God." It is an action— a *doing* of the Word of God. It is a creation of the gospel.

PARTICULARITY AND TEXTUALITY: DIALECTIC IN ARISTOTLE AND MILES JONES

Miles J. Jones used the language of particularity with ease and offered a course titled "Preaching and Particularity." I was not lucky enough to take the course, but I heard him use the semantics of particularity enough for the word to get embedded in my consciousness. Whether or not Miles Jones used Theodor Adorno's concept of "the partial is the true" as foundational to his thought, I can't say. But, I find Adorno's concept helpful. The particularity of the text is found not in its self-containment, but in its relationship with the wisdom and experience of the preacher. Miles Jones's correlation of preaching and particularity however came from his embrace of Paul Tillich's use of the word in his *Systematic Theology*, Volume 1 where Tillich's particularity is expressed vividly in his description of Jesus Christ as "Jesus *the* Christ," and Miles Jones always used the identical phrase which reflected the influence of scripture (Matt 16:16, Mark 8:27–33, Luke 9:18–22) upon his life. This is not my only focus here; however, the poetic nature of sermonic discourse is always relevant.

I am concerned about what appears to be the prevailing dialectic in Aristotle's thought between knowledge that comes from experience and knowledge and expertise that belong to skill. He sets this up in dialectic fashion as if experience and skill are contraries or binary opposites. This boils down to the question of theory and practice.[19] Is theoretical knowledge more important or valuable than practical knowledge? More precisely, the issue can be stated as follows: Does skill come from knowledge and expertise or does skill come from experience? This is an important question not only for theology and preaching (because they both are practical disciplines in service to the church), but also for theater and speech communication. Stage and television actors need to be competent communicators in their use of language and gestures. And, let's face it: the Black preacher is on the stage every Sunday participating in a theatrical event where she or he is the main character.

Aristotle says "experience is the knowledge of particulars and skill that of universals, and practical actions, like all occurrences, are concerned with particulars."[20] Yet he holds "that knowledge of universals is somehow higher or more valuable than that of particular things."[21] This seems to be an unnecessary dichotomy between the particular and the universal. I want to postulate that our understanding of the universal is achieved via particular experience. In other words, skill is not only constituted by knowledge and expertise but also by experience. Experience is the mother of skill, i.e., its nurturer and developer. Whether we are talking about acting on stage or screen, communicating through speech, textual analysis of a written narrative, poem, or play, experience is critical to success. Knowledge without experience can seldom be transformed into skill because skill is a consequence of practice, and practice is a necessary prerequisite for the development of skill. For example, a preacher should be undoubtedly very knowledgeable about the scripture text vis-à-vis the contours, chemistry and anatomy of the church and community; however, if she or he never actually preaches a sermon or serves as a pastor of a church, how can she be said to be a "skilled" preacher or pastor? I propose that in order for one to be considered skilled in any art or science, he or she needs to

19. Habermas, *Theory and Practice*.
20. Aristotle, *The Metaphysics: Book Alpha*, 5.
21. Ibid., 3.

have experience in the said art or science. The fallacy in Aristotle's thought is the inherent dialectic that skill and experience are opposites rather than correlates. In my view, only an "experienced" preacher can be said to be skilled enough, i.e., knowledgeable and expert enough to develop and construct meaningful sermonic discourse and hence teach others to do the same. And then another, more refined skill is needed to actually preach or deliver the sermon in the presence of a live congregation. The preaching part of the equation—the spokenness of the sermon is where most Black preachers are extremely gifted—experts in stylistics, gestures and other bodily interpretations of the word. It is the work that precedes the speech that I am most interested in. However, this does not diminish the import of meaning evidenced by those elements that accompany the spokenness of the word. The following words represent the source of the issue. Aristotle states:

> And yet we think that knowledge and expertise belong rather to skill than to experience, and we assume that the skilled are wiser than the experienced, in that it is more in connection with knowledge that wisdom is associated with anything. And the reason for this is that the skilled know the cause, whereas the experienced do not. For the experienced know the "that" but not the "because," whereas the skilled have a grasp of the "because," the cause.[22]

While I agree that causality is critical to metaphysics and epistemology in particular, I propose that experience vis-à-vis knowledge and expertise constitute skill in its basic form. Without experience, our knowledge is limited and our skill is suspect—even dangerous. Knowledge and expertise belong to experience as much as they belong to skill. Aristotle in the preceding quotation connects knowledge and expertise to skill; however, I submit that expertise is a byproduct of experience. Experience after experience after experience lead to knowledge of causality, especially in the modern world of science. Thus, all knowledge is grounded in particularity, the particularity of our own experiences. In the African American community, wisdom is not only associated with knowledge, but also with experience. Many Black preachers enter seminary or theology school with years of experience as pulpit preachers. They have as much experience as I do in the pastorate; however, they are in seminary to hone their skills and develop their knowledge base.

22. Ibid., 5.

INTERTEXTUALITY AND THE PLEASURE OF TEXTUAL PREACHING

There is very little that compares to the actual moment or event of preaching. While nervousness and jitters are preconditions and correlatives to preaching, the actual delivery of the sermon is also accompanied by a pleasure equal to that of other bodily satisfactions.[23] I am not suggesting anything sexual like ejaculation or orgasm. But, I am suggesting a comparative spiritual pleasure. That may be an apt or natural point of reference, but it is not sufficient to characterize the preaching experience. It is an experience of satisfaction that comes from love, struggle, and hope—struggling with interpreting and understanding the text, and the hope of explaining it in a way that both reflects its meaning today to people in a context very different from the context in which the text was written. Understanding is a necessary prerequisite to explanation, according to Paul Ricoeur. In this sense, the new text which is the sermon becomes the transforming gospel. And that sermonic text, not the biblical text, becomes the new Word of God, the current gospel that has been mined from the textual world of the Word of God. The gospel is being written and preached anew whenever the preacher mounts the pulpit in service to the love of God; thus preaching is an enactment of love. It is the embodiment of love and a reflection of God's love manifested in Jesus Christ.

Not only is the textual sermon based in the scripture text, but it too is a text. It is a creation of the author who in this case is the preacher. It was shaped in prayer and dialogue with the Holy Spirit. It is an irrefragable text as a written manuscript and as an oral presentation. So, it is both a written, oral, and aural text. This may be the only uncontrovertible attribute of the sermon: to wit, that it is a text grounded in a text and preached in a particular context. Again, as one of my mentors and teachers would say, "it is an interpretation of an interpretation." While Miles Jones was correct, he was not comprehensive enough in his description of a sermon, because not only is it an interpretation of an interpretation, it is an act of love. It is a gift, a gift of love that he later embraced as he expanded his definition of the sermon.

Contrary to Ferdinand Saussure and Jacques Derrida, sound in Black preaching does have a natural bond to meaning. There is a "phonic essence" to the language of the vocalized sermon. I have read, written, and performed hundreds of sermons and I have listened to and heard

---

23. Barthes, *The Pleasure of the Text*.

thousands more. Based on my direct experience and ethnographic research, I have concluded that there is an almost unbridgeable chasm that
exists between the written sermon and the spoken sermon. The written
sermon only becomes meaningful to the hearer when it is spoken. Some
even say that the sermon is not a sermon until it is spoken. The tone, cadence, and syncopation accompanied by the gestural and responsive nature of Black preaching help to create meaning. In reference to Saussure,
Derrida states: "He must now exclude the very thing which had permitted
him to exclude writing: sound and its 'natural bond' [*lien naturel*] with
meaning. For example: 'The thing that constitutes language is, as I shall
show later, unrelated to the phonic character of the linguistic sound.'"[24]

In preaching sound is critically coterminous with writing and in fact
trumps writing.[25] The orality and aurality of the sermon are the harbingers
of meaning especially in the Black church where the congregants are connected to the distant, though heartfelt, sound of the African drum. It is the
sound of the drum that speaks the language of the community. The drum
is a symbol of communications in Africa and in the African diaspora. The
sound of the drum signifies the mood of the community and the invitation to participate in certain rituals and activities. There is no community
event without an accompanying sound of the drum in continental Africa.
The drum speaks the language of the community and expresses the mood
of the people. The drum talks. The drum communicates meaning! It has
a spokenness that says "come and gather at the gates." The sound of the
drum conveys a message and meaning through the language of sound. The
"talking drums" in the chiefs' palace epitomize the language of drumming
as a tool of communications.[26] The certain sound of the sermon, the trumpet of consciousness, is pretty close to the heart and soul of Black preaching. While sound is not the heart of Black preaching, it houses the soul of
Black preaching.[27] Also, when I use the term "sound," I am not suggesting
a substanceless entity, but a spokenness that is grounded in a nexus of
style and substance. I am speaking of a percept that allows the speaker and
the hearer to connect on a deep spiritual, emotional, and cognitive level.
The sound of the spoken sermon does not exclude the written meaning

24. Derrida, *Of Grammatology*, 53.

25. Thompson, "Til Earth and Heaven Ring."

26. This explanation has been provided by Ghanian Minister Michael Alloteh who
has served as a pastor and leader in the Global Evangelical church. He is a freelance
Ewe musician and drummer. Interview held on April 5, 2011.

27. LaRue, *The Heart of Black Preaching* and Proctor, *The Certain Sound of the
Trumpet.*

of Black preaching, but rather facilitates such meaning. The sweetness of the word is augmented by the sound of the word bursting forth from the mouth of the prophetic Black preacher.[28]

THE PREACHER'S IDENTITY: CHARLES TAYLOR AND RALPH ELLISON

Identity is the dialectic of unity and difference, of closure and openness. I am fascinated by the thought of Charles Taylor's *Modern Social Imaginaries, The Ethics of Authenticity* and his essay on *Multiculturalism and "The Politics of Recognition."* These writings are even more fascinating when viewed alongside Axel Honneth's *The Struggle for Recognition,* and James Baldwin's novel *Another Country,* and Ralph Ellison's *Invisible Man.* I cannot do full justice to either Taylor or Honneth. I will focus only on their implications for identity as it relates to the African American experience of disrespect, which is characterized by insult and humiliation, the physical and mental abuse of slavery, and the residual experience of denigration and suffering. Identity, race, recognition and their relationship to invisibility and the ontological struggles of African Americans are surely beyond the scope and intent of Hegel's *Jena* lectures as well as Taylor's and Honneth's privileged disposition and point of departure; nevertheless, their theories have some practical applicability and can be carefully appropriated to the experience of African Americans vis-à-vis the nature of identity portrayed in the media. The invisibilization of African American women has been even more blatant and systematic, and unfortunately African American males have adopted some of the ways of white folk and applied these concepts and practices in fostering their own brand of invisibilizing Black women. The Black male preacher cannot escape the guilty verdict! In the blockbuster book and movie *The Help,* written and produced by whites, the Black male is the invisible one, but is implied and portrayed throughout as a violent and abusive partner to the Black domestic women. The Black women are invisible except when they are nursing white babies or cooking and cleaning—all in service to their white women and men bosses.

The struggle for recognition is connected to the issue of identity and is reflected in the African Americans' quest for survival. Their introduction to modernity was marked by the savage and tortuous journey across the Atlantic from the shores of West Africa to the ports of Richmond,

---

28. Harris, *The Word Made Plain* and *Preaching Liberation.*

Baltimore, and Charleston, South Carolina. This Middle Passage was designed to erase one identity and create an "other" identity, from freedom to bondage. This struggle for identity, or what G. W. F. Hegel and Axel Honneth called "The Struggle for Recognition," has had many roadblocks and much opposition, often posed by the architects of democracy: eighteenth-century theorists often grounded democracy in the notion of a uniform human nature that bleached out difference. Television often does the same thing today that art has done but it is much more egalitarian. The resistance to invisibility has fueled the struggle for recognition. The struggle culminated in the civil rights movement of the mid to late twentieth century, led by Rosa Parks and Dr. Martin Luther King, Jr. After many nonviolent protest marches, debates and speeches, Dr. King went to Memphis at the request of some local ministers to support the garbage workers' quests to be recognized as human beings who deserved decent wages, respect, and safe working conditions. Two workers had been killed on the job, and King went there to prick the conscience of the city leaders and to lead a nonviolent protest march. The march was sabotaged by looters and persons paid to precipitate violence. The march got out of control and King was heavily criticized by national politicos for fleeing from the scene—especially by the senator from West Virginia, Robert Byrd, who called him a coward and a plethora of other negative names on television. It was also because of television media that the world was able to associate Dr. King and the Civil Rights struggle with the need for social transformation.[29] This type of propaganda by Senator Byrd caused King to return to Memphis out of love and to set the record straight. In Memphis, on April 4, 1968, he was shot by an assassin's bullet. King's life came to an abrupt and untimely end while he was struggling to bring dignity to the garbage workers of Memphis. In this connection, Charles Taylor speaks of respect and dignity as the way we carry ourselves in public space. He states:

> Our "dignity" is our sense of ourselves as commanding (attitudinal) respect. The issue of what one's dignity consists in is no more avoidable than those of why we ought to respect other's rights or what makes a full life, however much a naturalist philosophy might mislead us into thinking of this as another domain of mere "gut" reactions, similar to those of baboons establishing their hierarchy . . . The very way we walk, move, gesture, speak is shaped from the earliest moments by our awareness that we appear before others, that we stand in public space, and that

29. Williams, "The Technology and the Society," 291–300.

this space is potentially one of respect or contempt, of pride or shame.[30]

Charles Taylor correlates one's sense of dignity with the minutiae of ordinary life, and in marching with the garbage workers of Memphis or poor Black people in Selma, Alabama or Jackson, Mississippi, Martin Luther King, Jr. was communicating his advocacy for human dignity and calling the nation and the world to respect the poor, Black disenfranchised American because it was the inherently moral, just, and right action to take. These "ordinary" citizens deserved respect and dignity. Just because someone's skin was dark or non-white was no ground for inferior treatment in a democracy where Jefferson wrote that "All men are created equal," in spite of the fact that he had slaves. The language of the Constitution is laden with patriarchal tones and semantic distortion. King sought to hold America to her stated and written treatises on noble democratic principles on the one hand while American embodied the attributes of oppression, patriarchy and Big Brother on the other.

In reading Charles Taylor's *The Ethics of Authenticity,* I am reminded of the character Rufus Scott in James Baldwin's novel, *Another Country.* Baldwin writes:

> The policeman passed him, giving him a look. Rufus turned, pulling up the collar of his leather jacket while the wind nibbled delightfully at him through his summer slacks, and started North on Seventh Avenue. He had been thinking of going downtown and waking up Vivaldo—the only friend he had left in the city, or maybe in the world—but now he decided to walk up as far as a certain jazz bar and night club and look in. Maybe somebody would see him and recognize him, maybe one of the guys would lay enough bread on him for a meal or at least subway fare. At the same time, he hoped that he would not be recognized.[31]

Rufus is ambivalent about the intersubjective concept of recognition. He wants to be recognized, yet he does not want to be recognized because he is not sure that this present self is one to be lauded or loathed. This present identity is on the verge of lostness, languishing in a state of limbo. How unlike the narrator character of Ralph Ellison's *Invisible Man,* who blatantly asserts his invisibility: "I am an invisible man." Ellison goes on to explicate this invisibility as a social and anthropological reality. He further states:

30. Taylor, *Sources of the Self,* 15.
31. Baldwin, *Another Country,* 34.

I am invisible, understand, simply because people refuse to see me. Like bodiless heads you see sometimes in circus shows, it is as though I have been surrounded by mirrors of hard, distorting glass. When they approach me they see only my surroundings, themselves, or figments of their imagination—indeed, everything and anything except me.[32]

Charles Taylor in his chapter, "The Need for Recognition," suggests that ones' identity is intimately connected, or more basically, formed "in dialogue with others, in agreement or struggle with their recognition of us."[33] He argues that this modern understanding of identity and recognition is highly correlated with the ideal of authenticity. This becomes an ontological issue—one's understanding of her being is correlated with recognition. And according to Ralph Ellison, one's visibility is placed in the hands of the other. People can act like one does not exist and in effect unrecognize one out of existence. Moreover, Taylor indicates that two changes, "the collapse of social hierarchies . . . intrinsically linked to inequalities,"[34] and the modern notion of dignity "where we talk of the inherent dignity of human beings' or citizen dignity"[35] have inevitably preoccupied the modern mind with identity and recognition. While Taylor may be theoretically correct, however, I submit that there has been no collapse of social hierarchies as it relates to African Americans and other people of color, and only in a marginal sense have ordinary non-white citizens been accorded dignity in the United States where democracy is still not equal in spite of Taylor's assertion that "democracy has ushered in a politics of equal recognition, which has taken various forms over the years, and which now has returned in the form of demands for the equal status of cultures and of genders."[36] The quest for equality is an ongoing process by Black males and females not only in the media, which is still overwhelmingly Caucasian, but also throughout the society. It is hard for Black folk to get a job, a mortgage on a house, or an educational loan. But, if you need a loan to buy a car there may be five banks willing to loan the money. Why? Because a car or any automotive vehicle loses its value by the time you drive it off the lot. But, an education's value is accretive.

---

32. Ellison, *Invisible Man, Prologue*, 15–18.
33. Taylor, *The Ethics of Authenticity*, 45–46.
34. Ibid., 46.
35. Ibid.
36. Ibid., 47.

Everyone needs to experience recognition because it helps to shape their identity and sense of self. Charles Taylor in his article "The Politics of Recognition" makes this point quite explicit. He states:

> The demand for recognition in these later cases is given urgency by the supposed links between recognition and identity, where this latter term designates something like a person's understanding of who they are, of their fundamental defining characteristics as a human being. The thesis is that our identity is partly shaped by recognition or its absence, often by the misrecognition of others, and so a person or group of people can suffer real damage, real distortion, if the people or society around them mirror back to them a confining or demeaning or contemptible picture of themselves. Non-recognition or misrecognition can inflict harm, can be a form of oppression imprisoning someone in a false, distorted or reduced mode of being.[37]

This is indeed the nature of patriarchy, slavery, and other more subjective forms of oppression in everyday life and work. Recognition is often as important as compensation because it is grounded in honor and appreciation, and the lack of it as Taylor says has the effect of an ontological reduction. Jesse Jackson's slogan to African American Youth "I am somebody" is an attempt to recognize and assert the value of those who are Black—those who are systematically unrecognized, overlooked and made invisible by those who simply "refuse to see me," to use the language of Ralph Ellison. Black folk deserve to be recognized and compensated for their work by each other if not by anyone else. We show how valuable our best teachers and preachers are to us and the world by recognizing their educational achievement and compensating them accordingly.

SERMONIC DISCOURSE: "UNEXPECTED ABUNDANCE"

When he had finished speaking, he said to Simon, "Go out into the deep water and lower your nets for a catch. Simon answered, "Master, despite laboring through the whole night we have caught nothing! But at your word, I will lower the nets." When they had done so, they caught so great a number of fish that their nets were beginning to burst. –Luke 5:4–6

A lot of times we have low expectations or quite frankly no expectations in our communications and relationships with others—whether they are

37. Taylor, *Multiculturalism and the Politics of Recognition*, 25.

our friends, our family members, our students if we are teachers. In other words, what we expect from others and even ourselves is often so low that it amounts to nothing at all. And, often when we expect nothing, we get nothing. And, sometimes when we expect a lot, we still get nothing.

To expect something is to anticipate or to look forward to something happening. It implies a high degree of certainty or at least that which is reasonable. We all have expectations regarding people, places and things. If you go to a five star restaurant, you expect to have a good meal. You also expect to pay a pretty penny for it. You go to McDonald's or Burger King, or Wendy's or Hardees, you expect to feed yourself and your two children for $25.00 or less. And, let's say, if you go there and one cheeseburger and fries and a coke are now $20.00, you'll be pretty tiffed and whiffed, pretty hacked and whacked, and ready to show another side of your church go-ing, praise dancing, sanctified personality. This unexpected price for what amounts to a kids meal is unreasonable. Your anticipation of the costs has been shattered because if you knew that you had to pay $20.00 for a cheeseburger and French fries, you would have gone somewhere else where you could get real steak and potatoes for that amount of money. You would have gone to Outback or Flemings Steakhouse or Ruth's Chris. So my beloved, expectation is highly correlated with anticipation and rea-sonableness. We could give countless examples, but the principle would be the same—to expect implies a degree of certainty, a degree of reason-ability and a degree of anticipating that the outcome will coincide with your logic. OK.

Now in the scripture text today we have an extraordinary situation that is compelling because so much is implied and unsaid, like so many other texts. Let me remind you that the situation in the text and the ser-mon are not the same. The text today points us to a context or to a circum-stance where Jesus is teaching a crowd of people the Word of God while at the same time embodying that Word. He is the Word and yet he teaches the Word. All of this is taking place in Galilee near Capernaum on Lake Gennesaret. This is the same as the Sea of Galilee or the Sea of Tiberias. Jesus saw two boats lying on the shore and the fishermen had gone out of the boats and were cleaning their nets. Jesus got in one of the boats and asked Simon to push him off the land a bit and he sat down and taught the crowd from the boat. Unlike Socrates, who would walk back and forth as he taught, the text says Jesus sat down and taught the crowds—he sat down. No calisthenics and histrionics. No paratactics. He sat down. No walking back and forth and jumping up and down as a substitute for digging deep and hard in teaching the Word. No, he sat down and taught. Standing and sitting is not as important as teaching the Word. Jesus is a pedagogical prophet; Jesus is a teacher. A God-certified teacher. A bona fide, qualified teacher. He was a bona fide teacher because he taught as one with authority. He was qualified because he had been tested by the powers of Satan and proven to be the Son of Man, the Son of David, and the Son of God. He was certified because when he was baptized in the River Jordan by John, the Holy Spirit descended upon him like a dove. He was touched by the Spirit, anointed by the Spirit. So he was certified by the power of the Holy Spirit. Now the text says that "When he finished speaking, he said to Simon, 'Go out into the deep water and let down your nets for a catch.'" Simon answered, "Master, we have worked all night long but have caught nothing. Yet, if you say so, I will let down the nets." "When they had done this, they caught so many fish that their nets were beginning to break." So they signaled their partners in the other boat to come and help them. And they came and filled both boats, so they began to *sink*. The only thing that's different between this scene now and what happened during the night is that Jesus is now on the scene and the whole narrative takes a powerful new turn. The expected has been replaced by the unexpected and nothing, catching nothing, has been replaced by abundance.

What does this mean to a people who ain't never been able to catch much of anything? What does this text mean to the church today? How are we to interpret this story to a community of people who have been hit hard by this recession—this economy where bleakness is everywhere? What do you mean, brother preacher, by unexpected abundance?

Well, let's look one more time at the text, verse 4—"When he finished speaking, he said to Simon, 'Go out into the deep water and lower your nets for a catch.'" We have got to be able to follow instructions. We have to allow the prophet to prophecy, to speak. "Go out into the deep water and let down your nets." He didn't say let down your nets again. We don't even know whether Jesus was aware of their all-night sojourn and if he was aware, it didn't mean much. What happened last night is past and while William Faulkner says "The past is never past," it is in this text. The prophet is more concerned about the proleptic vision than he is about what you did or did not do in the past. So instead of Jesus dredging up the past, validating their past failures, their all-night sojourn with disappointment, he speaks with prophetic authority: "Go out and let down your nets." His word is instructive and requires adherence. This means that we have to act according to his instructions. Jesus instructs Simon to do something and

Simon adheres to Jesus's word. Simon acts according to the instructions. He didn't go in a different direction. He didn't say no, my boat is docked for the rest of the day. He didn't say, "I'm tired and I've fished enough for now." We don't get any of the kind of stuff that we tend to say. From all indications, Simon adhered; Simon acted according to Jesus's directive instruction and put the boat out in deep water. Now, I'm not much of a fisherman but I think this deep water has some significance. This deep water is a semiotic reference to something. Deep water may be a sign of something. It may symbolize and signify the fact that as disciples of Jesus, not only do we have to follow his instruction, but sometimes that instruction will take us to places that look ominous, places that harbor inklings of the hopeless, places where only the deep levels of consciousness will enable us to successfully navigate the challenges of life. Go out into deep water is a call to surrender our own desires. Deep water is the place where doubt can be overcome by faith, and fear can be transformed into a follow-ership of Jesus. Today we need a deep water religion, today we need a deep water faith, today we need to adhere to deep water instruction where it may not feel as safe as it did in Sunday school. Deep water instruction may cause you to question what you are used to. Not only is Simon asked and instructed to "Go out into deep water and lower your nets for a catch." Not only is adherence important or the step toward unexpected abundance, but the text goes on to say that Simon answered, "Master, despite laboring through the whole night, we caught nothing. Yet, if you say so, I will let down the nets—at your word I will lower the nets."

Yet complaint often comes before compliance. Again, just because we cry and complain and object don't mean that we are going to shut the door to the presence of possibilities—because we know even if Simon didn't know—we as African Americans who have borne the heat of the day, as a people who have survived the Middle Passage from the West Coast of Africa to Richmond, Virginia, we know today, even if Simon didn't know, that God can reverse the course of human events and turn nothing into something so great that we will not be able to receive it. We know as a people burdened by all kinds of distractions and doubts, we know that in spite of the mountains that we have had to climb and are still climbing, we believe that in spite of our condition, in spite of our challenges and no matter how many times doors shut in our faces and we are discouraged by a perennial and resounding "No," we can still hear a "Yes" in the distant vistas, we can hear a word of hope because like the barrenness and surprising fertility of Elizabeth in Luke 1:37, "Nothing is impossible with God."

Listen, Simon was a fisherman by profession and he knew a little something about boats, currents, and fishing. That's why he complains to Jesus: "Master, we have worked all night long but we have caught nothing. We have worked *hard*—all night long and caught nothing." I suspect this is the nicest, most polite, public way that this can be said. I can imagine the body language, the resignation, the disgust, the tension. And, yet, Simon calls him "Master," which is the only reason he's willing to do what he is commanded. After complaining and objecting—Simon says, "But, if you say so, I will let down the nets. "But at your *Word* I will lower the nets." The *Word* is critical here. But at your *Word*. There is a clear understanding on the part of Luke that the *Word*, God's Word, is the source of prophetic power. The power of the Word is such that Simon's objection has to take a back seat. Simon is saying: I'm a fisherman, I do this for a living, I've been out here working hard all night long, I've tried this before, I've been unable to get my life together, I've been working hard and I'm still not getting anywhere, I've been praying hard, all night long and it seems that it all has come to naught. Can't you understand. In other words. I've been toiling trying to overcome the nothingness of my labor, I've been this place and that place trying to make a living—I've been up all night worrying, struggling, hoping, praying, trying with all my heart and soul and I have come up empty, nothing, no progress, no advancement, no further along than when I first started—but Master, at your *Word*, I will lower the nets.

When they had done so, they caught so great a number of fish that their nets were beginning to burst. They called the other boat to come and assist them. Remember there were two boats. The other boat and they filled both boats, so that they were about to sink. Unexpected Abundance. If we adhere to God's instruction and acquiesce or comply or submit to his Word, our blessings will be so abundant. We will have ample quantity; we will have more than enough. You'll have a plenty—a great plenty . . .

Chapter 5

Sermonic Discourse as Sign and Symbol of Freedom

We shall overcome, we shall overcome,
We shall overcome someday;
Oh, deep in my heart, I do believe,
We shall overcome someday.
The truth shall make us free, the truth shall make us free,
The truth shall make us free someday;
Oh, deep in my heart, I do believe,
The truth shall make us free someday.

—Negro Spiritual

Martin Luther King, Jr., in his "Letter From the Birmingham City Jail," said that when he walked past the white church with its steeples spiraling toward heaven, he would wonder, "who is their God?" The steeple is a sign of the institutional church and the religious beliefs and practices of Christians. It is a sign of those individuals who inhabit that sanctuary and believe that their ecclesiological rituals, doctrines, and spiritual community practices are in synchrony with the will of God, as it is manifested in their interpretation and practice of scripture. The statement by King is a sign of the need for a corrective reading of their beliefs and practices.

Like other liberation theologians, King's observation is intended to cause those who are a part of the white church to begin to correlate scripture with their actions and beliefs, i.e., practices within the church community. This question grew out of his own social ontology and his frustration with injustice and oppression. He was also critical of the Black church's eschatological message, which made it too accepting of the status quo. He further criticized the Black church, calling it "a tail light, rather than a headlight." This language suggested that the Black church was too passive on issues of oppression and injustice that were clearly grounded in racial segregation and hatred.

If the philosopher and religious scholar Peter Ochs is correct in defining Charles Sanders Peirce's pragmatism as a corrective reading of itself and others, then Black religion and Black preaching in America is the ultimate pragmatic corrective to traditional religious theory and practices. In his book *Peirce, Pragmatism and the Logic of Scripture,* Peter Ochs writes:

> My thesis is that pragmatic definition is not a discrete act of judgment or classification, but a *performance of correcting other, inadequate definitions of imprecise things* . . . It is a corrective activity . . . My thesis is therefore not a thesis in the usual sense. Since my claim is that to define pragmatically is to correct and that to correct is to read, my "thesis" is better named my "corrective reading."[1]

Ochs goes on to say that the aforesaid definition is lacking because pragmatism as correction is a complicated phenomenon that makes continuous correction normative. While preaching in the Black church is a form of continuous correction, and thus a form of pragmatism, I am more interested in the concept and practice of correction that characterizes and constitutes the homiletical and preaching enterprise. Black preaching has necessarily been practiced in an oppressed community of the faithful in a double context: in a microcosmic community of love and care and simultaneously in a macrocosmic community of hatred and disinterest. These two worlds constitute the context of the Black preacher. And, being caught in the metaxological reality of these two contexts, the preacher has had to use scripture as a corrective to both—with particular focus on the Black community. This Du Boisian dilemma has characterized the pragmatics of sermonic discourse from slavery to the present. Black preaching is compelled to be self-correcting: correcting the Other while at the same time being scriptural and *corrective of scripture as well.* There are scriptural texts

1. Ochs, *Peirce, Pragmatism and the Logic of Scripture,* 4–5.

that obviously reflect bias against Blacks, the poor, and women. These texts demand a corrective reading. For example, in Genesis 16:1–15, Hagar, without a consenting voice, becomes the solution to Sarai's inability to have children. Abram, Sarai's husband, goes along with the plan for him to father a child with Sarai's servant, Hagar. As soon as it is certain that Hagar is with child, the entire plan this couple has concocted falls apart because that which had no value (Hagar) is now suddenly a valuable commodity. The scripture text says that Sarai is being mistreated by Hagar because she is pregnant and Sarai is not, which leads the reader to believe that Sarai has a right to be angry with Hagar. Meanwhile, Abram has taken great pride in knowing that he will become a father; however, this drives a wedge between the couple, and instead of Abram standing by his "baby's momma" he allows his wife to send Hagar away as a way of resolving the new issue that they both were complicit in constructing. The point is that Hagar is not consulted—Abram and Sarai are complicit in exploiting her for their own satisfaction. Hagar has been used and abused as a surrogate mother and baby-making sexual object. She has been silenced and not given any choice in the matter. She is put out to fend for herself. She is not given the freedom or the opportunity to exercise her own free will. She has been used like a pawn at the will of her mistress and master. This story recalls elements of early American slavery and how women were summoned and used by the master and his wife in any manner they chose. Today, Black women are still trying to survive the "damned if you do and damned if you don't" syndrome that denies them self-determination. This brings to the forefront the fact that damage and harm are not perpetrated solely by men. White women particularly have been complicit in the oppression of Black women from slavery to the civil rights era. Ironically, they have been the chief beneficiaries of the civil rights laws, and they have achieved this by doing nothing to advance the cause of freedom and justice for the marginalized and the oppressed.

SPEAKING THE SERMON INTO EXISTENCE

Like the poem, the sermon is always a spoken text. It is written to be spoken and not read to the audience. The written form of the sermon is a prelude to its spokenness because the sermon on the page, when left on the page without being spoken, is a form of discourse that doesn't rise to the level of sermon in the Black church. Its orality and aural nature make it a real sermon. A sermon has to be spoken. If I were to come to church with copies of my written sermon for every parishioner, and when the moment came to preach, I proceeded to pass out the written manuscript and ask the people to sit and read it through and through while I sat and read it silently, smiling at them every now and then, there would be a mutiny at the historic Second Baptist Church. The people would swear that I had lost my mental bearings. Some would storm out of the sanctuary in absolute disgust, scratching their heads, mumbling unhappy complaints because they would feel that their attendance at church that day would have been wasted on the preacher's new experimental form of non-preaching. A form that would be constitutive of something foreign to the notion of preaching. And who would the preacher be writing to? Would this be Ricoeur's "unknown reader?"[2] How could that be and what kind of distanciation would that imply and confirm to the parishioners? And, what about those in the church who can't read? In this case, the semantic autonomy of the text which is intended to "create the audience of the text"[3] would be more destructive than creative. Ricoeur writes:

> It is the response of the audience which makes the text important and therefore significant. This is why authors who do not worry about their readers and despise their present public keep speaking of their readers as a secret community . . . It is part of the meaning of the text to be open to an indefinite number of readers and, therefore interpretations.[4]

There is a place for the sermon as written text, but not at the expense of the performative preaching and worship event. As event, it must be spoken. Its receptivity is even heightened if there is no sign of a written manuscript. Preaching without notes in the Black church is a virtue. However, if the preacher uses a manuscript, he has to master it to the extent that it becomes almost invisible, i.e., not limiting. And, some of the best preachers in my experience have used written manuscripts in the pulpit. That notwithstanding, the sermon is compelled to be a speech act. As a matter of fact passing out a written manuscript to the congregation would be construed as absurd and insensitive in the Black church, and I suspect that many in the white church would be incensed as well, because for the mainline protestant churches even the spoken sermons have already made the people drowsy and disinterested in the discourse. A written sermon even in these church settings would be anathema.

2. Ricoeur, *Interpretation Theory*, 31
3. Ibid., 33.
4. Ibid.

Ricoeur's most profound statement that "hermeneutics begins where dialogue ends"[5] is itself subject to interpretation, especially since preaching in the Black church is historically dialogical. This means that hermeneutics is a conversation between speaker and hearer. The preacher has been engaged in hermeneutics long before and during the development and delivery of the sermon, and then on Sunday morning the response of the audience helps to create the sermon, and at times restructure its message. So, while the writing of the sermon is an imaginary preaching event, it is something other than the actual preaching of the sermon. In this sense, writing the sermon is a virtual event.

Writing the sermon is also ritual on the level of preaching itself. Ritual in the sense that it occurs for the preacher as a weekly responsibility. For a period of three or four hours over four of five days every week, the preacher is in the process of constructing the written sermon. This construction process is itself sacred because the pastoral preacher is involved in a life or death enterprise—not simply a semantic exercise.

THE RHETORIC OF WRITING THE SERMON

The written sermon is a dialectic between writing and speaking, because when it comes to sermons, one has to speak the words onto the page and then speak the same words off the page. The preacher speaks truth to the page as a primal exercise in sermon writing. This means that in order for the sermon to sound like something profound when it is preached, it has to be spoken first as a part of the writing process. It has to be voiced and heard by the preacher as a precondition to its public spokenness. It is a lonely, private affair in its initial lexical state, but come Sunday, it makes its oral public debut. This happens every week like clockwork. It is an example of the dialectic that exists between the lexical and the rhetorical, i.e., the written and the spoken.

Hearing the sermon has meaning. The act of hearing, i.e., being present in the sanctuary while the sermon is being preached, has meaning. I take issue with Jacques Derrida's exclusion of the notion that sound has a natural bond to meaning. This exclusion is the very thing that I seek to include because in Black preaching sound potentially motivates the hearer and fosters meaning simply because of its sweetness and its inherent power to inspire. Augustine may have had this in mind when he speaks

5. Derrida, *Of Grammatology*. Also see Augustine's *De Doctrina Christiana*, Book IV.

of preaching and the sweetness of the Word.[6] The North African bishop preaching the Word in the Black church tradition is indeed a sweet thing to do and to hear.

Once the sermon has been spoken into existence as *ecriture*, it need not be written again, but it can be spoken over and over again. Each time it is preached, it becomes a new creation, not a new script or scripture reference, but a new sermon. Why and how is this possible? The best answer to that question is that the spokenness of the sermon takes on new form and content each time it is delivered because the audience or hearers are different and the mindset of the preacher is also different. And, unlike readers, their response is immediately heard, creating a dialogue between preacher and congregation. Moreover, the preacher is able to paint a brighter, more luminous picture each time the sermon is preached because he is being helped by the response of the hearers. And, in the Black church, this response is often audible, thus creating a new event—a new sermon. Verbalized words like "let the Lord use you" or "make it plain" or "preach" help to create a new sermon from the same manuscript.

Unlike Ricoeur, however, in his discussion of writing and iconicity, I submit that the spoken sermon has the power to bring about a metamorphosis in the universe. More than that, the sermon creates a new world via the preacher's imagination. That's why the slave preacher who was essentially illiterate could sense and feel the presence of evil in the words and actions of the slave master and declare to his fellow bondsman that "everybody talking 'bout heaven ain't going there." Ricoeur takes issue with privileging the denotative meaning over the connotative (which is classic Eurocentrism). Ricoeur is definitely not in the tradition of Rene Descartes. Ricoeur states, "For such a position [as Descartes's] only the denotation is cognitive and, as such, is a semantic order. A connotation is extra-semantic because it consists of the weaving together of emotive evocations, which lack cognitive value."[7]

The notion that emotive evocations lack cognitive value is not only an extreme ethical and psychological assertion, but seems to be a logical fallacy. The inherent dichotomization of emotion and cognition is an apparent hold-over from Descartes and the Enlightenment. It privileged thinking or cognition and suggests that this is the basis of ontology. Ricoeur, however, opposes such a view. Descartes's *cogito ergo sum* is no more valid than "I feel, therefore I am" or "I believe, therefore I am" or

6. Ricoeur, *Interpretation Theory*, 46.

7. Ibid.

"I cry therefore, I am." They are all ontological propositions grounded in the body. Emotion is a rational construct and the connotative aspect of the sentence is as significant as the denotative aspect. And, cognitive significance is not limited to one aspect of the sentence, but is seen in both the denotative and the connotative aspects of the sentence. Therefore, the logic of the sentence is both denotative and connotative.

PREACHING AS THE ART OF INTERPRETATION: AN ACT OF FREEDOM

The fusion of horizons as seen in Gadamer has to do with the coming together of the visions of the readers and the writer—much like what we see in Paul Ricoeur. For Gadamer, horizons overlap around subject matters. This means that horizons fuse around questions that emanate from an interest or understanding of the past, present, and future. Distance is often overcome by inquiry into the subject. This does not mean that historical understanding and historical consciousness are not constitutive of a horizon. The fusion of horizons is the process of understanding both the historical horizon and the future. This too is akin to Ricoeur's understanding of the meaning of the text as something that is not behind it, but always before it, i.e., in front of it—something being understood or something that will be understood. For me, this is one of Ricoeur's most liberating and powerful postulates. Gadamer says, "Every encounter with tradition that takes place within historical consciousness involves the experience of a tension between the text and the present. The hermeneutic task consists in not covering up this tension by attempting a naïve assimilation of the two but in consciously bringing it out."[8] Gadamer also says, ". . . understanding is always the fusion of these horizons supposedly existing by themselves. We are familiar with the power of this kind of fusion chiefly from earlier times and their naïveté about themselves and their heritage. In a tradition, this process of fusion is always going on, for there old and new are always combining into something of living value, without either being explicitly foregrounded from the other."[9]

For Gadamer every act of understanding causes or creates a new horizon. Understanding then becomes the foundation for a horizon being constituted anew. Gadamer states,

8. Gadamer, *Truth and Method*, 306.
9. Ibid.

> When our historical consciousness transports itself into his-
> torical horizons, this does not entail passing into alien worlds
> unconnected in any way with our own; instead, they together
> constitute the one great horizon that moves from within and
> that, beyond the frontiers of the present, embraces the historical
> depths of our self-consciousness. Everything contained in his-
> torical consciousness is in fact embraced by a single historical
> horizon. Our own past and that other past toward which our
> historical consciousness is directed help to shape this moving
> horizon out of which human life always lives and which deter-
> mines it as heritage and tradition.[10]

The "one great horizon" is constitutive of the fusion, the enmeshing of horizons, and the coming together of one world with another, overcoming their difference and their alienation. This is what constitutes genuine conversation and understanding of a text and of one another.

The issue of how one can come to grasp another's expression or message given distances of time and/or social, cultural, and political space is the chief hermeneutical problem that is addressed by Schleiermacher, Hans Gadamer, and Paul Ricoeur. I now move to a look at Ricoeur's dialectic of explanation and understanding as it relates to Gadamer's fusion of horizon (*Horizonverschemelzung*). Indeed, "the text is the mediating link in this process of horizon fusing," says Ricoeur. The text connects past with future because it is the subject matter of the conversation between the reader and historical author. Moreover, "there is a dialectical interplay between the text as a worldless entity"[11] and "the text as an orientation to a possible world."[12] Its meaning is that which is to be appropriated. The text is the center of discourse for the writer and reader such that the writer structures the text and the reader interprets the text. The interpretation by the reader may or may not capture the meaning of the writer—but it may capture the meaning of the text.

Ricoeur suggests that reading proceeds by understanding and explanation. He states, "It may be said . . . that understanding is to reading what the event of discourse is to the utterance of discourse and that explanation is to reading what the verbal and textual autonomy is to the objective meaning of discourse."[13] Understanding synthesizes explanation.

---

10. Ibid.

11. Ricoeur, *Interpretation Theory*, 81.

12. Ibid., 88.

13. Ibid., 71–72.

This means, in my view, that explanation is intended to create or foster understanding. Ricoeur states,

> Not the intention of the author, which is supposed to be hidden behind the text; not the historical situation common to the author and his original readers; not the expectations or feelings of these original readers; not even their understanding of themselves as historical and cultural phenomena. What has to be appropriated is the meaning of the text itself, conceived in a dynamic way as the direction of thought opened up by the text. In other words, what has to be appropriated is nothing other than the power of disclosing a world that constitutes the reference of the text. In this way, we are as far as possible from the Romanticist ideal of coinciding with a foreign psyche. If we may be said to coincide with anything, it is not the inner life of another ego, but the disclosure of a possible way of looking at things, which is the genuine referential power of the text.[14]

The issue of how one can come to grasp another's expression or message given distances of time or of social/cultural/political space is the essential hermeneutical problem. No theorist is any more provocative in his views of interpretation than Friedrich Schleiermacher, who states that the task of hermeneutics is "To understand the text at first as well as and then even better than its author." Since we have no direct knowledge of what was in the author's mind, "we must try to become aware of many things of which he himself may have been unconscious, except insofar as he reflects on his own work and becomes his own reader."[15] This gets back to Schleiermacher's interest in the reconstruction of meaning based on a psychological understanding of the author. This "reconstruction of a given statement"[16] is constitutive of imitating the meaning of the author. Paul Ricoeur is clearly against this view of interpretation when he states that *"The problem of the correct understanding can no longer be solved by a simple return to the alleged situation of the author."*[17] Yet, Ricoeur uses Schleiermacher's categories to explain his own dialectic—correlating what he calls "guessing" to what Schleiermacher called "divination," and "validation" to what Schleiermacher called the "grammatical." Understanding, for Schleiermacher, is the art of reconstructing the thinking of the author of the text through

14. Ibid., 92.
15. Quoted in Mueller-Vollmer, *The Hermeneutics Reader*, 83
16. Ibid.
17. Ricoeur, *Interpretation Theory*, 76.

interpreting his or her utterance. It seems that Ricoeur's hermeneutic of understanding is very much a take on Schleiermacher's hermeneutic. This means that Ricoeur's hermeneutic of explanation is more his own, i.e., a departure from the Romanticists whom he apparently respects and appropriates but does not imitate. Ricoeur states, "Interpretation is a particular case of understanding. It is understanding applied to the written expressions of life."[18] However, he later says, "Then the term interpretation may be applied, not to a particular case of understanding, that of the written expressions of life, but to the whole process that encompasses explanation and understanding." It is an acknowledgment of Schleiermacher, yet it goes beyond him to explicate Ricoeur's own concept of interpretation. Ultimately, the fusion of horizon is to make the text my own such that the to and fro of dialogue mediates, if not bridges, the possible chasm between text and interpreter and thereby creates understanding. Gadamer and Ricoeur are constantly dialoguing with each other and with Schleiermacher and others in an act of interpretation.

Before discussing the usefulness of Ricoeur's dialectic of explanation and understanding and his discussion of a "surplus of meaning" for describing problems of interpretation in "*The Metamorphosis*" by Franz Kafka, I am first of all struck by the opening line of the story: "When Gregor Samsa awoke from troubled dreams one morning, he found that he had been *transformed* in his bed into an enormous bug."[19] This line immediately draws me not to Ricoeur but to Gadamer, who defines transformation in his section on "Play as the Clue to Ontological Explanation." Gadamer provides a starting point by connecting the autonomy of play and the concept of transformation. He states that:

> Transformation is not alteration, even an alteration that is especially far-reaching. Alteration always means that what is altered also remains the same and is maintained. However totally it may change, something changes in it. In terms of the categories, all alteration (*alloiosis*) belongs in the sphere of quality—i.e., of an accident of substance. But transformation means that something is suddenly and as a whole something else, that this other transformed thing that it has become is its true being in comparison with which its earlier being is nil. When we find someone transformed we mean precisely this, that he has become another person, as it were. There cannot here be any gradual transition leading from one to the other, since the one is the denial of the

18. Ibid., 73.

19. Kafka, *The Metamorphosis and Other Stories*, 11.

> other. Thus transformation into structure means that what ex-
> isted previously exists no longer. But also that what now exists,
> what represents itself in the play of art is the lasting and true. [20]

Gadamer's assertion that transformation is something that is complete and cataclysmic—something ontological—captures that spirit and the essence of what seems to have happened to Gregor from the time of his dreams to the time of his morning awakening. But not only that. Gadamer's notion of transformation is very much a description of Paul's definition of an authentic encounter with Christ Jesus. One becomes a new creation such that baptism in Christ Jesus transforms one's existence into a new life (cf. 2 Cor 5:17).

Now, Ricoeur equates transformation with self-destruction in his discussion of metaphor and symbol as surplus of meaning. He states, "The metaphorical interpretation presupposes a literal interpretation which self-destructs in a significant contradiction. It is this process of self-destruction or transformation, which imposes a sort of twist on words, an extension of meaning thanks to which we can make sense where a literal interpretation would be literally nonsensical."[21] The fact that Gregor Samsa is now literally a giant bug, a species of vermin, is itself a contradiction because physiologically, biologically, and neurologically, we know that non-human animals such as bugs, no matter their size, do not have the ability to reflect and therefore cannot understand. This is a mode of intelligibility that an insect does not possess.

This makes me question Gadamer's definition of transformation as it applies to Kafka's use. Kafka asserts and leads the reader to think that Gregor has been "transformed," and Gadamer says that transformation means that "something is suddenly and as a whole something else, that this other transformed thing that it has become is its true being . . ."[22] Well, Gregor Samsa's transformation does not conform to Gadamer's dogmatic definition nor to Ricoeur's notion of understanding. Ricoeur writes that understanding has its origin in the human sciences "Where science has to do with the experience of other subjects/minds similar to our own."[23] Every kind of direct or indirect understanding has a common principle which is "empathy." This empathy is the transference of ourselves into the psychic life of another. This is something that Kafka does in his writing

---

20. Gadamer, *Truth and Method*, 111

21. Ricoeur, *Interpretation Theory*, 50

22. Gadamer, *Truth and Method*, 111.

23. Ricoeur, *Interpretation Theory*, 72.

about Gregor; however, more importantly, it is something Gregor himself does—*he understands and interprets!* Ricoeur says, "Then the term interpretation may be applied, not to a particular case of understanding, that of the written expressions of life, but to the whole process that encompasses explanation and understanding."[24] While Gregor's speech has been compromised in his transformation, his hermeneutical ability, i.e., his capacity to interpret and to understand speech and actions, has not been lost. Gregor is indeed human in his understanding and misunderstandings, but inhuman in his appearance and therefore is treated like an animal by his family, including his sister Grete, who gives him food with a certain degree of trepidation and condescension. None of the characters understand that Gregor understands speech and this leads to rampant misunderstanding. Misunderstanding is clearly the mode of operation for all involved. Understanding on Gregor's part does not prevent misunderstanding on his part as well as the other family members. This misunderstanding on the part of the father precipitates violence and threats inasmuch as the father wanted to kill Gregor. In interpreting Gregor everyone is somewhat biased against vermin. The difference in form (his appearance) and substance (his human intelligence) is so pronounced that misunderstanding is inevitable. Gadamer says that "The important thing is to be aware of one's own bias, so that the text can present itself in all its otherness and thus assert its own truth against one's own fore-meanings."[25] Moreover, for Schleiermacher, the operative word in hermeneutics is "misunderstanding," which seems to be normative and is evident throughout *The Metamorphosis.* For Schleiermacher, misunderstanding is inevitable, not occasional but systemic and pandemic. "Thus Schleiermacher even defines hermeneutics as the 'art of avoiding misunderstanding.' "[26] However, this is something that Gregor cannot do, because in his present state, he cannot explain his state of being which is referred to by his family as an "illness." The lack of the ability to explain facilitates misunderstanding.

This brings me to the point of asserting that everything said and done regarding Gregor Samsa, including the conversations between the host of folk trying to get him out of bed, was a matter of what Ricoeur called "guessing" and Schleiermacher called "divination." Guessing is the first act of understanding a text. Ricoeur says, "the text is mute"[27] and in the case

---

24. Ibid., 74.

25. Gadamer, *Truth and Method*, 269.

26. Ibid., 185.

27. Ricoeur, *Interpretation Theory*, 79.

of Gregor Samsa and the rest of the family, there is clearly an unequal and imbalanced relationship between them. This "asymmetric" relationship fosters misunderstanding and impedes any true semblance of "fusion of horizon" or "empathy." The family is utterly unable to transfer themselves into the psychic life of Gregor. He is no longer of any use to them. He has become a burden—an unbearable burden.

Because the symbol has its roots in something other than language, Gregor Samsa, the bug, is the perfect symbol/sign of the unnatural ontological self-understanding of Franz Kafka. Moreover, the estrangement between Gregor and his family, especially his father, who is totally disconnected with the bug, can be understood as a symbol of the chasm between being and non-being. This story is about interpreting death, self, other, suffering, estrangement, deception, survival, play, relationships, courage, etc. *The Metamorphosis* is an interpretation nightmare, and yet, some might call it "a joy" to interpret! Nevertheless, I have found it to be very challenging and exciting because interpretation is a ubiquitous act for the preacher.

SERMONIC DISCOURSE: "NO MORE OUTCASTS"

Once when He was in one of the cities, there was a man covered with leprosy. When he saw Jesus, he bowed with his face to the ground and begged him, "Lord, if you choose, you can make me clean." Then Jesus stretched out his hand, touched him, and said, "I do choose. Be made clean." Immediately the leprosy left him. And he ordered him to tell no one. "Go," he said, "and show yourself to the priest, and, as Moses commanded, make an offering for your cleansing, for a testimony to them." But now more than ever the word about Jesus spread abroad . . . —Luke 5:12–16

There is a tendency in the course of human events to cast people aside; to use people up and then throw them away. And, the reasons for this behavior are as varied as the seasons of the year or the pages of a book. We naturally separate people based on our own biases, our own limitations, or own prejudices, our own weaknesses, our own sense of security, our own sense of superiority. We tell ourselves that we are better than others, we think we are brighter than others, we are more deserving than others because we have not been victimized by the weakness of the human mind or the frailty or the human spirit; or even the pain and agony of the human body. We have a proclivity—a tendency to isolate and separate ourselves from those who are not like we are—those who are oppressed, mentally ill, physically ill, or those for one reason or another who have suffered a setback.

An outcast is a person who is refused acceptance by the community, by the church, by the family. This text presents us with a man who has leprosy. Leprosy was a chronic, infectious disease that affects the skin and the nerves that may lead to paralysis or deformity. The leper is in a terrible position because I imagine people whispered and snickered when they saw him. I suspect people crossed over to the other side of the street, or got up and moved to another seat or were just plain uncomfortable in his (the leper's) presence. And, yet Jesus had no such concerns.

We need to learn how to make humble request of the Master with the recognition that Jesus has the power to heal regardless of the disease. Jesus is a healer of broken bodies, broken promises. Jesus is a healer of broken hearts and broken families. If Jesus can heal a man with leprosy, a man with sores covering his body, a man with skin nodules that could disfigure, skin deformed by disease, then I submit to you today that Jesus's healing has no limitations. Jesus is not just a dermatologist, but he's a heart fixer and a mind regulator. He's a cardiologist and a psychologist all wrapped up in one. His healing is not limited to the outside appearance of the body—but he is an internist with sub-specialties in every area of anatomy, physiology, and medicine. Jesus is a healer. But wait. We play a role in our own healing. We have to have the drive, the initiative, the desire to be healed. So healing is highly connected to our own faith initiative. The leper approached Jesus. He didn't sit in silence. No, he didn't saturate himself in self-pity. He didn't allow his condition to defeat and destroy his will. He didn't go and curl up in a corner or become too depressed to get out of bed. No, he went to Jesus and said, "Lord, if you choose, you can make me clean." Oh, isn't that a powerful petition on the part of the patient? Lord, if you choose, you can make me clean. Listen at the language—Lord, you can make me *clean*. Lord, you can free me from contamination; Lord, you can free me from internal and external flaws. Lord, you can make me clean. Make me clean. Lord, you can free me from offensive and oppressive treatment. Lord, you can free me from violation and vilification. Lord, you can make me clean. You can free me from the grip and grasp of grease and grime and crime. Lord, if you choose, you can make me clean. You can free me from the demons that darken my soul and destroy my dreams. Lord if you choose, you can make me clean—Lord you can cure me of my disease, my leprosy; my disease, my hopelessness; my disease, my troubles, my biological, my psychological, my social disease of the body and mind. Lord, if you choose, you can make me clean.

Jesus stretched out his hand, touched the man and said, "I do choose. Be made clean." And immediately the leprosy left him and he ordered him to tell no one. Jesus's actions say that the time and place for outcasts have been overcome.

This is a defiance of social, ethical and religious norms and practices and codes. This man with leprosy was an outcast in every way. He had been relegated to non-being; his humanity, his dignity, his somebodiness had been taken away from him by the people in the community. The community can be mean. The church people can be mean and ugly—banning some folk and embracing others. And . . .

Jesus demonstrates the meaning of resurrection and the possibility of new life by instilling in this man with leprosy a testimony of transformation. Jesus shows through his actions toward the leper that change—drastic change and total transformation are always on the precipice of possibility. Resurrection means new being. It means bringing to life that which is dead, that which is without hope. Resurrection means that there is a moon rising. Resurrection means that there is a new sun rising in our souls every day. Resurrection means new life and a new being in Jesus Christ. It is what Paul Tillich calls a "New Being" and the Apostle Paul calls a new creation. "'Lord if you choose, you can make me clean.' Then Jesus stretched out his hand, touched him and said, 'I choose, be made clean.'" He touched him. He touched a leper. This is radical. This is worse than plucking grain on the Sabbath. This is worse than healing on the Sabbath. This is radical. This is an abomination. This is an act of heresy. This is a violation of the cultural norms and practices. He stretched out his hand, touched the leper, and said, "Be made clean." I choose to make you clean. Be clean. Be healed. Be redeemed. Be restored. Be made whole. Be healthy now. Be somebody. Your nothingness has been replaced with absolute, pure somebodiness. Those who relegated you to a heap of ashes outside the city can know now that you have been resurrected. Be clean is a testimony to resurrection—show yourself to the priest. Be clean is a testimony to transformation. Show yourself to the priest.

The spirit of this text is that Jesus's actions and words have the power to transform the oppressed, the outcasts, the dejected, the despised, the unclean, the unwanted, the diseased, the distant, the dirty into the acceptable. There are no more outcasts. In the final instance this is evidenced by the directive to tell no one, but go and show yourself to the "priest."

Sometimes silence is golden, actions speak louder than words: Go show yourself—don't say anything now, you have talked enough now—just go and show yourself—don't just show him your hands and your face—show yourself—not your body—but show yourself—you have been ashamed of yourself—now show yourself. You have been embarrassed (by) of yourself—now show yourself—you have been emotionally unstable—now show yourself. The self is a compendium—a confluence of all that we be. The self is the isness of our being—the self is the mind and the body, the spirit and the soul; the self is the union of emotions, body, thought and sensation. The self is a nexus of experience and hope; the self is a coming together of good and bad, right and wrong, strength and weakness. Show yourself is also about Jesus' understanding of himself—healer yes, but more than that. Show yourself was to say don't talk about me in the limited language of your understanding; show yourself—don't limit my identity to healing; show yourself is a clarification and testimony to the community about Jesus's identity and the leper's identity. It's a double identity statement. Show yourself to the Priest is about a new being—show yourself, there is nothing they can say to refute your transformation. Don't say anything, don't tell nobody nothing. Don't say a word, just show up. You are no longer an outcast. Show yourself to the Priest and he'll interpret this for himself. He may scratch his head in wonder and bewilderment. He may come to a new understanding of Jesus as the Son of God, the Healer, the Lamb of God, the Redeemer, the Messiah. Go show yourself and when people see that your skin is smooth; show yourself and when people see that your hair has grown back; show yourself and when they see that your eyes are clear and bright; *show yourself* and when they see that you are walking tall, *show* your*self* to the Priest and when they see that your*self* is new, your*self is* sober; your*self* is clean—the word about Jesus will spread abroad. The word will get out. Folk will start talking and testifying about the power of God through Jesus—show yourself is the meaning of identity and showing yourself is the wordless speech of resurrection. Show yourself says, "Look at me, see what God can do!"

Chapter 6

Black Church Preaching, Culture, and Counter-Culture

"All subjects are linked to each other."
—Michel de Montaigne

"The price of culture is a lie."
—Du Bois, *The Souls of Black Folk*

My sister-in-law, a native of Greenwood, Mississippi, tells a story of her great grandmother, who was born around the turn of century in 1896 in the Mississippi Delta. She says that when she was a young girl, she would ask her great grandmother for money and her great grandmother would respond by saying, "I don't have no money. Go and ask your *mammy* and daddy for it." This story confirms the fact that the word "mammy" was a holdover from slavery and Blacks imitated the language of the slave system by using the term used to refer to their mothers. It was the practical, that is, safe, thing to do. Lawrence Levine explains:

> The rewards of imitating whites were never very certain. "I was once whipped," a freedman in New Orleans told David Macrae, "because I said to Missis, 'my mother sent me.' We were not

allowed to call our mammies 'mother.' It made it come too near the way of white folks." The world of the whites, attractive as it might appear at times, offered little but the certainty of arbitrary and perpetual enslavement and inequality. In slavery the surest way of attaining those things that would alter life positively, short of escape or rebellion, was not outside but through black culture itself. Thus profound dissatisfaction could be an inducement to enter more fully into one's own culture, which seemed to offer the only promise of amelioration and change.[1]

Culture by its very nature is an eclectic phenomenon, a potpourri of ideas, beliefs, and practices of a community—a people. Clyde Kluckhohn offers a comprehensive definition of culture as (1) "The total way of life of a people;" (2) "The social legacy the individual acquires from his group;" (3) "A way of thinking, feeling, and believing."[2] It is everything that people say and do. It is experience, understanding, interpretation, practices, beliefs, etc. For Black people in America who are products of chattel slavery, "religion is culture and culture is religion."[3]

Raymond Williams, in his book *Keywords: A Vocabulary of Culture and Society*, says that "culture is one of the two or three most complicated words in the English language."[4] Yet it is so much a part of our lives, our thoughts, and practices. Although culture is difficult to define, all of us think that we know what it is. Larry Bouchard's definition hits the nail on the head: "culture entails every aspect of the social, artistic, and linguistic environment humanity receives from the past and creates for the future . . . we speak both of particular cultures and of culture as a universal human condition."[5]

In speaking of culture, anthropologist Clifford Geertz says, "It denotes an historically transmitted pattern of meanings embodied in symbols, a system of inherited conceptions expressed in symbolic forms by means of which men (sic) communicate, perpetuate, and develop their knowledge and attitudes toward life."[6] Moreover,

> For Geertz, religion is a "cultural system" of symbols that serves a fundamental human need: to unite a people's vision of what

1. Levine, *Black Culture and Black Consciousness*, 4.

2. Kluckhohn and Kroeber, *Culture*, 32.

3. Stuckey, *Slave Culture*, 33:4.

4. Williams, *Keywords*, 87.

5. Musser and Price, *The New Handbook of Christian Theology*, 121.

6. Ibid., 115.

reality is (their "world view") with their vision of how life ought to be lived (their "ethos"). This synthesis of "is" and "ought" serves a basic need for meaning and coherence and it resists the basic threat of chaos or "bafflement." Religion would be then a function within culture from which it is clearly inseparable. By this view, theologians must acknowledge that their tools—language, ideas, images, texts and so forth—are themselves products of culture and that their own situations in history are thoroughly cultural. Culture is thus an aspect of the "hermeneutic circle" within which theology and other disciplines must work.[7]

It is unfortunate that culture as expressed by philosophers and theologians has generally been exclusionary and narrow in its focus—equating both theology and culture with German Idealism, Romanticism, and the Enlightenment or some other Western perspective that masquerades as universalism. Even modern and postmodern perspectives on culture and theology are similarly constrained by a Western or European bias.[8] For example, H. Richard Niebuhr's *Christ and Culture* suffers from such a bias in my view. Theologians seem to have a narrower view than some anthropologists, who tend to value the life experiences of all groups, not just white or Eurocentric perspectives. T. S. Eliot captures a viable perspective that religion and culture are quite interconnected. He states ". . . from one point of view religion is culture, and from another point of view culture is religion . . ."[9] Moreover, T. S. Eliot postulates that religion and culture are different aspects of the same thing. He states:

> Anyone with even the slightest religious consciousness must be afflicted from time to time by the contrast between his religious faith and his behavior; anyone with the taste that *individual* or *group* culture confers must be aware of values, which he cannot call religious. And both "religion" and "culture," besides meaning different things from each other, should mean for the individual and for the group something towards which they strive, not merely something which they possess. Yet there is an aspect in which we can see a religion as the *whole way of life* of a people, from birth to the grave, from morning to night and even in sleep, and that way of life is also its culture.[10]

7. Ibid.
8. Tanner, *Theories of Culture* and Tillich, *Theology of Culture*.
9. Eliot, *Christianity and Culture*, 104–5.
10. Ibid., 103.

BLACK CHURCH RELIGION AND CULTURE

The Black church and Black religion remain the embodiment of the cultural life of African Americans. In spite of acculturation and adaptation of too much of what exists in the wider society, the Black church remains a place where a confluence of activities, beliefs, and practices represent the cultural life of the community. As an institution, the Black church represents freedom and independence more clearly than any other institution with which Blacks are associated. It is the only American institution that is owned, operated, and controlled by Blacks. There is nothing else in Black life that is as ubiquitous as the Black church and Black religion. Black life is an imbrication of both religion and culture.

Historically, the Black church has been the center of life and culture for the African American. The church and culture are so intermingled that any effort toward the dichotomization of the two would be a false and fruitless enterprise. The Black church is a harbinger of the ways, beliefs, and practices of African American people. These practices—both secular and sacred—come together in the lived religion, i.e., particularly the church life of Black folk. To some extent, the church in the power of the Spirit (cf. Jürgen Moltmann) and the church as a moral community (cf. James Gustafson) is an integral part of Black cultural life. Preachers and ministers know how difficult it is, however, to get their particular local church to embody the essence of spirit (*pneuma*) and community (*polis*) that W. E. B. Du Bois describes in *The Souls of Black Folk*. Few people have expressed the essence of Black religion and culture with the critical and descriptive accuracy of Du Bois, who wrote that "the problem of the twentieth century is the problem of the color line, the relation of the darker to the lighter races of men in Asia and Africa, in America and the islands of the sea. It was a phase of this problem that caused the Civil War."[11]

The correlation between slavery, religion, and skin color permeates the history of Blacks in this country. As a matter of fact, Black religion and culture are directly related to the Du Boisian "double consciousness" and to the issue of race, which is a ubiquitous issue in American life. One's Blackness forever impacts any lived understanding of philosophy, theology, ethics, and social reality. Du Bois writes:

> From the double life every American Negro must live, as a Negro and as an American, as swept on by the current of the nineteenth century while yet struggling in the eddies of the fifteenth

11. Du Bois, *The Souls of Black Folk*, 10.

century—from this must arise a painful self-consciousness, an almost morbid sense of personality and a moral hesitancy which is fatal to self-confidence. The worlds within and without the veil of color are changing, and changing rapidly, but not at the same rate, not in the same way; and this must produce a peculiar wrenching of the soul, a peculiar sense of doubt and bewilderment. Such a double life with double thoughts, double duties, and double social classes, must give rise to double words and double ideals, and tempt the mind to pretense or revolt, to hypocrisy or radicalism.[12]

The ethical paradox of African Americans has changed very little since the publication of this book at the dawn of the twentieth century. In a lecture presentation given at Virginia Union University, James H. Cone argued that the issue of race and racism toward the African American is as pronounced today as it was when he first wrote *Black Theology and Black Power* as an expression of the theology of the oppressed.[13]

Black people were not only stolen from their homeland and sold into slavery, but even after hundreds of years of chattel slavery in America and after the Reconstruction Era, Blacks continue to suffer from the vestiges of legal segregation and racial hatred that have characterized all of American history, from Columbus's "discovery of America" to the election of President Barack Obama. Moreover, the land that many of our forefathers labored to purchase from sunup to sundown with their sweat and blood was often stolen from them by "hook and crook" and other economic and legal maneuverings. There is a direct correlation between land ownership in the South and the lynching of black people. Much of the land now owned by large corporations, country clubs, and white individuals can be traced back to black ownership and the unethical tactics used to steal the land from them. In a documentary about how Black Americans have lost family land over the past one hundred sixty years, the Associated Press writers Delores Barclay, Todd Lewan, and Allen G. Breed wrote:

> The Tuskegee Institute and the National Association for the Advancement of Colored People have documented more than 3,000 lynchings between 1865 and 1965. Many of those lynched were property owners, said Ray Winbush, Director of Fisk University's Race Relations Institute. "If you are looking for stolen

12. Ibid., 142.

13. James H. Cone lectured at Virginia Union University (presented the Ellison Lectures, 2004), where he argued that white racism is still alive and well. See also Cone's *God of the Oppressed* and *Risks of Faith.*

black land" he said, "just follow the lynching trail." Some white officials condoned the violence; a few added threats of their own. "If it is necessary, every Negro in the state will be lynched," James K. Vardaman declared while governor of Mississippi (1904–1908). "It will be done to maintain white supremacy."[14]

Black people have inherited a legacy of injustice, domination, hatred and invidious discrimination, despite the Constitution and other documents claiming that all people are equal and entitled to liberty and justice. In my view, this includes the Bible, the Koran, the Bhagavad Gita, etc. The issue of race permeates religion and culture to the extent that one cannot extrapolate one from the other with any degree of authority or definitiveness.

Interpreters of black religion, from theologians to pastors to sociologists, recognize that there is no monolithic, undifferentiated social institution that can be labeled "the Black church." They argue that there are varieties of Black congregations that share a common core culture. In a case study of black congregational culture, anthropologist Melvin D. Williams summarizes the functions of a black congregation as:

> . . . a huddling place where members take refuge from the world among familiar faces; a source of identity and a matrix of interaction for the members it recruits; a subculture that creates and transmits symbols and enforces standards of beliefs and behavior; it allocates social status, differentiates roles, resolves conflicts, gives meaning, order, and style to its members' lives, and provides for social mobility and social rewards within its confines.[15]

The Black church is constantly in the process of clarifying its ontological status and reexamining self-imposed and externally bestowed definitions. However, the term "Black church" is understood, scholars have historically and consistently agreed that the Black church is the most dominant institution within Black society. The religion of the Black church has provided the organizational framework for most activities of the community—economic, political, and educational endeavors as well as spiritual ones. The Black church is unique in that it was organized and developed by an oppressed group, shut off from the institutional life of the larger society. During and after slavery, this invisible, often clandestine convocation of believers used their church and religion as a way of coping with the realities of injustice: invidious discrimination and abject racism manifested in

14. *The Richmond Times Dispatch,* December 3, 2001, A8.
15. Williams, *Community in a Black Pentecostal Church,* 259.

customs and laws. As a result of society denying Blacks the institutional access and outlets necessary for normal social existence, the Black church became a vehicle for the pursuit of freedom, justice, and equality in society at large.[16]

The unique historical development of the Black church requires a study that devotes attention both to the beliefs as well as the practices that engage the congregation. In his book *Speaking the Truth*, theologian James Cone raises the question: What is the relationship between a theology of the church and a sociology of the churches? He is critical of theologians who give an inordinate amount of attention to the doctrine of the church and little attention to the sociology of the churches:

> This clever ecclesiological sophistry enables pastors and other church officials to justify existing church institutions without se-riously inquiring about their historical faithfulness to the gospel message that they claim as the foundation of the church's iden-tity. By focusing their attention on a doctrinal understanding of the church that has little sociological significance, theologians can ignore obvious historical contradictions and shortcom-ings of empirical churches. This abstract theological maneuver makes it possible for theologians to speak of the church as the "body of Christ" without saying a word about its relation to bro-ken human bodies in society.[17]

James Cone is correct in identifying the flaws in theology that often elevate the theoretical over the practical and thereby creates an unnecessarily bi-furcated religion. Black religion is not dyadic, but nexeological.

Based upon their own observations and study of the Black church, C. Eric Lincoln and Lawrence H. Mamiya have constructed what they term the "dialectical model" of the black church. According to them, the dialectic holds polar opposites in tension, constantly shifting between the polarities in historical time.[18] Their model, a revision and expansion of the Nelson and Hart model, consists of six main pairs: *(1) The dialectic be-tween priestly and prophetic functions.* Priestly functions involve activities concerned with worship and maintaining the spiritual lives of members. Prophetic functions refer to involvement in political concerns and activi-ties in the wider community; *(2) The dialectic between other-worldly and this-worldly.* Other-worldly means being concerned only with heaven and

16. Morris, *The Origins of the Civil Rights Movement*, 5.
17. Cone, *Speaking Truth*, 112.
18. Mamiya and Lincoln, *The Black Church in the African American Experience*, 15.

the world beyond. This-worldly refers to involvement in the affairs of this world, especially politics and social life; *(3) The dialectic between universalism and particularism.* This refers to the tension between the universalism of the Christian message and the particularism of the black churches' history. As institutions they emerged out of the racism of white Christianity and the larger society; *(4) The dialectic between the communal and the privatistic.* The communal orientation refers to the historic tradition of black churches being involved in all aspects of the lives of their members. The privatistic pole means a withdrawal from the concerns of the larger community to a focus on meeting the religious needs of adherents; *(5) The dialectic between charismatic and bureaucratic.* Black churches tend to lean toward the charismatic pole when compared to white mainstream churches, which tend to have more bureaucratic forms; *(6) The dialectic between resistance and accommodation.* The pole of accommodation means to be influenced by the larger society and to take part in aspects of it. The pole of resistance means to struggle against the forces and pressures of the American mainstream.[19] Some Black churches will be closer to one of these poles, some to the other. Lincoln and Mamiya maintain that the dialectical model of the black church is helpful in explaining the pluralism and the plurality of views that exist in Black churches and Black communities.

This empirical study demonstrated that the Black church is an extremely complicated cultural, sociological, and theological institution. This complexity is exacerbated by the fact that the Black church at large is also multi-denominational and socially diverse. It is constituted by seven major denominations, which include 80–85 percent of all Blacks who profess to be Christians.[20] Moreover, as I found in an earlier study, it remains overwhelmingly Baptist, African Methodist, and Church of God in Christ. This examination, which can be found in my first book *Black Ministers and Laity in the Urban Church*, came to the same conclusion. This dialectical reality is endemic to the black church. The polarities, while not absolute, do offer real insight into the organic nature of the church. For example, the research conducted for this study shows that a small percentage of respondents felt that preaching was mainly entertainment, while others felt it to be teaching on a biblical text. In the local church, there are also persons within a single congregation who subscribe to both of these beliefs. However, the practice of ministry in the local church is often an

19. Ibid., 1, 12–14.
20. Ibid., 1, 411.

effort to synthesize these polarities in order to keep the inherent tension from becoming so implosive that the church will end up a mangled and fragmented entity.

The fact that the Black church continues to be overwhelmingly middle class and female is consistent with previous research and suggests that women ought to play a more prominent role in the leadership and ministry of the church. While women remain on the fringe of leadership in the black church, there is a growing recognition among some pastors and laity that there is an inherent bias and unfairness, if not blatant injustice, perpetrated against women. The Black church remains a very male-dominated institution, although males constitute only about one-third of its membership. My discussion of patriarchy and identity in Black church culture appears in the book *Walk Together Children*, edited by Dwight Hopkins and Linda Thomas.[21]

The dialectic that exists within the Black church as an institution also exists in a more microcosmic form, i.e., in individuals and groups within the church. As a participant observer, actively involved in the practice of ministry, I have gained insights that are virtually impossible to achieve through any other research methodology. This means that my observational activities are quite unobtrusive but never really concealed, because people in the church are aware of the minister's presence no matter how well he or she becomes integrated into the group.

In observing individuals and groups, I have seen the tension between good and evil, love and hate, justice and injustice, caring and indifference manifested in the local church, small church groups, and individual behavior. This is similar to the dialectic I talk about in later chapters on *Huckleberry Finn*. For example, this dialectic is represented by Sarah, a church member who sits near the front of the church and every Sunday shouts vigorously when the choir sings. However, if the pastor asserts a perspective on an issue that she and others do not agree with, the shouting ceases, and Sarah suddenly becomes overcome with a spirit of resistant quietude. Moreover, I have observed other persons display the same emotive disposition during the worship service, and as soon as the church service is over, some initiate an argument, use profanity, and literally get into a fistfight with other church members. The aforesaid examples are indicative of the dialectical ways of church folk and not necessarily representative of a pattern of behavior.

21. See Harris, "Patriarchy in the Black Church."

IN THEIR OWN WORDS: VOICES FROM THE
UNDERSIDE OF RELIGION & CULTURE

The Black church helps to form the social world of its participants. In activities and worship, persons come together to relate, reflect, and review each others' behaviors and practices. In ministry meetings, worship services, church school classes, fellowship dinners, and choir rehearsals, people struggle to understand themselves and their cohorts. They try to be themselves, to free themselves from oppression and injustice, from guilt and pain, from fear and doubt. The ways of church folk is about the culture of a people, their beliefs, feelings, gestures, expressions, their use and understanding of language, and theology as praxis. Because I am interested in the everyday, ordinary church person—the person who has no specific leadership position in church or society, no necessary reason to be in church other than a genuine faith and commitment to God—I will offer the reader the heartfelt and genuine, almost verbatim and unfiltered feelings, expressions and beliefs of representative church folk.

In this section, the reader will hear the voices of particular church members, mainly women whose beliefs and practices constitute, to a large degree, their culture, their ways. Participants in a patriarchal church and culture, these women were asked to speak for themselves. This type of ethnomethodology allows the voices of those speaking to be heard as directly as possible. Accordingly, I have sought not to distort the language of the respondents and have left their words intact as much as possible. Transcribing their words into print, unfortunately, diminishes their impact to some degree.

However, I have tried to reproduce the spontaneity of speech, the call and response of other listeners, and the laughter and unsolicited interruptions of other interviewees. Ethnography seeks to capture the dialogue between the interviewer and the respondent and to learn from those doing the talking.[22] For example, by listening to folk in the local church, I have learned a great deal more than the theory in books and articles could ever teach. For example, I remember when I first began to serve as pastor, I learned about Christian ethics and theology from the everyday practicing Christians in the local church community. Many of them were marvelous examples of love, truth, fairness, and justice. They displayed attitudes that showed respect and family solidarity, compassion and kindness, Christian loyalty, and devout spiritual living. I will forever remember how church

22. Isasi-Diaz, *En la Lucha*.

officers took me under their wings and nurtured my undeveloped and embryonic theology and spirituality. This helped my self-understanding and enabled me in time to minister to them. In the words of ordinary church folk, I hear and feel the pain and agony, the strength and stamina, the doubt and convictions of those whose lives are a constant struggle to negotiate between good and evil, joy and sorrow. The dialectics come through in the voices that are heard—voices that speak of commitment to Jesus Christ, church, and community on the one hand, and fear, anger, and frustration on the other. These voices have seldom, if ever, been heard because the world of professional theologians, philosophers, and pastors is often outside their purview. I have no doubt that church people talk to each other, but this talk is usually among themselves, largely ignored by preachers and theologians. Some of the voices of church folk are heard only by the pastor and even then they disguise their true feelings and personalities. They are the voices from below, from the underside of culture. Voices from the margins. These are the people whom I love because they have done so much to make me a pastor and minister. They are the ones who come to church on Sundays and Wednesdays to pray and sing while I preach from the Scripture text, weaving their context into the sermonic event—an event characterized by the dialectic embedded in the life of the church and in their personal lives. Their lives are filled with binary oppositions that are sometimes so glaring and so deep that the sermon only touches the surface of providing healing. And, whatever little help the sermon does provide, it must be driven by love for the people. The song writer expresses my sentiment as a preacher in the Black church: "I got nothing but Love for the people."

First, I describe the participants in psychological, social, and theological terms and then provide their responses to questions designed to garner insight into the praxeological nature of Christianity.

- Hilda is an only child, sheltered and protected by her parents. She is a schoolteacher who participates in various church activities. She also likes social activities and is struggling to exert her independence. She lives in a working-class neighborhood and is extremely articulate and has grown up in the church. Hilda likes herself but displays unnecessary doubt about her abilities. She wants her parents to be proud of her and shows a cautious attitude toward new people and new ideas.

- Louise is a retired factory worker. She is an active leader and supporter of the church's ministry and is very much interested in social activities. She can be very overbearing and presumptuous at times. Although status may be one of her strongest yearnings, she seems to be very concerned about helping others.

- Sandra is a seemingly shy young lady who exerts an enormous amount of time, energy, and money trying to keep up with the latest fashions, clothing, hairstyles, and shoes. On the surface, she seems rather materialistic and naïve, but her life experiences continue to force her in the opposite direction. She desires step-by-step guidance to assure her that she is doing what is expected of her. She respects persons in leadership roles and is eager to learn from and please others. She lost her father at an early age.

- Denise is very articulate and expresses her views with candor and unending confidence. She is extremely decisive about what she wants; however, she is overly cautious or skeptical in some of her opinions. Nevertheless, she sees life as a challenge, a continuous cycle of wins and losses. She seems to have a strong and rapidly developing view of ministry in the local church.

- Bonnie is a mother of two who usually keeps quiet until something said or done cuts to the core of her being. She speaks softly but candidly and forthrightly: she shares her beliefs with conviction. She is a compassionate person. However, this compassion is often obscured by her strong beliefs and opinions, which tend to alienate and frustrate others.

- Wilma is a young widow who has been active in the church all her life. She is well educated and articulate, and has a tendency to speak her mind. She grew up in the inner city and now devotes her time to caring for the sick. She is about forty years old and sings in the church choir and works with several church organizations. She is a very caring and progressive-minded person.

- Gloria is a very self-assured, assertive, and almost overbearing woman who is devoted to God and the church. She is a wife and mother who works hard to teach her children to be responsible leaders and thinkers. She seems to be very serious about making an impact on the community and the church.

- Carolyn is a hard-working businesswoman who has a great deal of nervous energy. She is very interested in the work of ministry and tries to encourage and support her children. Her interest in personal spirituality, prayer services, and other religious activities is evident. She is very devoted to her family and cares for others with extraordinary devotion.

- William is a very studious gentleman in his early fifties. He loves to teach church school, participate in community outreach, and do whatever he can to promote the church's ministry goals. He is a strong family man who reaches out to do whatever he can to develop and sustain positive self-esteem in young people.

- Camelia is the mother of five and has been divorced for nearly twenty years. She is a teacher in church and works very hard with children and youth. She often expresses concern for black males and the problems that they face. She is a student of the scripture and is very committed to church life and ministry.

- Mary is a woman who is connected throughout the congregation. She has family and friends in her network. She is very faithful with the use of her networking system and can be successful at contributing either to the demise or the success of a project. She is from the "old school," wanting to keep things the way they have always been. Although she did not practice Christian discipline, she was reared in the church and has never lived outside of the city she was born in. In her younger years, she was extremely active in the church while maintaining her worldly ways. Though she does not have the health and strength she once enjoyed, her social relationships keep her abreast of what happens throughout the community. She doesn't seem to have a systematic way of dealing with issues because every issue is judged based on the participants. Many church folk, however, have an *ad hominem* approach to the issues of life. Mary has little formal education and tends to be suspicious of those who have formal education, often creating tension between the two groups. She willingly facilitates gossip-like conversations among the membership and throughout the Christian community.

- Jean is a mild-mannered woman who is kind and giving. She is very confident in her ability and displays courage and faithfulness. She can readily be found trying to do that which the Bible illustrates for her life. She is most capable in planning church activities. Her cooperation is such that she commits herself to each task that is assigned and works hard to accomplish it. When asked, she orchestrates many functions around the church and implements them to the best of her ability. She seems to be a model for Christian living and is a great observer of everything around her. She knows that she is not perfect, but she tries to be an example to others.

- Wanda is generally indecisive and shy, especially in a group. However, she is most exuberant when confusion is present. Confusion seems to excite her and to facilitate her ability to distort the position of people in any setting. This causes those with whom she works to really be very leery of her. She has not always been in the church, but she loves the recognition that church participation brings to her. She abuses drugs and alcohol, and she has been known to come to church intoxicated. Wanda is very concerned about the hereafter, such that her life focus seems to be more eschatological than existential, except when it comes to personals pleasure and being the life of the party.

The following are responses that stem from the questions posed to these everyday church folk shared in their own way. This is but a limited theological summary of the themes that have emerged from the very candid discussions. It is only fair to note that other themes did emanate from the discussions, but this is an attempt to summarize the prevailing thoughts particularly as they relate to preaching in the Black church.

Sunday after Sunday, we come and listen to the preacher. Most often we are encouraged to share what God has given us; every good sermon encourages Christian practitioners to share what God has endowed us with. Paul in 1 Corinthians 12:21–31 suggests a rudimentary church organization in respect to the various gifts that its members can offer the community. Indeed we are all gifted and we are all a part of the body—whether we accept the responsibility or not.

The church is the body of Christ and is made up of various parts. Every organ in the body was created for a function and that function is to serve the whole body in an excellent way. In every church, the recognition of the simple truth that in such a divinely appointed organism as the body of Christ, a variety of functions mark the beginning of vital and effective service, community empowerment, and life-changing ministry. Therefore, the strong beliefs that we harbor about the existence and infinite power of God manifest themselves in service and sacrifice to others. This leads to the following questions: *How does preaching affect your life? What is the meaning and importance of preaching to you?*

<u>*Camelia*</u>

"Well, I thank God personally for a church [uh huh], because when I was young, I could sit and listen to the preacher preach. He would say something that I would take home. I would open the Bible and read it. Like the sermon was Sunday, I went back home and read the Scripture and I knew more than what I knew before. When I come to meetings like this and hear the minister talk about whatever his subject is, whether I agree with it or not, I listen and I go home and read about whatever it was that he preached about. I'm just so much more aware of what is going on now than when I came in. Sometimes you think you understand and you do, to a degree, but when you are instructed and taught and you teach one another, you get so much more out of it. I'm thankful to be able to be here among you all and to listen and to have a group of people to share ideas and thoughts with. I'm fortunate and thankful!"

<u>*Wanda*</u>

"What shapes my Christian conduct is fear of missing the mark. Every single day; every time I say something I shouldn't—like holler at the kids or do something wrong—I say, 'Lord, if I died this minute, I'd be in trouble.' It's the fear of missing the mark that is constantly shaping my conduct."

<u>*Carolyn*</u>

"I learned early to fear God [that's right] and then I learned that the only way I could live is by faith, so my actions are strictly by faith, because I'd never know where something is coming from or what I'm gonna get tomorrow and I've learned that whatever He tells me to do, I do. Sometimes I seem to be real strange to people. I've noticed that about myself, but I can't help this, you know. I just can't help this, but I listen, just like I listen to the preacher. I look for God's approval, whether you see me doing wrong or not, God is there watching, listening . . . and that's important!"

<u>*Camelia*</u>

"I listen to God all the time. For example, today we had an unpleasant experience on my job, and I prayed and asked God to help me to be patient. I remember the other fruits of the Spirit in Galatians, but patience is what I need. One of my students had to be taken out of class by the police today because he threatened to shoot all of us. We

147

were calm and patient. The counselor and the other children were very cooperative. My responsibility was to keep the class calm and I also prayed for that student because he's already on house arrest. Today he just had a terrible day, and I asked God to help me to lead them and be a light for them because I try to please God. That was a good sermon you preached yesterday, *'How To Please God'* [uh huh]. I try to put God first, and I ask Him to help me every day. It's a song we used to sing, 'Let Jesus lead you, let Jesus lead you, let Jesus lead you all the way; He's a mighty good doctor, He's a mighty good lawyer, He's a mighty good teacher,' so I let God lead me all the way."

Jean

"Sometimes I'd rather see a sermon than to hear somebody preaching all the time. I slipped in this church to see who was preaching. I am sorry I didn't come to join the church . . . but I love you anyway."

Louise

"Well frankly, I think at times it might not be a word in the preaching. I might have heard the music and the music has uplifted me. So frankly, I don't even care what the pastor is saying because I am still thinking about that 'good number,' or maybe the lyrics of the hymn. I might have had something happen in my life and then when I hear that hymn or song, I might not hear what the pastor says that Sunday morning. I might shut him out completely. When somebody says, 'What was the subject of the sermon this morning?' or 'What did the pastor say?' Well I was back there still hearing the music."

Sandra

"I think that when someone preaches that they are giving you the Word of God and they are giving you the Word of God through the actual Scripture; it should be scripturally based. The Scripture is brought into focus through illustrations of someone else's life and how that affects you. If the sermon does those things, it is well . . . Even if I feel that what he talked about today I understand, I know and it doesn't hit me, I feel that it must be hitting somebody, right? Sometimes I need to reexamine myself by asking, 'Is he trying to talk to me?' I'm just so hardheaded that I am not listening but that's the purpose of it. The only thing about it is that everybody has a different style of preaching. It's one style that certain people like and another style that someone else likes . . . but as long as they are genuine and called, I don't care if the preacher is a hooper. I consider a hooper one who yells and 'tunes up' all the time. Others are so eloquent that you have to look up half the words they use because you really don't understand them . . . but as long as they are called by God they are fine."

Hilda

"I feel that the preacher should show that he has gotten authority from God to preach his Word. Something might be going on in society that forces him to change the Scripture or you know, just talk about a topic. The sermon was good yesterday; it was very textual and helpful. I'm going to be one of those people who will support the message. You're not going to have to worry about me . . . because it taught us something. We were given some points that we need in order to please God."

Camelia

"I think a good sermon is insightful. It causes you to pause and to think and reflect about something in your life, something that's going on. If a sermon can connect in some way you may be able to follow the whole thing through. I find myself sometimes getting stuck on one point and just meditating on that one point because that's what I needed. That's what I needed on that day because that's what I was going through. The sermon often connects with my experience or what I'm going to be facing. Sometimes it comes back to me a few days later, and I say, 'Oh, that's what that was about.' A good sermon is insightful and it does interpret the Word of God. You can sit and read the Bible, especially the King James Version, and you can go to two or three other versions to try to gain understanding, but a good sermon helps you to understand and interpret the Word, and to apply it to your own life."

Gloria

"Then too, it depends upon your feelings that particular day. Some days you feel uplifted and you want to listen. Sometimes you feel 'kind of down' and when you listen, it will lift you up. It depends upon your feelings."

William

"Sometimes we need challenges in our life too in order to hear a good word. There is a large number of people in our society who don't want to sing hymns in church anymore and who really think that church should be an extension of what's going on in secular society. That is, there is more concern about entertaining and entertainment than anything else."

Gloria

"I don't think there is nothing (sic) any better than an old-fashioned hymn. That is what I heard from the beginning and that is what I was brought up listening to."

Denise

"I believe that preaching is all those things that folk have said. Jesus is a comforter, as I say all the time. This means to me that the sermon should have some uplifting points *for me*. I can come and listen to any preacher because I like all preaching, but I strongly feel that if Jesus was a comforter then there should be some times when we are comforting people. So I believe in putting emphasis on it because most of us come to church already down, feeling bad. Something is in our lives that is bad. If it's not our personal life, it's someone in our family who is sick or somebody in the family who is not doing as well as you would like. If you are not praying for yourself you have prayers for your people. Therefore if you are not 'standing' in the prayer line for yourself then you are standing there for someone else and, at that point, I think you need something inspiring. I know there are a lot of negative things going on in the world, and we have a lot to say about the negativity, but through it all Jesus inspired us to keep on moving and keep on believing in his word. He instructed us to study more and to pray more. I think that when you hear someone who is inspiring as well as telling you about yourself, it helps me . . . although I really don't need it at this point in my life because I have already been inspired, but it helps. It does help."

So, do you think that the sermon should be based on the Bible or something else?

Mary

"I think it should be based on the Bible."

Gloria

"It has to be based on the Bible because that's what we are coming to church for."

Wilma

"It has to be based on the Word of God, but it also should give you some insight on how that Word affects you today. It's got to give you that."

Carolyn

"When you are grounded in the Word, then you realize that even though you are in this fix, God is going to see you through it. He saw this person and that person through it in the past. Even if you are on drugs, there is still hope. So I think it should be like that even though you are in a terrible predicament, you can pray on it and have faith and eventually you will see something happening. Sometimes it doesn't take as long as you think. God has never let me down."

Camelia

"We really don't come to church to be entertained. I come to hear the Word of God whether it is through music, song, preaching, or whatever. We come to hear the Word of God. There is a time and place for everything. The church is not the place for entertainment."

How do you feel about having a female as pastor?

Jean

"Would I follow a female pastor? Indeed I would, no problem."

Bonnie

"I feel that in this day and time God has to call whoever he can get. And if enough men aren't listening to him to do his will, then that's what he may need. But, I feel a man should be the head of the church, that's always been my personal opinion. God made man to lead so man should be head of the church, and man should be head of the family; that's just how I feel. But if the men give out and women give out, then He may start using horses, I don't care. The song says, 'even the rocks will cry out.'"

Denise

"Well, ministry is a very suffering type of job, so I believe that a man should do it. But I think we should support each other. We do have our ministry as we go along every day."

Sandra

"I attended this small Methodist church in North Carolina, and this lady was the guest speaker there. The pastor would not let her in the pulpit. He told her that she had to stand on the outside of the pulpit. She couldn't come in the pulpit because she was female. I felt awful; I was upset and couldn't understand why at that time, but after I thought about it and talked about it, then I could see his point. Still, I didn't like it; that's just his way of doing things and he was the pastor of the church, you know."

Louise

"But does that mean he's saying that women can't be called?"

Sandra

"That's what he was saying to me. They were just not called to preach!"

Gloria

"God calls who he wants to when he gets ready. God does exactly what God wants to do!"

Mary

"If God calls a woman, it's not for us to say that this person should not lead. This person could have a vision, 'OK, this is my call; this is where God has sent me to be,' and who are we to say a person should not be . . .'"

Wilma

"I just feel that God touches women as well as he touches men."

Denise

"He touches everybody to do something; everybody's got some work to do."

Camelia

"I know when I first got the calling to my ministry, my Father was sick and I told him of my calling and he said to me, 'you know, a lot of people in society think there are not women ministers,' so I told him in a positive way, I said 'with a lot of our black men in jail and a lot of black men don't have jobs in the city area, God has got to call somebody [uh huh] and he has called me to preach.' And I thought about what he said and I waited for a few years and then I answered my calling."

Jean

"And if the men cannot get the people to rally or come to Christ, if the men cannot get the people to change their life or something like that, maybe God has decided that now is the time for him to use women to see what they can do about winning souls to Christ. Maybe it's the time that he wants to use both, to win souls collectively, not in a disturbing manner though. I don't believe God is a forceful God. That's my opinion. I don't see him forcing you, except that one story we had, but other than that I don't see him as being forceful. I think he wants us to come together to agree on that so that when you see a woman preacher, you won't be angry or, like you said, you won't put her off the pulpit. I don't think he wants to throw that in there like that. I think it should be a smooth transition where you're accepted and you're not fighting each other, i.e., the men are not fighting the women and the women are not fighting the men. You have to realize that there's a place for both and you're going to do it together and not separately, you understand what I'm saying? You know, ministry can be done collectively. We shouldn't be cutting each other's throats. We should work this thing out together. I think that's what God wants us to do. Together we should work out our problems and differences, and that's why I don't see it as something to be forced. I don't see the women coming in real fast; it's a slow process. When you start saying I want to be a pastor; that causes concern. God's calling you slowly. When he does move us like that, I think that's better than forcing the issue.

Is there a need for the church to have forums on affirmative action, equality, and/or race relations?

Carolyn

"Well, racism is a genealogy issue . . . and you know that God has said, that if parents are sinful, then their offspring will be sinful. So when you see persons who have been practicing racism for generations, then that is a form of evil and it goes back several generations. You want to know why there is so much crime? This is the former capital of the confederacy; and there has been so much crime and injustice done for centuries, for generations, and somebody is going to need to take a stand and try to cleanse our city of its past history and deliver those evil spirits that have been passed on from generation to generation to generation. Injustice is rooted in racism. So to answer your question, yes, racism is in existence in society; it's in existence in our government, businesses, and worship today. Why is it that black folk and white folk segregate themselves on Sunday morning? You see . . . and you look at the news and see those black Jews from Ethiopia in an uproar, fighting in Jerusalem . . . and even the Israeli army could not contain them. Why? Because these Ethiopian Jews, these descendants of Moses and Abraham, donate their blood, and white Eurocentric Israelis discard the blood! You should have seen those Black Jews fighting. They looked like we did in the United States in the '50s and the '60s. That is wrong. They admitted, [last night on television] that this goes way back before the time of Christ. Racism is alive and well right now . . . you see! Now once you have been delivered from this type of thinking, this type of practice, this type of injustice, God will help you. Well, God will deliver you and you will be free of this. So through prayer and through confession and forgiveness . . . through God's forgiveness, white folk can overcome racism. They can be delivered from the oppressive evil of racism. It is possible with God's help."

Carolyn

"I say yes, it is possible with God's help, but until that time I think minorities, whoever they are—women, blacks, or a new minority— I think affirmative action is important and should stay put, because through that vehicle and through that vehicle only, we were able to advance. Before, it was only a small segment of us who were able to advance, but through affirmative action, more of us have advanced."

Wanda

"I don't know what God is calling us to do because we are finding ourselves with the help of affirmative action, being able to get a job but being miserable on the job. I don't think that the Lord wants us to be in misery either. So, through coming to him like we did years ago, and praying and asking for a way out, is what I think is necessary for us as a group of people. I'm not too much on thinking that affirmative action is the answer to black people's prayers. I'm thinking that we have to start something new among ourselves, because if you're not happy when you get the job, you're going to have to sue to stay on the job or be treated unfairly because you are not wanted in the first place. What's the use? I can't see any sense in having a job that you're not happy with.

That causes you to come home in the afternoon and be mean and ugly to your wife. The wife is fussing with her children, and everything is going on under the sun because you're not happy with what's going on at your job. Then, sometimes you try to cover it (unhappiness) up with alcoholism, drugs, or something else. I don't see the point in all that. I don't think that's what God has intended for us as a people. I think he wants us to come to him together in prayer. He is going to help us to pull ourselves up. I do believe that, like we did years ago, everybody turned to God for an answer. Then the Lord showed us something different. But if we don't ever go to him, as a group of people, how is he going to show us anything different? We keep thinking that somebody else has to give us something. So I think that we need to pray more as a group of people and look to God for our guidance and deliverance."

Mary

"I agree with that, but I want both of them in place, i.e., affirmative action and togetherness while we are praying and working."

Camelia

"I believe that if it is intended to be, then God is going to keep it in place. He will keep affirmative action in place because that is the Lord's will. He said that everybody has to ultimately come unto him. That's his will. I always say that we can go fighting or we can go in peace. You will still have to come before God. He said he is going to draw all men unto himself and that's what he meant! You know I went to a Martin Luther King program in January, and I met a seminary student who was white. I had a chance to talk to her before the program. She shared with me that her father is very prejudiced, that he does not like black people at all. She was raised that way, but she said, when she was called by God to preach, that feeling of racism and prejudice left her. She mentioned that her father had to go to the dentist and because of the snow, he had to see a black dentist. He called her and said that he had the funniest feeling because this black dentist had to look down his mouth for about two hours. She said that she doesn't feel that way since she has been called by God. I feel that prayer will help change the racial situation we face in this country."

Denise

"If I can look at it from a more secular perspective, racism in this society is so insidious that it permeates every single aspect of our society.

White folk don't even realize that they are racist. They don't even own up to it . . . to their own racism. I'm in and out of Juvenile Court, all the time. Who do you think is there? It's black folk. The poor black kids. I'm not talking about custody or child support. I'm talking about being in court for crime. You go to the jail, who is there? It's black folk. There are things that black kids do, which quite frankly, are just a part of growing up; yet, they end up with permanent criminal records. Now you have conservative and racist politicians trying to open up even the juvenile records and holding it against these kids until they are sixty years old. White folk do the same kinds of criminal things and their community protects them. They don't end up in the judicial system."

Mary

"But those are the same kinds of things that Black folks are going to have to start doing for Black people. God is calling us, and we can't necessarily look to affirmative action to do those things for us. But you are right; we need affirmative action to combat injustice and racism, which are rampant."

William

"I'm dealing with racism right now. But racism is so built into the system. It's just built in there. In terms of practical ways to try to make people sensitive to the fact that they are racist—I don't know because they don't realize it. They certainly act like they don't realize it! When you look at their lack of support for welfare, often suggesting that the whole system be thrown out without setting up any training programs. Sometimes they will give you a little bit of money supposedly to set up a program. This is really more lip service and a smoke screen, because when you look at the criteria for the program there is no way in the world for it to succeed. The program will be set up to fail from the inception! So two years down the road, when all these Black people are out on the street, they are going to be bitter, and our community cannot absorb their bitterness. Cutting out affirmative action means fewer Black people in jobs, houses, etc. I think that it is all a scheme! The big picture is ultimately genocide of Black folk."

Hilda

"A lot of folks are saying that the obsession to eliminate affirmative action is a plot to keep the money in the white community. Over a long period of time, if you keep Black people in jail, then who are the workers? We can talk about them and see what they are doing, but until we come together and realize our plight, we are not doing anything except talk about it like we have done for years. Now we have to go to the preachers, teachers, and come together in some kind of prayer forum. Like she said about the evil spirits, you have to dismiss them so you can go on with your life and work because you know they are there. Their presence is unavoidable. We can't keep on saying why are you do-ing this to us? This is like slavery. God delivered us from that through prayer and discipline. All of a sudden we were delivered. Well, not so suddenly. It took over two hundred years, but it happened."

Louise

"That works for those of us who are operating on a spiritual plane, but how do we bring the rest of us in?"

Chorus of Voices

"That is the whole thing; that's the issue!"

William

"We have to deal with an economic base. This is an economic issue and a moral issue."

Bonnie

"No, it's spiritual and economic. It's also political and social."

William

"Right now we are living in a time that is pretty much the same as it was with Moses. We have to make more bricks with less straw. Conse-quently, as we deal with this whole issue, we need to remember that the slaves had to make more bricks with less straw, and they overcame it by being obedient to God's word and by exposing the infirmities of their oppressors to God. Right now, I would say that if we had to, we could use that same idea and premise that Moses did. If they want to put more of us in jail, they need to save themselves the trouble. Give me the thirty thousand-dollar job, rather than pay me to sit behind bars. Put the thirty thousand dollars that you will pay me for being incarcerated to better use. Let me build a bridge, let me build a skyscraper, let me do the will of the Lord as I work towards doing what is right. The sad part about it is that we as a people tend to miss the mark. We need to be able to look at the pastor's vision in a serious way and rally behind that cause and deal with the issues in our community in terms of making more bricks with less straw!"

I have concluded that it is hard to get church folk to understand and accept the notion that there should be a strong relationship between being a Christian, belonging to a church, and treating others with love and respect. There seems to be a strong desire to "belong," and the church meets the need of folk to feel wanted and accepted. To the extent that persons do not listen to the church's teachings or read its literature or feel that it is a transformative institution—to that extent, it is much like any other social organization or convocation of individuals. However, for others, it is the long association with the people and the institution that makes them remain a part of the church. It is integral to their being, because there has never been a time in their lives that they were not associated with the local church. Still others speak of the church as a "change agent," i.e., a facilitator of spiritual growth, a place where redemption is facilitated and actualized. One respondent in relationship to church attendance and its impact on her life said, "I feel like I am getting more redeemed each day." This process of redemption becomes an actuality through relationships with others who are also struggling to understand the meaning of church and world.

There are mixed feelings about the importance of the local church in the lives of some folk. Some felt, quite to my surprise, that they did not have to come to church (i.e., to a house of worship) in order to grow spiritually. This is represented by the response of one woman who said, "I can have church by myself." This ascetic notion of church, divorced from the presence of other believers, represents a personal spirituality that rebuffs the organized church. Yet this introverted view of church and the practice of Christianity is not in synchrony with the New Testament view of "ekklesia," which suggests a gathering of believers—not an isolated, meditative practice of spiritual aloneness. For others, the church is a place to network, to meet friends, and to find fellowship. This is all good and in keeping with the findings of E. Franklin Frazier, Kenneth Clark, and others who have suggested that the church is very much a social organization. While this is true, it is not necessarily ideal. The tension between the real church, which is often laden with problems of faithlessness, cynicism, doubt, egoism, and fear, and the ideal church, where persons are bold and faithful, is difficult to reconcile, because each person represents a microcosm of the dialectic. When this dialectic microcosmic entity grows into an entire congregation, the complexity of the problems associated with the practice of ministry is almost unimaginable to the novice pastor and to the theologian. I am always learning, oftentimes more than I want to know, about the ways of Black church folk and about myself as preacher, teacher and theologian.

SERMONIC DISCOURSE: "COMMISSIONED (COMPELLED) TO PREACH THE GOSPEL"

"Yet when I preach the gospel, I cannot boast, for I am commissioned to preach. Woe is me if I do not preach the gospel" (1 Cor 9:16).

There are a lot of things that we have to pay for—almost everything I can think of carries a price tag—Nikes, Adidas, jeans and jerseys, iPods, cell phones—all entertainment; going to a show where the rappers and hip-hoppers are performing. Some of the music is nasty—the lyrics are point blank graphic—bordering on the pornographic. I'm worried because while the praise songs are being sung, some of our young people are texting and listening to the Top 10 Rap songs that they pay for in one way or another. The downloads are free, but the price is high.

H #	Title	Artist
1	"I'm On One"	D.J. Khaled *featuring* Drake, Rick Ross & Li'l Wayne
2	"My Last (Finally Famous)"	Big Sean *featuring* Chris Brown
3	"How To Love"	Li'l Wayne
4	"Super Bass"	Nicki Minaj
5	"Give Me Everything"	Pitbull *featuring* Ne Yo
6	"Look At Me Now"	Chris Brown *featuring* Li'l Wayne & Busta Rhymes
7	"Party Rock Anthem"	LMFAO
8	"Out of My Head"	Lupe Fiasco featuring Trey Songz
9	"All of the Lights"	Kayne West
10	"Roll Up"	Wiz Khalifa

This is the environment of preaching today. The sermon, the preacher in the Black church, is in competition with Rap and Hip-hop that has our youth on "Lock-down." They say "it ain't serious, it don't mean nothing"—but it does. Study after study on the impact of sexually explicit lyrics and lyrics that are about drugs and violence show that those who listen to a steady diet of sex and violence go out and imitate what they hear and see

159

on the videos. Every young person in here—male and female—can cuss like a sailor, and they know stuff about sex that would make some of the older people look like Tibetan Monks and celibate priests. These fourteen to nineteen year-olds are "off the chain," and some of it is due to social media. This is not a total indictment of the culture or the youth, and neither is it a blanket condemnation of social media—but it is a realization that the ministry and its two thousand years of tradition is under siege. The church, which used to be the chief educator of the culture, first had to yield its influence to the university in the Middle Ages, and now the media has replaced both the church and the university as the chief teacher and influencer of our youth. The media, social and otherwise, have become my chief rivals. I feel like the early Christian preacher John Chrysostom.

Since I've been pastor here for the past twenty years, desktop computers, laptops, notebooks, iPads, iPods, cell phones, facebook, texting, sexting, emailing, on-line dating, matching, friendships, and a host of other postmodern terms and phrases have become a part of the social and cultural life of our young people. And, I tell you the truth, I'm struggling against the odds, I'm swimming upstream, I'm fighting an almost losing battle by trying to correct the things that I see captivating our youth and young people. I'm troubled because everybody (youth advisors, youth ministers, choir leaders, dance instructors, teachers, and preachers alike) all think that the answer to addressing the needs of young people is to imitate them, to placate them, to accommodate them with one gimmick after another—to speak their language—broken English and all; to write like they write in their text messages and emails—all lower cases, no capitalization to start a sentence, small I's, phonic spelling, incomplete sentences, no subject/verb agreement: we *was,* I *been,* she *don't,* we *be,* and on and on. No wonder the principals and teachers in public schools have been changing the answers on the SOL tests so their schools can get a 100 percent pass rate. And, it "ain't no different" here in the Richmond area. It's no way these schools can be accredited claiming that everybody passed. When no one can write clearly or read properly. And some folk think it's cute—telling me that I shouldn't correct the youth. I'm embarrassing them in public, they chide. Well, I'm not embarrassing them; they are embarrassing themselves to me. My job is to correct. That's what the preacher is called to do. It is my duty to correct, to repair, to help, to train, to educate, to call a spade a spade, and to tell people how to act, how to dress, how to speak, how to pray, how to walk, and how to talk.

That's what Paul is up against in the Corinthian church—freely preaching the gospel, addressing those in the church who thought he should act like everybody else regarding eating meat and being paid. Paul was on to something because he didn't want anyone to deprive him of his ability to boast in the Lord. And, sometimes when folk pay your salary they think that they can control what you say—and make you walk easy around certain issues. If that be the case, then you are not compelled or commissioned to preach. You can't be a called preacher and allow yourself to be dangled and wrangled by the powers and powerbrokers in the church and society.

What does it mean for us in this particular community, at this moment in history, to be commissioned to preach the gospel?

First, the preacher is commissioned by God, not by the church, the people or the council, but by God. The decision to preach doesn't come from within but from without—not from within, but from above. Look at the text in 9:16 "yet, when I preach the gospel, I cannot boast, for I am commissioned to preach." My brothers and sisters, Paul is saying that he doesn't want to preach, but he has no say in the matter. He preaches out of necessity. Necessity has laid this compulsion to preach, this commission to preach upon him. He has to preach because God has made him a preacher. God has commissioned him, God has called him, God has told him what to do and he cannot do anything else. He is not his own. He is God's agent. God has certified him, and he is authorized to preach as God's agent. He preaches by the authority God has placed upon him. He has a duty to preach "what thus says the Lord." This means that the preacher can't be worried about being accepted by everybody—not offending anyone, not addressing the issues of today, the issues of the church—evil and ugliness in old people, young people gone wild, sex and violence, reading and writing, big words, little words, cuss words, partying, clubbing, drinking, swilling, wheeling and dealing. You name it, and if it affects Black people, church people, young people, then the preacher is compelled to address it—not boastfully but compassionately and boldly. "When I preach," Paul says to the church at Corinth—"when I preach the gospel, I cannot boast, for I am commissioned to preach" (1 Cor 9:16). And, my commission has no expiration date—unlike the notary or the magistrate, or the judge— my commission to preach the gospel does not run out—as long as God strengthens me, as long as God authorizes me, as long as God certifies me—not the church or the Baptist denomination, not the university, or the Academy of Homiletics—but God has commissioned me to perform a duty on God's behalf, and I tell you I must do it. I have no choice . . .

And, finally as a preacher, if I don't do what God has commissioned me to do then my life will be full of regret, full of deep suffering and sorrow. That's why Paul says, "Woe is me if I do not preach the gospel." It will be a terrible act of rebellion against God. That the regret would be so deep and sorrowful that he could not proceed . . . Woe is me if I don't preach. I won't be able to go on. My life will be an agonizing hell—my joy will be dried up like the brook with no water to cool my parched lips—my suffering would be unbearable if I couldn't tell folk about the love of God and the goodness of his grace and mercy. Woe is me if I could not declare the gospel. If I didn't proclaim the gospel—woe is me. I'd be pitiful. I'd be a pained, puny, pundit unable to find solace because I'd be soaked in sorrow. Church, let the preacher preach; young people, let the preacher preach. Pull up your pants, turn off your iPods, stop texting, and talking, and listen to the preacher preach.

Chapter 7

The Place and Problem of Race in Literature, Theology, and Preaching

*"I am free, praise the Lord, I'm free. No longer bound
No more chains holding me . . ."*

—Negro Spiritual

"The soul, long pent up and dwarfed, suddenly expands in new-found freedom."

—Du Bois, *The Souls of Black Folk*

Life itself is larger and more basic than any dominant religious perspective. Our place in life, however, impacts religious perception as well as socio-cultural and economic understanding. By this I mean that context, i.e., the Black church community, is a critical determinant in understanding the meaning of God, self, and other. The Christian life is as much a social construction as racial identity. This is to suggest that religious understanding and race are highly correlated: you can't talk about one without the other. In the United States, one cannot extract one's religious or Christian practice from the reality of racial identity because of the legacy of slavery and its architectonic structure as developed and constructed by the architects of the social structure.

Richard Glaubman's book *Life Is So Good* is a personal history of a Black man named George Dawson who learned to read at the old age of ninety-eight. The story begins in a Texas town in 1908 with George and his father witnessing the hanging of a seventeen-year-old Black boy named Pete for impugning the virtue of a white girl. A cardinal sin. He was wrongly and deliberately accused of rape. This is the stuff of novels such as *To Kill a Mockingbird*, where a Black man named Tom is wrongly convicted of rape. In the novel the narrator is a six-year-old white girl named Scout Finch. She lives in the Great Depression era in the fictive town of Maycomb, Alabama. Her father, Atticus, defends Tom Robinson, a Black man on trial for raping a white woman, Mayella Ewell. An all-white jury convicted him despite attorney Atticus Finch presenting compelling evidence of Tom's innocence. Tom testified that Mayella tried to seduce him and upon her father's discovery, she cried rape. Her father beat her up, thus causing the bruises on the right side of her face. Atticus proves that Tom was disabled on his left side, making it virtually impossible for him to inflict her wounds. The culpability of the father was beyond doubt. But no. Black men are guilty regardless of proof of innocence. This novel looks at an old racist trope: that a Black man with his animalistic behavior could not contain himself in the presence of a white woman. In reality there is no evidence to support this unfounded myth. However, there is evidence of an unjust justice system in which Black males are guilty until proven innocent. This is the African American's story in the United States. And that story is a part of the Christian story. To be a Black Christian in America is to be oppressed and marginalized—to see life, the church and the meaning of God from the underside of culture.

The following scene from *Life Is So Good* depicts the dialogue of a young Black man who was accused of raping a white girl in Texas during the early part of the twentieth century. His fate (the death sentence) was predetermined by his racial status as an African American:

> "It wasn't me, I didn't touch her," Pete screamed. "Lord, let me go."
>
> "Kill the nigger boy, Kill the nigger. They can't be messing with our white women. We gonna keep our women safe . . ."
> "Make that boy pay and show all the niggers that they can't get away with this . . ." "I swear to God it wasn't me. Have mercy, you've got the wrong man. I didn't touch her . . . I didn't do nothing." Pete cried in a voice that rang without hope. Desperate and

nihilistic. "Pete's neck broke instantly . . . When they did a lynching, they made us leave the body hanging to put terror in the colored folk." About six months after the lynching, Betty Jo had her baby. It was a boy, a little white boy. No one said nothing. I guess by then most folks, white folks anyway, had all forgotten. [1]

Like Tom in *To Kill a Mockingbird*, Pete was hanged for the sins of the white community. The painful memory of one Black man is the story of Blacks in America. And it's a story that we are compelled to remember until "death do us part." The "inner history" of the believer is what H. Richard Niebuhr calls, "The Story of Our Life." Likewise, the Apostle Paul in telling the story of Jesus connects his own life to the Jesus Christ story. Accordingly, I too feel that the story of Black people—chattel slaves, lynched in the American public square, traded and sold on the auction block and still able to sing the prophetic spiritual song of hope: "There Is A Bright Side Somewhere"—is the prism through which Black folk see God and humanity. Any conception of Black religion is grounded in the historical experience of race, including the use of the word "nigger" by whites as a vile racial epithet.

Narrative expressions, stories, myths, practices, and experiences constitute much of what the academic theologian George Lindbeck describes and analyzes as a cultural-linguistic approach to religion. He states that "a cultural linguistic approach is preferable to the traditional cognitivist and experiential-expressive approach, provided the aim is to give a non-theological account of the relations to religion and experience."[2] This "non-theological" approach, "shaped by ultimate theological concerns,"[3] is a viable and meaningful interpretive tool for an African American whose inner history has passed through American slavery. This is the story of Black religion in America such that any explication of its origin and post-colonial significance is highly correlated with race and slavery. This means that the Black church, in its brush harbor origins, was in some significant respects a response to White racism—a socio-structural grammar realized in the institution of slavery. Certainly, it was more than that, but in America racism loomed large in every dimension of Black culture. From the beginning, the slaves' Christianity was something more and something less than traditional Christianity, as Gayraud Wilmore asserts in his now classic book *Black Religion and Black Radicalism*.

1. Glaubman, *Life Is So Good*, 5–6.
2. Lindbeck, *The Nature of Doctrine*, 31–32.
3. Ibid.

Since the majority of Blacks in America were transported here via the transatlantic Middle Passage, the most heinous example of modernity gone awry, it seems to me to be a virtual impossibility to dissociate black religious experience from slavery, oppression, racism, and the quest for freedom.

While Lindbeck's "non-theological account" of religion is probably directed against the liberal theology of Schleiermacher, Wilhelm Hermann, Martin Kähler, Adolph von Harnack, Albert Schweitzer, Ernst Troeltsch, and others (a theology grounded in socioeconomic and cultural elitism), it is nevertheless not a godless theology. It is, however, a theology whose god is more a reflection of the theologian's hegemonic contextual and biased acculturation than anything else. I think Lindbeck's category of a cultural-linguistic approach to religion is quite theological, but the theology is not very synchronous with the hubris inherent in traditional liberal theology. At the very least he seems to be making some overtures to diversity while simultaneously holding on to the sacredness of historical doctrine, originating from the Councils of Nicaea and Chalcedon. At certain points, because of his own privileged, mainstream philosophy, Lindbeck's cultural-linguistic model pulls him back in line with the liberal theologians whom he appears to struggle against. My view of his complicity is buttressed by his own statement that:

> Nicaea and Chalcedon represent historically conditioned formulations of doctrines that are *unconditionally* and *permanently* [emphasis mine] necessary to mainstream Christian identity. Rule theory, in short, allows (though it does not require) giving these creeds the status that the major Christian traditions have attributed to them, but with the understanding that they are permanently authoritative paradigms . . .[4]

I think that even Ernst Troeltsch would find some of this problematic, and liberation theologians James Cone, Dwight Hopkins, Katie Cannon, Gayraud Wilmore, J. Deotis Roberts and other Black pastors, theologians and ethicists like myself, would suggest that it is not Nicaea and Chalcedon that are permanent and unconditional, but rather that the "liberation of the oppressed" is a *necessity* for Christian identity. In this sense, the scriptural witness in the Gospel of Luke bolsters the theology of freedom argument: "The spirit of the Lord is upon me, for he has anointed me to bring Good News to the poor. He has sent me to proclaim that captives

4. Ibid., 96.

will be released, that the blind will see, that the *oppressed will be set free,* and that the time of the Lord's favor has come." (Luke 4:18)

Lindbeck makes a more explicit gesture toward valuing those who are non-European and non-white when he ventures to assert that the condemnation of slavery by Christians has now attained quasi-doctrinal status. He writes:

> The condemnation of slavery, which now has at least informal doctrinal status in all the major Christian traditions, would seem to be an example. Christians at first shared the consensus of classical cultures that slavery was an inescapable institution (although they differed from many others in thinking of it as unnatural, a result of sin). Once historical developments taught them, however, that societies without institutionalized chattel slavery are possible, they came to think, despite the absence of scriptural commands, that the logic of the biblical story demands not only humane treatment of slaves but struggle against the institution itself. Assuming that history is sufficiently cumulative so that awareness of the possibility of slaveless societies will not disappear, the Christian obligation to oppose slavery is irreversible even though conditional.[5]

The condemnation of slavery as an example of an irreversible conditional doctrine is in itself quite scary, inasmuch as the conditionality seems to obviate the irreversible nature of the doctrine. Chattel slavery in the United States was in existence three times longer than Blacks have been free—especially if we consider the fact that "Jim Crow" laws made slavery a *de facto* reality for nearly one hundred more years following the Emancipation Proclamation signed by Abraham Lincoln. Lindbeck thinks the end of slavery is irreversible, but I think it has to be actively opposed. Consequently, I am a bit leery about Lindbeck's example, which demands skepticism if not a blatant correction.

In the next section, I explore the role of one's own story in preaching and in the understanding of Christianity. This approach is discussed by H. Richard Niebuhr in *The Meaning of Revelation,* and is employed by preachers, theologians, and ethnographers to suggest the importance of the lived experiences of ordinary church folk in the construction and practice of theology.

5. Ibid., 85–86

THE STORY OF MY LIFE AS TEXT

I was agitated by the sharpness of my own memory and the pain of my own experiences. I thought to myself: *Memory is a perpetual pursuit of content and past transgressions. An untold mystery. A scathing, hideous bringing back to life of all that was dead and buried.* It is like a resurrection of Satan—Dante's *Dite.* Like the Apostle Paul's evil, which is always raising its ugly head in the presence of the good and the beautiful. Paul says "when I try to do good evil is always at hand" (Rom 7:21). Memory is full of tears and sorrow. Sometimes, even joy unspeakable, but more often than not it is painful.

There are some experiences and words that we never forget. Michel-Rolph Trouillot's book *Silencing The Past* is an incredibly illuminating treatise on the production and content of history. His statement that "the past has no content"[6] is provocative but existentially absurd. My own past is full of content. It is what H. Richard Niebuhr called "inner history."[7] In my view there is no contentless past. A past without content is as bleak as a future without hope. It is like an ontological void. A violation of memory's power to imagine a future. It is an oxymoron because time is always constitutive of some content, i.e., memory itself is qualified as content. Allow me to speak for myself: *There are certain things that I never forget,* and these experiences are the inner history of an individual and community. They constitute the meaning of revelation and the meaning of freedom.

In other words, I'll never forget the kindness and graciousness of my parents towards relatives and friends. Our house was an open door to those in our family. People were always coming and going, talking and telling stories. My uncles and aunts were like my parents in the sense that everybody felt free to correct and encourage. My Daddy was a sage whose spirit was represented by compassion and love. My own love of reading and studying came from Daddy's devotion to reading the newspaper and the Bible. My remembrance of these experiences revealed unto me a new understanding of my own family and my concepts of community. This is one aspect of my inner history that allows me to long for the closeness of family that I feel is desperately missing in my own life and the lives of so many in our community.

6. Trouillot, *Silencing The Past,* 15.

7. Niebuhr, *The Meaning of Revelation,* 16

THIS IS MY STORY: METANARRATIVE AND INNER HISTORY AS THEOLOGICAL DISCOURSE

I am surprised. No, somewhat bitter, but not really surprised. I remember the sweltering sun shining bright in a cloudless sky on that particular Monday morning in late May. I was six years old, about to turn seven. It was the spring of 1959 on a narrow road in Southern Chesterfield County—just a half-mile from our small two-room clapboard house in Matoaca, Virginia. Across the road was a large white plantation house sitting almost a half-mile off the road, perched on a bluff, surrounded by hundreds of acres of corn, wheat, and barley. That side of the road was very pale and rich looking. You could tell by the sight of several palomino horses grazing, of irrigation waters flowing over the crop fields and the manicured lawn. The white folk driving their glistening new Pontiacs and Cadillacs. They were the Driscolls, whose houses, land and jobs represented white privilege. On the other side of the same road, the side where we lived, you could tell the difference in a moment's glance. We lived in a box; a two-room barn–like structure built by my father's own hands.

Anyway, my cousin and I were walking to the corner store during the coolest part of the scorching hot day. But, in order to get there, we had to pass through a clump of houses where several white children were playing in their yards. We were always told to stay on the public road and not to veer onto anyone's property because white folk didn't need much of an excuse to shoot and kill you, or cause some other bodily harm to a black boy, not during those days of Jim Crow. This was the year of fourteen–year-old Emmett Till's murder for saying, "Hey Baby" to a white store owner's wife in the backwater Mississippi Delta. Two white men went on trial and were acquitted by a jury of their peers in less than an hour. For much of the nation, their verdict sparked the modern civil rights movement. I remember these things because my daddy used to read the newspaper like it was the Bible, and he kept up with the evening news faithfully. Religiously. As a matter of fact, my daddy insisted that we not leave the "home place" while he was off to work. But, because boys will be boys, I was eager to join my cousin in our mile walk to Sadler's country store. It was just over the hill at the end of the road. So close to where we lived; yet, it was a whole world away. That's how blatant and blurred the racial lines were.

As soon as we reached the top of the hill we knew that we were in white folks' territory. Over the hill was dangerous for us because it marked the space between leaving the area where Blacks lived and entering into the white zone. As we passed the little cluster of houses where poor whites lived, three of these little rascals, playing in the yard, saw us walking on the main road. They moved to the edge of their property to taunt and harass us. "Niggers go home." This was my first exposure to the word *nigger*. "Niggers go home," they yelled and stuck up their middle fingers as we slowly came in full view. A double insult. With hand and mouth, racism and vulgarity spoke with a unified voice. My cousin, who was a few years older than I, whispered to me, "Just don't say a word. Ignore the little bastards, unless they come on to this road. And if they do try to hit us, then we will fight like hell. No white boy is going to get away with hitting me." My older cousin was bad. Tough. Fearless. I was naïve.

"I'll kick their ass," said my cousin in bold anger and determination. I was empowered by his blind courage. I didn't wear my feelings on my shirt sleeve, but internally I was just as angry as he. I think. Maybe, I was a bit more scared than angry. The fact is Blacks were made to stand in fear, and I was a child. The sad truth is I was too young to run up against this iron wall of American prejudice. Can you imagine this?

"Niggers, black niggers go back to Africa," they said over and over again, until we passed by and got out of their sight. We were now almost at the corner store, where Matoaca Road intersected with River Road. This was the heart of Ku Klux Klan country. I later learned that their local headquarters was just up the about a half mile down a long foot path. We had twelve empty Coca-Cola bottles to redeem for one or two cents each. This was enough for us to purchase some candy and to buy ourselves a soda. At the time, a bottled coke was six cents and most of the candy, like a "jaw bone breaker" or a "Sugar Daddy" or "lollipop," was one or two cents each. A dollar could purchase a lot back then. For a poor boy like me, a dollar might as well have been a hundred. On that day I certainly did walk a mile for a dollar, although it cost me more than it was worth.

We made our purchases and then headed back down what seemed like the long road towards home. We had almost forgotten that we again had to pass by the same little white boys until one of them yelled, "niggers, go home," and began to spit at us and throw rocks at us. All we could do was speed up and walk faster as we held onto our sodas and candy. God knows we didn't want to do anything to make us drop our goodies. These were times when blatant hatred toward Blacks was embedded everywhere in the culture. It was especially vivid in small Southern towns in Virginia, the Carolinas, Georgia, Alabama, and points south. Nowadays, racism is often more subtle and masked, but equally pandemic. It has mutated and adjusted to the new laws. The civil rights and desegregation laws. The Fair

Housing Act. The Equal Employment Act. The law has changed, but what about the heart and mind? They are not as easy to change as the law. And even that's not easy.

I got a terrible butt whipping that night because my daddy was adamant about us children staying put when he was at work. My mother told him about my little adventure of mischief and disobedience. I can hear her even today as she told Daddy, "Richard, James Henry walked to the store today. He knew he was supposed to stay in the yard, but he was hard headed." My daddy was furious and, without asking any questions, ordered me to get the "strap"—or was it a "switch"—so that I could receive my just punishment. After that awful whipping, I seldom disobeyed Mother and Daddy again. But, I could not figure out why such harsh punishment was rendered for such a small, insignificant infraction. In my eyes, the punishment far outweighed the crime. But what could I possibly know at such a young age about America's "liberty and justice for all?" About the mind of the South? If I didn't know anything else, there is one thing I did know. That was the day when I was first called a nigger.

That very day I had learned one of life's worst lessons—that Black people are hated because of the color of their skin. Nothing more. Nothing less. This, I think to myself, is not only profane, but sinful. And, my learning it so early was searing and profound. I came to self-consciousness by realizing that otherness can never be escaped because of one's Black skin. It slapped me squarely in the face that hot summer day. Equality is always suspect to me. It sounds like doublespeak. Propaganda. "It just don't seem equal if you are Black." It might eventually come to be. Still, I refuse to be too cynical or hopeless. Beautiful Black chocolate colored skin, smooth as a milkshake, and yet, so hated. For what reason? I appeal to Socrates, Plato, and Aristotle. I appeal to the daughters of Zeus. No, I state my case to Zeus himself. I appeal to YHWH. To *Elohim*. To *Adonai*. I appeal to the God of Abraham, Isaac, and Jacob: Please tell me it isn't so. It's an illusion. It's a dream. An awful dream. I ask myself, Why? What drives this insanity? What propels this irrationality by the architects of Enlightenment's rationalism and empiricism? Tell me. I ask Mark Twain and Joseph Conrad: *Why do you use the word "nigger" so much?* So *flippantly. So cavalier-like. So wrenchingly and unashamedly.* Somebody tell me. Explain it to me so that, maybe, I too can understand. Is that too much to ask for? To hope for?

In the next chapter, I will continue to show how the story of my life impacts preaching, theology, and culture by focusing on Mark Twain's use of the word "nigger" in his most acclaimed novel *Adventures of Huckleberry Finn*. But first, I share these words of freedom and inspiration.

SERMONIC DISCOURSE: "WRITE THE VISION"

"Write down the vision, make it plain" or "Write down the revelation and make it plain on tablets." —Habakkuk 2:2

For over twenty years now, I have been writing down what God has revealed to me through prayer, meditation, and study. There is a record in sermons and books; there is a record in programs and activities. God is a God of revelation—a God who discloses God's self in ways clear and unclear, seen and unseen, ways that are discernible by the Spirit. God's word doesn't say *see the vision* and yet we associate vision with seeing. We cannot deny the language, the semantics, the wording: Write. Write the vision. The textual language is not recite the vision, not memorize the vision, not explore the vision, demonstrate, orchestrate, pantomime, or mime the vision—but write the vision. Write the *apocalypsis*. Write the revelation. Write the vision. Put it on tablets, i.e., put it down on paper and make it plain.

If we consider our text to include everything that leads up to this verse, all of chapter one and the first four verses of chapter two, then we see the prophet complaining to God twice, and Yahweh twice answers. The first complaint tells of wrongs and violence, "O Lord, how long will I cry for help and you will not listen? (v. 1) "It is hard to say whether this complaint is a reference to oppression by enemies within or enemies without" (Gerhard Von Rad). But God is not impressed with the complaints. As a matter of fact, God's answer to Habakkuk's complaint is to say that things will get worse before they get better: "Look at the nations and see! Be astonished. Be astounded! . . . For I am rousing the Chaldeans [the neo Babylonians] that fierce and impetuous nation . . . Their justice and dignity proceed from themselves . . . They sweep by like the wind, they transgress and become guilty; their own right is their god" (Hab 1:5–11). God's divine words catch the prophet completely by surprise, and this leads to a further complaint: How can God allow so much evil, so much iniquity and not do anything about it? How can God not intervene on behalf of the righteous? These complaints by the prophet seem legitimate. They seem reasonable. They seem fair. It is clear that in this text one complaint begets another. But we, like the prophet, must do something other than complain. Some of us are chronic complainers—we are walking negativity, negativity on two legs, negativity on crutches, negativity on medication, negativity on life support. We are obsessed with questioning God about everything that befalls us. We pine and mope; we cry and sob; we allow our complaints to lull us into complacency so much so that we conspire with our doubts to the point of depression and disease.

When the prophet complains the second time, God says, "Write the vision." The text says, "Then the Lord answered me and said, "Write the vision; make it plain on tablets so that a runner may read it. For there is still a vision for the appointed time; it speaks of the end, and does not lie. If it seems to tarry wait for it; it will surely come, it will not delay. Look at the proud, their spirit is not right in them, but the righteous live by their faith." (Hab 2:2–4) What does it mean to write the vision? How does this text speak to us here as we embark upon an unknown year—a brand new decade?

Write the vision. Write the future. God says write the word down. Write the revelation. Write the vision, write the future because its fulfillment is a process, not a cataclysmic event. Write the vision and allow it to unfold as time passes. The Lord hears our complaints but his response to our complaints is: "Write the vision." In other words, *stop complaining and start writing.* I confess to you today that one of the easiest things in the world for us to do is to complain. We lament and cry unto God about everything wrong in our lives, in our churches, in our marriages, in our relationships, in our homes, on our jobs; you name it, and we can complain about it. But God doesn't seem to be moved by all of our self-pity and self-interest. I speak from experience because I have complained to God about every possible human concern: children, family, school, my students, the church. You name it. I have complained that it seems that the more, the harder I try to do God's will, the harder life becomes. I complain about the fact that the church doesn't seem to be growing no matter how hard we try to evangelize, to do outreach, to help the poor and feed the hungry. I complain, you complain, we complain to God year in and year out. For some, the word "complaint" is our middle name, and for others "complaint" is our maiden name. And, this time when we complain, God answers "with a word which is to be written down because it is not to be fulfilled at once: Write the vision." In other words, write the future and make it plain. Write it down so that everybody can see it. Write it down so everybody can understand it. Write it down. Write the vision and make it plain—so plain that you will not need a college degree to understand it; so plain that everybody in Second Baptist will understand it and be able to interpret it; so plain that the birds that fly over the roof of the church will be able to sing it; so plain that children and the youth will be able to read it; so plain that the men and the women, the diaconate and the choirs, the ushers and the missionaries will be able to see it, to read it, to hear it and to write it over and over again. Claim the vision!

To write the vision is an act of liberation and imagination. I say this because writing the vision means moving from the complacency of complaint to an act of planning for the future. This means that we must deliberately move from death to life. Rather than sit back and allow ourselves to be devoured by the Chaldeans or the Babylonians, or to question the power of God or God's sovereignty—rather than ask God like the prophet: why do you look on the treacherous and why are you silent when the wicked swallow those more righteous than they? Rather than continue to complain, do as God commands us: Write the vision with the understanding that this is not just an act of obedience, but it is an act of making the future happen. We can't afford to sit back and complain, but we are called to get up and do something—"For there is still a vision for the appointed time; it speaks of the end, and does not lie" (2:3).

Write the vision and wait faithfully for the revelation itself. That's what Habakkuk had to do, and that's what we have to do. The text says, "If it seems to tarry, wait for it; it will surely come, it will not delay. Look at the proud! Their spirit is not right in them, but the righteous live by their faith." (2:3–4) Living by faith is the mark of the people of God. The righteous are able to survive by remaining steadfast, reliable, unperturbed, unfazed, unwavering, faithful. Faith is the saving power of the people of God. Our faith allows us to believe that postponement of fulfillment is a part of the nature of writing the vision. Writing the vision means that it may not happen at once, but whatever happens, the righteous shall live by faith (2:1–4). Writing the vision is an act of faith. Faith and the future go hand in hand. Our future is directly tied to our faith—our ability to believe that God will not leave us or forsake us . . .

Chapter 8

The Disembodiment of Language in Literary Texts and Culture

"Death is over," he said to himself. "There is no more death."
"He drew in a breath, broke off in the middle of it, stretched himself out, and died."
—LEO TOLSTOY, *THE DEATH OF IVAN ILYICH*

"Every work of literature has both a situation and a story."
—VIVIAN GORNICK

IN MANY WAYS THE use of the word "nigger" by Mark Twain is the obviation of personhood. It is the objectification of the Black body. This means that the depersonification of the other is symbolized and actualized in Twain's disembodied language.

Twain's novel *Adventures of Huckleberry Finn* is not only about two people in search of freedom, it is also an archetypal instance of dialectical thinking and phonological discourse. More particularly, the novel represents the dialectic of good and evil, right and wrong, justice and injustice, love and hate, white and black, freedom and oppression, slave and free, consciousness and unconsciousness. The fundamental dialectic is ultimately established by the two protagonists Jim and Huck; Jim is the adult runaway slave, and Huck is the white boy running away from his abusive father. At least this is a first naïve reading of the text, which is layered and laden with symbolism that reveals the failure of the Civil War's efforts to grant Blacks equality, and white America's determination to keep the concept of "nigger" alive, not only in literature and art, but in life. The language of the novel is a part of a cruel unknowing system of oppression signified by the use of the racial epithet "nigger," which is a dominant trope in the novel—more dominant than the Mississippi river. This chapter, dominated by *Adventures of Huckleberry Finn*, is a critique of the disembodiment of language and helps to describe the multicultural situation which is quintessential to the preaching enterprise.

I will use cultural theory and criticism, postcolonial theory and criticism, anamnestic reasoning, and reader-response analysis to examine the racial epithet "nigger" by Mark Twain in his *Adventures of Huckleberry Finn*. I seek to develop the argument that the ubiquitous use of "nigger" by Twain is the basic reason why his novel has attained the status of an American classic. "Nigger" is an American invention and its use by whites is inseparable from the nature and meaning of American democracy, constitutionality, and culture. In short, white Americans' use of the word "nigger" is tantamount to describing what makes America American. I am arguing that Mark Twain knew this, and he too capitalized on it. It made him a wealthy man. This made him complicit in American racism.

Both language and "style of life" are critical components of culture, and it is my belief that the language of "nigger" is constitutive of white folk's style, which is to express their hatred and bigotry toward others, especially Blacks. The word "nigger" is a complete sentence. It seems uncontroversial to postulate that no other race in America has endured the violent and dehumanizing forces of hatred as Blacks. And for Blacks, like the Confederate flag, the word "nigger" needs no predicate to be referential.

Culture is "notoriously hard to pin down," according to cultural critic Raymond Williams. Accordingly, as another writes, "Cultural studies is composed of elements of Marxism, new historicism, feminism, gender studies, anthropology, studies of race and ethnicity, film theory, sociology, urban studies, . . . postcolonial studies: those fields that focus on social and cultural forces that either create community or cause division and alienation."[1]

---

1. Guerin, et al., *A Handbook of Critical Approaches to Literature*, 290.

The mistreatment of Blacks, embedded in the laws and customs of American democracy and in the construction of capitalist and colonialist theory and practice, helps to define and describe the nature of America. From slavery to Jim Crowism to the postmodernism of today, the word "nigger" spoken by whites has no semblance of the positive, i.e., no empathic or salvific value, but represents the meaning of the hated Other. My interest in the book is more Sausserean and Ricoeurian such that there is a dialectic between *langue et parole*, i.e., between coded language and message.

The derogatory use of the word "nigger" is engrained in the language of American history and culture, and this cannot be erased from the consciousness of Blacks. There is no positive way for whites to use the word "nigger," because the understanding of the word when used by whites is blatantly clear, i.e., independent from the one who uses it. No amount of good intentions could possibly lighten the weight of history that the word carries. It is inherently pejorative and indicative of racial hatred and bigotry. The use of the word in American culture is indicative of the everyday evil and the iniquitous behavior of whites towards Blacks during and after slavery. Mark Twain is a type of "preacher" for whom preaching is not an act of love and preaching without love is a failure of the preacher's embodiment of Christ, an I-it embodiment.

It is a part of white Christianity and culture to embed racism in their religion. The white church has historically been complicit with racism. It has been a symbol of evil especially as it related to Blacks before and during slavery and even today. It has provided the theological justification for making slaves less than human by theorizing that slavery was ordained by God. This was one of the concerns Mark Twain expressed in *Adventures of Huckleberry Finn*. For example, the feud between the Shepherdsons and the Grangerfords vis-à-vis their religiosity is indicative of Twain's view that white folks' religion was a sham, created to accommodate their cultural biases, prejudices, and hatred toward one another and the Other. Going to church was a civic duty disconnected from any ethical or Christian responsibility. Twain describes a church scene:

> Next Sunday we all went to church, about three mile, everybody a horseback. The men took their guns along, so did Buck, and kept them between their knees or stood them handy against the wall. The Shepherdsons done the same. It was pretty onery preaching—all about brotherly love and such-like tiresomeness, but everybody said it was a good sermon, and they all talked it over, going home, and had such a powerful lot to say about faith,

and good works, and free grace, and preforeordestination, and
I don't know what all, that it did seem to me to be one of the
roughest Sundays I had run across yet.[2]

While all of these folks went to church and tolerated the sermon, there was
no correlating "free grace"[3] with the freedom of Blacks. Going to church
and the use of "nigger" are both as American as apple pie. In the same
chapter, Huck describes the false aristocracy of the Grangerfords by saying, "Each person had their own nigger to wait on them—Buck, too. My
nigger had a monstrous easy time, because I warn't used to having anybody do anything for me, but Buck's was on the jump most of the time."[4]
Twain demonstrates how the word "nigger" was engrained in the language
of white American culture such that the presumption of white supremacy
is clearly correlative to the language of nigger.

Black religion and the religion of whites are quite different today
and were different during slavery. For whites, religion and church were
designed and practiced in a way that served their racial and cultural biases—biases represented by coloniality or colonization, i.e., dominance of
the Other. Religion was grounded in the ontological and anthropological
negation of others, particularly Black slaves. This is why whites saw no
disconnection between their practice of slavery, economic exploitation
of the slave "nigger," and their faith in God. Black folk saw God as the
opposite of how whites constructed God. God is simply a philosophical
construct created to accommodate Kant's religion of reason and rationality. Black religion has always been something more and something less
than what whites constructed as religion.[5] So for Blacks, religion is more
than rationality. It is a memory of past transgressions by the architects of
modernity. It is spiritual, social, emotional, and quite holistic such that it
speaks to the totality of one's existence, which includes the past, present,
and the transcendent.

2. Twain, *Adventures of Huckleberry Finn*, 147.

3. Ibid, 143.

4. Ibid.

5. Wilmore, *Black Religion and Black Radicalism*.

THE LITERARY TEXT: THE SURPLUS OF MEANING AND MESSAGE IN ADVENTURES OF HUCKLEBERRY FINN

It is the ubiquitous use of the vile and white supremacist racial epithet "nigger" that makes Mark Twain's novel *Adventures of Huckleberry Finn* an American classic. It started out as the "veriest trash" for whites and now it is almost universally acclaimed as an American classic. The word "nigger" is derogatory towards Blacks, and Twain did not use the word to describe anyone else in the book except Blacks. Its use is fundamentally and ultimately racial. But this is not what white society objected to. It was the satirizing of white religion, aristocracy, etc. that caused a stir. In March 1885, the *Boston Evening Transcript* newspaper reported that *Huckleberry Finn* was excluded from the library by the Concord (Massachusetts) Public Library committee. The committee pondered its immorality, humor, coarseness, and inelegance. One member of the committee regarded the book as "veriest trash."[6] Likewise, the Springfield *Republican*, in March 1885, responded in agreement with the Concord Public Library's banning of *Huckleberry Finn*, calling it "trashy and vicious."[7]

Also in a letter to the *Omaha World-Herald*, August 23, 1902, a citizen wrote that Huck Finn's new adventure "is doing much harm. It has started a number of hitherto spotless people to reading 'Huck Finn,' out of natural human curiosity to learn what this is all about—people who had not heard of him before, people whose morals will go rack and ruin now."[8] I believe this suggests that for whites the novel is trash because of their objection to how they were being portrayed by Twain—murderers, liars, racists, duplicitous religious hypocrites, and the like. It exposed their inner feelings by one of their own. However, to Blacks like John Wallace, the NAACP and the Urban League, the chief objection was to the ubiquitous use of the racial epithet "nigger," and to the audibilization of the word in mixed race public school classrooms where the opportunity for miseducation and misinterpretation is as prevalent as the opportunity to advance the educational process.

Twain's use of "nigger" seems to flow from his pen with a frequency unsurpassed by any other adjective or noun in the text. Because the word was so embedded in the psyche of America it seems to move beyond irony

---

6. Champion, *The Critical Response to Mark Twain's Huckleberry Finn*, 13–14.

7. Ibid.

8. *Omaha World-Herald*, August 23, 1902

to the level of commonality, which suggests that Twain, like his readers, used the word without forethought. More precisely, "without forethought" as I am using it here means that Twain's use of the word *nigger* so often suggests to me a natural use—one that is so much a part of one's being that he does not have to think twice about its use. The idea that the slave Jim, a thirty-something Black man with a family, is considered inferior to Huck, a thirteen or fourteen-year-old white boy of questionable moral character and low social class, was engrained into Huck, and for that matter Jim's cultural self-perception. Unfortunately, the colonized too often take on the attributes and character that the colonizer ascribes to him. Frantz Fanon is correct when he says that "it is the racist who creates the inferiorized."[9]

American chattel slavery was the most dehumanizing form of colonization practiced during the modern era. It was grounded in economic exploitation and the belief that Blacks were inhuman. It was a project of creating the hated Other, grounded in redefining the nature of being and non-being. Blacks' lack of human status was constitutionalized by the Dred Scott decision of 1857, and before that in the three-fifths clause. It was easy for Twain and Huckleberry Finn to model the current cultural practices of white American racism. Fanon says, "Once and for all I will state this principle. A given society is racist or it is not."[10]

DIALECTIC BETWEEN GOOD AND EVIL

Because *Adventures of Huckleberry Finn* is set in a racist topographic location during a time when colonialist ideology was entrenched in the structure of American democracy, the word *nigger* could be used with ease. The casual use of the racial epithet leads me to think that both Twain and his protagonist, Huck, were as racist as the next white person. They were products of colonialism and endowed with a type of superiority that accompanied their white racial status. This does not mean that Twain was necessarily unsympathetic toward the cause of Black freedom, nor does it mean that Twain was not troubled or torn by his white racist tendencies. However, it does mean that he could not totally extricate himself from the colonialist culture from which he was a beneficiary. This inability to extricate himself from the desires and needs of his society keep him writing "nigger" on nearly every other page of his *Adventures of Huckleberry*

9. Fanon, *Black Skin, White Masks*, 73.
10. Ibid.

Finn. Twain's own being was caught up in the dialectic of good and evil, right and wrong, cultural critic and beneficiary of colonialist and capitalistic practices. I think that he was ambivalent toward Blacks and whites. Twain had to keep one foot in both worlds. This put him in a position of betweeness, caught in the middle. This dilemma accounts for Huck's use of the racial epithet "nigger," his apparent love of Jim, and yet his acts of evil against Jim, evidenced by his not so compassionate tricks. William Desmond explains this philosophical construct:

> If univocity stresses sameness, equivocity difference, dialectic the appropriation of difference within a mediated sameness, the metaxological reiterates, first a sense of otherness not to be included in dialectical self-mediation, second a sense of togetherness not reached by the equivocal, third a sense of rich ontological integrity not answered for by the univocal, and fourth a rich sense of ontological ambiguity not answered for either by the univocal, equivocal, the dialectical.[11]

Clearly, I think that Twain expresses this ambiguity through his protagonist Huck, who vacillates between truth and lie, good and bad, serious friend and youthful prankster. This is particularly evident in the relationship between Huck and Jim. In an example, when Huck is thinking about telling on Jim, Twain writes that Huck says:

> I was paddling off, all in a sweat to tell on him; but when he says this it seemed to kind of take the tuck all out of me. I went along slow, then I warn't right down certain whether I was glad I started or whether I warn't. When I was fifty yards off, Jim says: Dah you goes, de ole true Huck; de on'y white genlman dat ever kep' his promise to ole Jim. Well, I just felt sick . . .[12]

And, later in the same chapter, Huck continues expressing his feeling:

> They went off, and I got aboard the raft, feeling bad and low, because I knowed very well I had done wrong, and I see it wasn't no use for me to try to learn to do right; . . Then I thought a minute, and says to myself, hold on, s'pose you'd a done right and give Jim up; would you felt better that what you do now? No, say I, I'd feel bad—I'd feel just the same way I do now . . . I was stuck.[13]

11. Desmond, *Being and the Between*, 379.
12. Twain, *Adventures of Huckleberry Finn*, 92.
13. Ibid.

This being "stuck" is indicative of the similar position that Twain found himself in—stuck in a culture and society grounded in colonialist ideology and practice, and his belief that there was something "awful" wrong with this culture. This notion of being stuck in the between suggests that one is in a perpetual ethical dilemma that impinges on the self with a tension and pressure that makes one feel "awful" bad at times.

Laurie Champion in her book, *The Critical Response to Mark Twain's Huckleberry Finn*, describes Ted Koppel's ABC News Nightline segment, "*Huckleberry Finn*: Literature or Racist Trash?" on the one hundredth anniversary of the novel. The news analysts are Ted Koppel, host, and Jeff Greenfield, ABC Correspondent. Koppel sets the tenor of the conversation by acknowledging that the novel is an American classic and has been historically regarded as a classic work of literature by some, and as racist trash by others. The declaration by Ernest Hemingway that "all modern American literature comes from one book by Mark Twain called *Huckleberry Finn*" is not the issue. The issue or the question according to Koppel "ought to be whether the pain it causes to some children and their families provides sufficient reason to remove it from our schools and perhaps even from our libraries."[14] Ernest Hemingway has declared that *Huck Finn* is the classic from which all American literature flows. I feel that it is a classic because it speaks the language of racism symbolized by the over use of "nigger." However, this declaration by Hemingway and others also makes it difficult for Blacks and whites to attack the novel because its now classic status tends to blind people to its shortcomings.

Dr. John Wallace, a Chicago educator, has led the public crusade against the use of the book, arguing that the frequent references to "nigger" and Twain's use of rural Black dialect is demeaning and insulting to Blacks.[15]

Lenny Kleinfield, a drama critic, and Jack Saltzman, an American literature professor, both defend the book. Kleinfield argues that Mark Twain is using irony to expose how the minds of white people have been poisoned towards Blacks. Saltzman, however, is more direct. He says, "The problem erupts because readers fail to understand why a writer would use a term like 'nigger Jim' to expose racism." Saltzman locates the problem in the hermeneutical failure of the reader rather than in the failure of the writer or the text itself. Meshach Taylor, the actor playing the role of the slave Jim in the dramatic version of *Huckleberry Finn* at the Goodman

14. Koppel, ABC News *Nightline*. (Date unknown.)
15. Champion, *Critical Response*, 147.

Theater in Chicago, read the book and felt that it was "one of the best indictments against racism . . . I had ever read."[16] On the other hand, John Wallace says that "the book is certainly the most racist book, among many, that is printed in the United States of America."[17] Wallace argues that the book's use of the word *nigger* disqualifies it as a source to be used in the public schools. He repeatedly labels it "racist trash." Ted Koppel questions the necessity of banning the entire book, but says, "If I had a child in a school, and I was black and the child was required to read from that book and repeat the word 'nigger' several times, I can see how that would be painful, how that would be offensive."[18] Nat Hentoff, a novelist and syndicated columnist, joins the panel and essentially suggests that the use of the novel in junior high and high school is okay because it demystifies language by its use of the term *nigger*. Moreover, he indicates that John Wallace unwittingly underestimates the intelligence and learning ability of Black kids by trying to ban the teaching of the book. All parties agreed that every English literature teacher is not qualified to teach such a novel to youth.[19]

The Otherness of Black Religion, Race and Culture

James Baldwin in *The Fire Next Time* offers poignant advice to his young nephew and all African Americans when he states that "You can only be destroyed by believing that you really are what the white world calls a *nigger*. I tell you this because I love you, and please don't you ever forget it."[20]

Postcolonialism is a sub-category of cultural studies which is the broad hermeneutical approach to analyzing texts from a perspective outside the dominant white Anglo-Saxon culture. The truth is that colonialism is not over yet. As long as there is domination and imperialistic actions, colonialism still pervades the mind, heart and soul of some nations, e.g., the United States and Great Britain. Cultural studies then is constituted by the "Others" who are not white Europeans or white Americans. Persons who have given voice to the field are writers and thinkers such as Frantz Fanon, Gayatri Spivak, Edward Said, Alice Walker, Henry Louis Gates, and Toni Morrison, to name a few. Cultural studies have three

16. Ibid., 148.
17. Ibid., 149.
18. Ibid., 150.
19. Ibid., 152–54.
20. Baldwin, *The Fire Next Time*, 18.

main approaches to literary theory: postcolonialism, African American criticism, and gender studies.[21] These subaltern writers, critics and thinkers "provide new ways to see and understand the cultural forces at work in society, in literature, and in ourselves."[22]These writers were labeled subaltern by the Marxist critic Antonio Gramsci, mainly because of their subordinate status in a culture dominated by whites "who have historically sought to relegate the views of others to subservient status."[23]

In short, the subaltern peoples are the oppressed, the marginalized; those who have been violated geographically, politically, economically, socially, and often physically and mentally. The cultural hegemony of whites is the foundation of universalism—a universalism grounded in Eurocentrism or patriarchy. Moreover, a central issue for postcolonial theorists and critics is to attack and deconstruct nationalism and provincialism that masquerades inevitably as universalism.

The privileging of Eurocentric ideology and according it normative status is constitutive of colonialism's intent to dominate and subordinate other peoples and cultures. K. M. Newton states several facets of postcolonial criticism. He says, "Postcolonial critics and theorists attack the explicit or implicit claims made for Eurocentric art and literature as having universal application, thus relegating non-Western cultural forms to the margins."[24] The marginalization of everything non-Western constitutes the vertical nature of the problem and becomes the foundation for the justification of violence and pathological hatred of the Other. Moreover, the delusion of superiority on the part of the colonialists (the desire for every culture to make an axis through the West) metonymically and metaphorically constitutes the essence of the colonialist mentality. This tendency of colonialists to denigrate other cultures and to morph their own into something described as "universal" is the very practice that postcolonialist theorists seek to interpret, critique, and deconstruct: "Cultural difference is therefore a central preoccupation of post-colonial critics and theorists."[25] They feel an obligation to attack Eurocentrism and the practices of cultural imperialism propagated by Western theology, literature and art—all represented in this section by words Mark Twain places in the mouths of his characters, especially Huck, and by the minstrelsy and

21. Bressler, *Literary Criticism*, 199.

22. Ibid.

23. Ibid.

24. Newton, *Twentieth Century Literary Theory*, 283.

25. Ibid.

stereotypical depiction of Blacks by Twain's illustrator, E. W. Kemble. There is a persistent racial and cultural hierarchization that permeates the written and visual texts of *Adventures of Huckleberry Finn*.

There can be no discussion of postcolonialism without looking to Edward Said's book *Orientalism*, which explains Europe's deeply ingrained practice of othering—especially the doctrine of ruling over Orientals. The Orient is a place, the Far East mainly, but Orientalism is also a constructed philosophy—a practice of subordinating, defining, knowing, and dominating those in the Orient. Professor Said says that Orientalism has many facets, but more particularly, it is "a style of thought based upon an ontological and epistemological distinction made between 'the Orient' and (most of the time) 'the Occident.' "[26] This ontological distinction, in effect, says that Europeans have made themselves into superior beings who see their teleological goal as domination and oppression of the oriental (Other) because of their knowledge of him. The Europeans claim to know the Other—the Egyptian (African), the Indian, the Chinese, the Japanese. This knowledge then presumes conquest and superiority. Said cites a speech that British imperialist Arthur James Balfour gave in June 1910 to the British House of Commons where he spoke with authority about Europe's knowledge of Egypt, saying: "We know the civilization of Egypt better than we know the civilization of any other country. We know it further back; we know it more intimately. We know more about it."[27]

This epistemological arrogance suggests that knowledge of the other is power, and it necessarily justifies supremacy and domination. Said further explains:

> To have such knowledge of such a thing is to dominate it, to have authority over it. And authority here means for "us" to deny autonomy to "it"—the Oriental country—since we know it and it exists, in a sense, as we know it. British knowledge of Egypt is Egypt for Balfour, and the burdens of knowledge make such questions as inferiority and superiority seem petty ones. Balfour nowhere denies British superiority and Egyptian inferiority; he takes them for granted as he describes the consequences of knowledge.[28]

The dialectic between ontology and epistemology is nowhere more evident than between colonizer and colonized, and while this is clear when

26. Said, *Orientalism*, 2.
27. Ibid.
28. Ibid., 52.

viewing the relationship between the British and the Orient (or the Occident and the Orient) it is not as blatant or as clear as the American form of
colonization represented by American slavery and the "deontologizing" of
African Americans as chattel slaves.[29] This "taking for granted" is exactly
the way Twain uses the word *nigger* in *Huck Finn*.

He normalizes the term in a way that takes for granted the fact that
Blacks are all "niggers" inferior to whites in every conceivable way. Twain
uses "nigger" in the mouths of his characters in a way that reflects American racism and culture, a culture that he was an integral part of such that
it was his major benefactor, and the members of this cultural society made
him a wealthy man because he so effectively used their language of racial
supremacy typified by the use of one word: *nigger*. The Americans inherited this attitude and posture from their forebears, the British. I shall say
more about this later. But, for now, the British seem to believe that their
knowledge of the Egyptian is constitutive of who they are, i.e., the colonizers' very being is predicated upon their knowledge of oriental history and
culture. This ability to speak for the Other, as if the Other has no voice
or no thought, is the essence of colonialization. By elevating this sense of
self and superiority, the colonizer stamps out the very being of the Other,
especially as a *human being*. Thus colonization is a form of ontological negation. These European masters of epistemology and ontology used their
knowledge to oppress the others.

The psychology of the colonizer is such that it rationalizes its domination and oppression as a duty, a form of "help or assistance" to the lower
being, who in actuality is the non-white (Anglo-Saxon), non-European.
Said quotes Balfour once again showing the depth and scope of the colonizers' pathological practices of domination:

> If it is our business to govern, with or without gratitude, with
> or without the real genuine memory of all the loss of which we
> have relieved the population [Balfour by no means implies, as
> part of that loss, the loss or at least the indefinite postponement
> of Egyptian independence] and no vivid imagination of all the
> benefits which we have given to them; if that is our duty, how
> is it to be performed? England exports our very best to these
> countries.[30]

29. What I mean by "deontologizing" is the negation of the Black self or the ontic
denial of Black humanity. I use the term to mean dehumanize. I do not use the term
here to mean the theory or study of moral obligation, which is the denotative meaning
of deontology.

30. Said, *Orientalism*, 33.

The arrogance and the logic are astounding. They are the gods of the universe—the rulers of the world. It is their duty (Kant) to speak for themselves and everyone else—the West and the entire civilized world. For the colonizers, Egypt, Africa, India, etc. are "a subject race, dominated by a race that knows them and what is good for them better than they could possibly know themselves. Their great moments were in the past; they are useful . . . only because the powerful and up-to-date empires have effectively brought them out of the wretchedness of their decline and turned them into rehabilitated residents of productive colonies."[31]

The European colonialists had a dyadic view of life and the world. They made everyone outside of the West essentially uncivilized and unimportant as human beings: "There are Westerners, and there are Orientals. The former dominate; the latter must be dominated, which usually means having their land occupied, their internal affairs rigidly controlled, their blood and treasure put at the disposal of one or another Western power."[32] This mentality was so extensive in scope that it encompassed almost the entire world during the period of European expansion. During a one hundred year period "from 1815 to 1914 European direct colonial dominion expanded from about 35 percent of the earth's surface to about 85 percent of it. Every continent was affected, none more than Africa and Asia."[33]

Postcolonialism, as described by French philosopher and postmodernist theorist Jean-Francois Lyotard, is a remembering and recovering the meanings of past life situations. The postcolonial critic Homi Bhabha says that "Memory is the necessary and sometimes hazardous bridge between colonialism and the question of cultural identity. Remembering . . . 'is never a quiet act of introspection or retrospection. It is a painful re-membering, a putting together of the dismembered past to make sense of the trauma of the present.' "[34] This is why the terroristic nature of America's past should never be forgotten, particularly as it relates to the vile and dehumanizing treatment of Native Americans and African Americans. And, it is the Black preachers' responsibility to liberate the oppressed by interpreting scriptural texts and cultural texts in a way that will foster understanding of the inner history of a people—their persistent pain, struggles and fears in speaking truth to power. The voyage to America, the Middle Passage, the haunting journey to hell was itself traumatic,

31. Ibid., 35.
32. Ibid., 36.
33. Ibid.
34. Gandhi, *Postcolonial Theory*, 9.

and then to be auctioned to the duplicitous defenders of individual liberty and justice for all, must forever be made to loom large in the consciousness of Black Americans. Unlike George Washington, for example, it is generally believed that Thomas Jefferson traded his slaves.[35] This made him a much more callous and vulgar capitalist than those slave owners who theoretically and practically sought to be more humane in a very inhumane culture of slavocracy. The language of slavery and humaneness is a true oxymoron. The history of slavery is present in those who continue to oppress the poor and discriminate against people of color. And, it is present in the memories and the painful reality of those African Americans who are able to sense injustice intuitively and even today can still feel the pain of the lynchings and the lashings of those Black slave brothers and sisters, who were caught trying to escape to freedom.

I partially reject the argument advanced by two of the leading postcolonialist therorists, Albert Memmi and Leela Gandhi, that there is complicity on the part of the colonized in their colonization.[36] This is too much like blaming the victim. Unless the colonizer is himself colonized, he will find someone to victimize. This, in my view, does not mean complicity between the two, but there is a "strange and relentless reciprocity" between the two as seen in the relationship between Huckleberry Finn and "Miss Watson's nigger Jim,"[37] and in the fact that the colonized generally outnumbered the colonizers. There is indeed a perverse and inexplicable relationship between the oppressed and the oppressor. This is related to the concept of desire. The oppressed are almost always seeking acceptance by the oppressors, or if not acceptance then some strange form of validation. This desire to be associated with the oppressor permeates American culture—business, education, theology, etc. Now, this has some logic to it because our society is still controlled by colonialists who themselves seek to maintain some continuity between the past and the present. This simple fact seems to corroborate Jean Paul Sartre's and Albert Memmi's view of the "mutuality" that exists between the colonizer and the colonized. I agree

---

35. Terry Oggel. Lecture, "Major Works Seminar on Mark Twain's *Adventures of Huckleberry Finn*," Virginia Commonwealth University, Spring, 2006.

36. Gandhi, *Postcolonial Theory*, 12–14ff.

37. Memmi, *The Colonizer and the Colonized*. Memmi ties the colonizer and the colonized together in a strange connectedness. I think "complicity" is too strong a term because it implies some degree of equality and autonomy that, in my view, does not exist between colonized and colonizer. Moreover, Jim and Huck seem to have a mutual need for one another, although Jim is much more honest and upright than Huck who is a habitual liar who feels, like all whites of this era, that he is better, smarter, more logical, etc., than the "nigger" Jim.

that there is a strange and almost inexplicable relationship, but complicity is too strong a term to describe the relationship between the colonized and the colonizer.

Albert Memmi makes this point even more emphatically when he asks, "Who can completely rid himself of bigotry in a country where everyone is tainted by it, including its victims?"[38] While there may be some truth in this statement, it should not mean that victims and victimizers or the colonizers and the colonized bear the same degree of responsibility for bigotry. As victims, whether Indians, Native Americans, Africans, or African American, we have maybe learned too well the lessons taught by colonization for the purpose of never again becoming slaves. Jean-Paul Sartre in his introduction to Albert Memmi's book *The Colonizer and the Colonized* says,

> Colonialist practice has engraved the colonialist idea into things themselves; it is the movement of things that designates colonizer and colonized alike. Thus oppression justifies itself through oppression: the oppressors produce and maintain by force the evils that render the oppressed, in their eyes, more and more like what they would have to be like to deserve their fate. The colonizer can only exonerate himself in the systematic pursuit of the "dehumanization" of the colonized by identifying himself a little more each day with the colonialist apparatus . . . Oppression means, first of all, the oppressor's hatred for the oppressed . . . The impossible dehumanization of the oppressed, on the other side of the coin becomes the alienation of the oppressor.[39]

"The Negro," Fanon writes, "wants to be like the master; therefore, he is less independent than the Hegelian slave. In Hegel, the slave turns away from the master and turns toward the object. Here the slave turns toward the master and abandons the object."[40] Again, Fanon and Gandhi seem to corroborate the view held by Albert Memmi and Jean-Paul Sartre that "a relentless reciprocity binds the colonizer to the colonized—his product and his fate."[41]

While there is a strange connection between the colonizer and the colonized, it is imperative that the colonized, whether African, Egyptian, or African American, never forget the pain of the Middle Passage,

38. Ibid., 23
39. Ibid., 27–28.
40. Gandhi, *Postcolonial Theory,* 20–21
41. Memmi, *The Colonizer and the Colonized,* 28.

European expansionism, American chattel slavery, Orientalism or the Holocaust. This anamnestic posture is critical to the continued survival of the oppressed.

REMEMBERING, RELIGION AND CULTURE— POSTCOLONIALISM AND IDENTITY

The problem with almost all systematic theology and philosophy is that it is speechless regarding African Americans and their condition of existence. It is devoid of the sermonic such that its focus is too abstract and unrelated to Black existence. Its talk of universalism is a form of violence that perpetuates the modern project of religion and rationality without understanding that human beings are more emotional and social than anything else. From Descartes, Kant, and Hegel, and others, this is a religion that is based on identification with power and its concomitant idols—money or capitalism, Europeanism, Americanism, and white supremacy.

The book *Religion and Rationality* by German philosopher and critic Jürgen Habermas suggests a tension between religion and rationality, God and reason. The opening essay, "The German Idealism of the Jewish Philosophers" gives examples of this dialectic: the assimilated Jewish intellectualism of a marginal minority on the one hand, and the masses of Jewish people on the other. Or by rationalism on the one hand and the kabbalah/mysticism on the other. Out of this assimilated intellectual strata "emerged the spokesmen for turning back of the German Jews to the origins of their own tradition."[42] The Jewish intellectuals from Martin Buber (*Ich Und Du*), Franz Rosenzweig, Herman Cohen (head of the famous Marburg School), Ludwig Wittengenstein (Cambridge, Vienna Circle and Logical Postivism), Gershom Scholem (historian of Jewish mysticism) to Edmund Husserl (phenomenology) found themselves caught in a world skewed more toward idealism than the evil reality. Even Husserl's profound statement to his student Helmut Plessner expresses the deep dialectical tension that exists in the hearts and minds of Jewish philosophers. He said: "I have always found German Idealism in its entirety disgusting. All my life, I . . . have sought reality."[43] And yet, he too was co-opted or overcome by German Idealism in thinking that he could overcome fascist oppression and irrationalism by erecting a "renewed rationalism." This, to me, is the

42. Habermas, *Religion and Rationality*, 38.
43. Ibid., 46.

collapse of reality back into the German idealism from which he sought to escape.

Secondly, the essay by Jürgen Habermas entitled, "Israel or Athens: Where does Anamnestic Reason Belong? Johannes Baptist Metz on Unity Amidst Multicultural Plurality" also helps to put the process of remembering into perspective. There are certain things like three hundred years of chattel slavery and the Holocaust that should never be forgotten. The Greeks separated the Old Testament God of creation from the God of salvation, creating what Habermas calls, "this idealistic dilution of suffering."[44] Against this notion Johannes Baptist Metz "invokes a culture of loss, a culture of remembrance which could keep open, without false consolation, the existential relentlessness of a passionate questioning of God."[45] This intersubjectivity creates a necessary chasm between God and the question of theodicy. While Habermas, Primo Levi, and other philosophers and writers use Auschwitz as the measuring rod of human suffering, I, as an African American, offer the transatlantic slave trade and the economics of violence, the slave auction block, and the extirpation of one's native language as another paradigm of terror and barbarity. Derrida's dictum in *Monolingualism of the Other*, that "I only have the one language and that language is not mine" appropriately describes the condition of African Americans in the United States, who are clearly, in my view, the most blatant examples of the "excluded." This is also evident in Mark Twain's *Adventures of Huckleberry Finn* where we see "niggers" are excluded from the human race/species: "Good gracious! Anybody hurt? No'm. Killed a nigger." "Well, it's lucky; because sometimes people do get hurt."[46]

This is probably the most blatant example of irony in the entire novel; however, the language is also the most callous and nonchalant indicator of ontological negation in the entire novel. These words by Aunt Sally reflect the cultural mindset of white American racism and the absence of any connection between Americanism and concern for the Other. Irony or no irony, African Americans, like the Jews in regard to the Holocaust, must never forget the violence of slavery, the bondage, and the colonialist culture represented by the words of Aunt Sally in the novel.

In this context, the Other is not the one who imposes language, but the one who has had language imposed upon him. The monolingualist speaks a language of which he is deprived, and the African American

44. Ibid., 133.
45. Ibid.
46. Twain, *Huckleberry Finn*, 279.

speaks a language of deprivation and imposition—an otherness beyond the description of Jacques Derrida. We cannot even remember our own African language. It has been erased fully from our memory by violence and hate. It is a forced amnesia. African Americans all suffer from amnesia caused by the violence of slavery. The words of the Negro spiritual: "*Oh freedom, oh freedom over me . . . Before I'd be a slave, I'd be buried in my grave and go home and be free*" express the resolve and determination to never again be in bondage.

This brings us back to the issue of anamnestic reasoning and the univocal nature of the Enlightenment. As the historian of religion Charles Long suggests, multicultural plurality is a misnomer. It is for everybody else except those who are writing the history and making the decisions. In a recent lecture Charles Long stated,

> Theology is always trying to show the logic of or the reason for . . . religion during the Enlightenment, as a style of thought, was against religion because it was designed as a critique of religion . . . The Enlightenment believed that one day religion would all be gone. The one country that comes into being as an atheistic country is now the most religious country.[47]

America has never been any more religious than her self-serving, capitalistic philosophy and economics would allow. This is exactly what Mark Twain lampooned throughout his novel *Adventures of Huckleberry Finn*. The white folks' religion was a joke to Twain! An abomination. A travesty. A contradiction.

Similarly, Charles Long's critique of the Enlightenment is a critique of colonialism, American religion, and culture. He also says, "being an American is a religion. America is a belief system."[48] And this system is structurally extraordinary. From this perspective, it is neither "Israel nor Athens," but America. Long suggests that being an American excludes one from being anything else. This exclusion obviates any notion of multicultural plurality and asserts that unity is grounded in Americanism. It is then illogical and unreasonable to be an African and an American. [49] But it is very logical and American for a Black person to be called a "nigger." This issue of multiculturalism and plurality is for others, not white Americans. Long states:

47. Charles A. Long, Virginia Union University, Richmond, Virginia, unpublished lecture, October 7, 2004.

48. Ibid.

49. Ibid.

The American church is falling apart because race is at the heart of the American church. When white people say "diversity and pluralism" they are talking about Asians, Indians, Blacks, etc. They don't relativize themselves. Being white means that you don't ever admit you got messed up. James Baldwin says that it is not the color of your skin. It's in your head. They call themselves white because it's a sign of purity. Baldwin says, I don't know where white people come from. They leave England, Germany and France, etc. and land on U.S. soil and say that they are white. In America people are "white." You can "make like" you are Irish, German, or French etc. but you are "white."[50]

According to Long, multicultural plurality is something for other people—non-white people. It is another form of othering by the colonialists and their progenies. Moreover, if persons are not careful, their identity will be signified out of existence by white Americans. This means that Jews, Blacks, Asians, Latinos, etc. will have their identity collapsed into white Americanism. And this collapse or multicultural plurality becomes a form of assimilation that obstructs any anamnestic understanding of particularity and cultural identity, thereby eliminating the possibility of the ideal of authenticity.

This is very different from what Habermas asserts in "The German Idealism of the Jewish Philosophers." Quoting Ernst Jünger, the chapter begins with a statement that is *prima facie* as anti-Semitic and deprecatory as much of what I heard growing up in Central Virginia, the former capital of the Confederacy. Unlike in the United States, where assimilation is encouraged and everyone's (except Blacks') identity is collapsible into Americanism, the process of assimilation is put in question by Jünger. Habermas quotes him saying:

> "To the same extent that the German will gain in sharpness and shape, it becomes increasingly impossible for the Jews to entertain even the slightest delusion that they can be Germans in Germany; they are faced with their final alternatives which are, in Germany, either to be Jews or not to be." This was in 1930, when those who could not adapt to a dubious politics of *apartheid* were already being offered the menacing promise that was so gruesomely kept in the concentration camps.[51]

50. Ibid.

51. Habermas, *Religion and Rationality*, 38.

Habermas also mentions the tension between the cultural Jews and moneyed Jews and describes this as an intra-Jewish anti-Semitism. He states:

> The fantasy of Jewish scholars in general was sparked by the power of money—Marx, especially the young Marx, was an example of this. In this regard the intimate enmity of the cultured Jews toward the moneyed Jews—that sublime intra-Jewish anti-Semitism against the stratum whose *imago* was minted by the Rothschilds—might have been a motive. Simmel, himself the son of a salesman, wrote a blatant "Philosophy of Money."[52]

It seems that the Jews were definitely caught between "a rock and a hard place." Their very being was threatened by adaptation. If they put their anamnestic notion in practice they were doomed, and if they assimilated into German culture they were doomed. This alternative ("to be Jewish or not to be") was in fact a violent threat to their ontological status.

I now return to the issue of multiculturalism and plurality in the church and in Christianity. I take a theological perspective that sheds light on this domain of church politics. Habermas asserts, without equivocation, that the Christian church is constituted by a cultural multivocity and that Christian doctrine is constituted by an authentic search for truth. I have some reservations about the accuracy of both these claims, especially in light of the pervious assertions made by Professor Charles Long. Moreover, the Christian church seems to me to be more culturally univocal than anything else. This does not mean that this unity is absolutely devoid of otherness, but that it is a unity mediated by sameness. One of Martin Luther King's observations about the white Christian church over forty years ago was that it was a leader in the segregation ideology and practices of exclusionary American democracy and Christianity. Habermas offers some perspective in his discussion of the polycentric world church when he states:

> A church, which reflects on the limitations of its eurocentric history, seeking to attune Christian doctrine to the hermeneutic departure points of non-Western cultures, cannot start from the idea of a historical, culturally unbiased and ethnically innocent Christianity. Rather, it must remain aware both of its theological origins and of its institutional entanglement with the history of European colonialism. And a Christianity which takes up a reflexive attitude to its own truth claims in the course of dialogue

52. Ibid., 53.

with other religions cannot rest content with an "inconsequen-
tial or patronizing pluralism."[53]

Habermas suggests that the polycentric church both internally and externally offers a model for dealing with the political problem of multiculturalism.[54] He connects this with identity and a shared Christian
self-understanding as he correlates multicultural societies with the polycentric world church. Regarding the church he states, "A shared-Christian
understanding must emerge within it, one which no longer coincides with
the historically determining traditions of the West, but merely provides
the backdrop which enables the Western tradition to become aware of
its eurocentric limitations and peculiarities."[55] This type of thinking by
Habermas seems to me to be a lapse back into an idealism that is itself as
Eurocentric as the Enlightenment philosophy that describes and shapes
modernity. While Habermas and Metz both gesture toward inclusivity
and "recognition of the other in his otherness," there is in fact little hope
for such a recognition on a global scale.

In the discussion of the "preferential option for the poor" Habermas
speculates that the G-8 nations could take global responsibility for transforming the world by eradicating poverty based on John Rawls's second
principle of justice, which he states as: "social and economic inequalities
are to be arranged so that it is reasonably expected that they will bring the
greatest advantage to the least well-off."[56] This postcolonial, anti-imperi-
alistic posture in and of itself would be a just action beyond abstraction.
Yet, Habermas seems to dance around the question of moral responsibility
and places it in the realm of the political, as if he had no part in it. He says:
"The burning issue of just global economic order poses itself primarily as
a political problem. How a democratically responsible politics can catch
up with globalized markets that have outpaced it is, in any event, not a
question for moral theory; social scientists and economists can contribute
more to it than philosophers can."[57] While Habermas is right on one level,
he seems to distance himself on another regarding this question. It is the
responsibility of philosophers and theologians to at least imagine a world
where there is an eradication of social and economic disparities for the

53. Ibid., 135.
54. Ibid.
55. Ibid., 137.
56. Ibid., 166.
57. Ibid.

"Other," a world where Christian love becomes the praxis. Habermas is right when he says,

> The call of liberation theology in its quests to lend a voice to the downtrodden, the oppressed, and the humiliated, does indeed stand within this context. I understand it as the active outrage against the inertia and the insensitivity of a status quo that no longer appears to move in the current of a self-accelerating modernization.[58]

It seems that modernity is not too modern when it comes to issues of parity and justice for the poor around the globe. But when it comes to global issues of war and the destruction of the poor, modernity is a full blown reality, where colonialism and its ideology is practiced, through repackaging its tenets under the banner of globalization. Colonialism is always a part of the seemingly postcolonial world.

READER RESPONSE ANALYSIS OF TEXTS

Much of what has heretofore been said is an effort to theorize about the nature of coloniality, anamnesis, and otherness as it relates to American and European domination. I have sought to locate and expound upon correlatives regarding the use of the word *nigger* by Twain and the nature of American culture.

My mind moves towards a feeling of anxiety and anger every time I read the word *nigger* in Twain's *Adventures of Huckleberry Finn*. When I was in high school, a segregated public school in Chester, Virginia, this book was not on the reading list, and "I's mighty glad it warn't." The reading of *Huckleberry Finn* remains a very difficult task for me, mainly because of the American stereotypical and condescending way that Blacks are portrayed. I find no humor in the vastly exaggerated images of the Black body throughout the novel. The art by E. W. Kemble, the illustrator, is as demeaning as the linguistic use of the racial epithet "nigger" on almost every page of the book.

While I recognize some elements of literary genius in the novel, I do not accept the irony and satire as simply literary devices devoid of the author's biases and presuppositions. Moreover, there seems to be no corresponding or correlative equivalent to "nigger" in describing the colonialist behavior of whites. When it comes to whites, they are "Kings and Dukes,"

58. Ibid.

"Phelp's plantation" owners, "Shepherdsons and Grangerfords" and the like, while all Blacks are "niggers": nigger Jim, nigger women, nigger children, nigger boys and nigger girls. Twain writes:

> A nigger woman come tearing out of the kitchen, with a rolling pin in her hand, singing out "Begone! You Tige! You Spot! Be-done, Sah!" and she fetched first one and then another of them a clip and sent him howling and then the rest followed . . .
> And behind the woman comes a little nigger girl and two little nigger boys, without anything on but two-linen shirts, and they hung onto their mother's gown, and peeped out from behind her at me, bashful, the way they always do. And here comes the white woman running from the house, about forty-five or fifty year old, bare headed, and her spinning-stick in her hand; and behind her comes her little white children, acting the same way the little niggers was doing. She was smiling all over so she could hardly stand.[59]

This was a perfect opportunity for Twain to refer to the poor white trash children as "niggers" inasmuch as they were "acting the same way the little niggers was doing." But Twain's language reserves the term "niggers" for Blacks only and by implication reflects the racist views of the time period as well as today, and possibly his own subliminal views.

It is pretty clear that Twain is spoofing white culture and its false sense of superiority through many of the novel's characters, but the use of *nigger* throughout the novel has more than tropic use: in other words, is "nigger" a figure of speech or is it more than figurative and more than speech? Moreover, Twain does inadvertently provide us with a metalanguage in his use of the racial epithet "nigger." So how is he using the term in the text even if it is a trope or figure of speech? I believe that the ubiquitous use of the term is indicative of the extent to which Twain himself was a part of this colonialist culture such that he, as a white man of privilege, had internalized the language of colonization in a casual, matter of fact way. This fusion of his own colonialist culture and his literary skill help to confound his metalinguistic use of the term *nigger*. Satire can be used to obfuscate the writer's own biases and prejudices. As a literary device, the author's own feelings, prejudices and beliefs can be shielded by the mask of the literary device. At minimum, there seems to be a level of equivocity in Mark Twain's use of the racial epithet "nigger."

59. Twain, *Huckleberry Finn*, 277.

The use of "nigger" by white Americans permeated the culture and whenever the term was/is used by whites, it is derogatory in both intent and interpretation by Blacks. There is no agapeic or loving way that whites use the term. Its history and current cultural usage is laden with the colonialist intent of domination and condescension. Because the term is grounded in racial hatred and a presumption of superiority on the part of white Americans, it is unlikely that there exists an African American today who will tolerate being called a nigger by a white man or woman. The word has become the most blatant audibilized taunt and invitation to physical violence in American culture. All of my own understanding of the etymology of the word suggests that racial hatred, bigotry, and offensiveness are inherently intended when it is used by whites or those with Eurocentric ideologies. During an argument between Huck and Jim about the way French people talk, Huck concludes via his own irrationality that Jim is incapable of logical argument, and the cause of this incapability is grounded in Jim's race. Then Huck makes a gigantic leap that bestows Jim's incapability upon the entire Black race. He states: " '*Well*, den! Dad blame it, why doan' he *talk* like a man?—You answer me *dat*!' I see it warn't no use wasting words– you can't learn a nigger to argue. So I quit."[60]

This is universalism in Huck's voice. It is irrationality on Huck's part. This blanket indictment of the logical and rational inability of Blacks, i.e., niggers in Huck's language, is an excellent example of racism and bigotry and clearly demonstrates Huck's presumption of superiority and the nature of racism and colonialism embedded in his character and voice. The dialectic of fellow-feeling and presumed superiority that Twain displays in Huck, however, is also expressed in the strange nexus that exists between Huck and Jim and Jim's perfect logic in other places throughout the novel. For example, Jim is still a "nigger" in chapter twenty-three when he concludes through reflection and logic that his daughter was "plumb deef and dumb."[61]

Again, I reiterate my hypothesis that Twain's use of the racial epithet "nigger" makes *Adventures of Huckleberry Finn* an American classic. Whether satire, irony or metaphor, the word "nigger" is an American literary trope that Twain used so effectively that *Adventures of Huckleberry Finn* remains an American classic. This word, this racial slur, this bigoted epithet in the minds and mouths of whites is constitutive of the heart of Americanism.

60. Ibid., 98
61. Ibid., 202.

Mikhail Bakhtin also helps us in interpreting the word nigger or nigga. While his use of the word *heteroglossia* or many meanings inherent in words will be helpful to us in understanding the historical and current word usage, we must also recognize the complexities of any hermeneutical enterprise. Hermeneutics is the effort to overcome distance between the speaker and the text, the community, the word, and any existential or transcendent reality. This is a tough task, replete with difficulty and disagreement, because interpretation is ultimately a subjective phenomenon, i.e., a discussion of a subject by a subject. This means in my view that the interpretation of a word, an event, a book or song grows out of experience. And, because we all have different experiences, our interpretations will inevitably be different, and rightfully so. Also, *heteroglossia* means that we always speak with more than one voice because our voices are inhibited and inhabited by other voices even when we don't know it or realize the depth of it. This means that we bring multiple meanings and understanding to the use of words. Inasmuch as the unit Bakhtin is concerned with is the utterance, i.e., the word which can be as microscopic as the word "nigger" or "nigga" or an entire song, poem or novel, the word deserves exegetical or hermeneutical exploration. For Bakhtin, the utterance is socially constructed and constituted. Translated, this means that heteroglossia plays voices against each other, such as when comedian Chris Rock plays the word "Black" against the word "nigga" saying "I love Black people, but I hate niggas." In heteroglossia, meaning is both semantically and symbiotically expressed through language. Bakhtin states:

> The linguistic significance of a given utterance is understood against the background of language, while its actual meaning is understood against the background of other concrete utterances on the same theme, a background made up of contradictory opinions, points of view and value judgments—that is, precisely that background that, as we see, complicates the path of any word toward its object. Only now this contradictory environment of alien words is present to the speaker not in the object, but rather in the consciousness of the listener, as his apperceptive background pregnant with responses and objectives.[62]

The use of the word "nigger" or "nigga" has linguistic significance in today's culture because many of the entertainers—poets, writers, comics, and rappers—have placed the word or its hybrid in the public domain such that it is now heard on television, radio, DVDs, CDs, etc. a million

62. Bakhtin, *The Dialogic Imagination*, 281.

times a day in a thousand different cities and countries throughout the world. With satellite television and radio, I would venture to hypothesize that Asians, Africans, Europeans, Middle Easterners, etc. probably hear the word "nigger" or "nigga" over and over each day from comedians and hip-hop and rap music that envelops the world and its myriad cultures. Yet, most people are probably not aware of the semantic or phonetic distinction made in the current use of the word by rappers and some comics. The history and etymology of the word's usage is known only by a few Western Europeans and Americans, who have developed the word and implemented its negative usage and meaning. African Americans have used the word mainly to signify kinship and identity formation. But this, too, has not always been the case as heretofore mentioned. This is complicated by the fact that the word is bandied about by the Black stars such as Tupac, Notorious BIG, Ice Cube, Chris Rock, Kanye West, and 50 Cent in a nonchalant way. Moreover, the word enjoys a certain amount of applause when used by comics such as Richard Pryor, Chris Rock, Cedric the Entertainer, or Wanda Sykes. But this type of response by the listener, i.e., acceptance and applause, suggests that the hearer understands the meaning and interpretation of the word. But does he? Certainly, Bakhtin says, "Understanding comes to fruition only in response. Understanding and response are dialectically merged and mutually condition each other: one is impossible without the other."[63] True, I believe American audiences who have been nurtured on the word "nigger" or "nigga" for more than three hundred years probably do in fact have the ability to sift through cultural biases, racist modes of thinking and semantic usage, and socio-cultural contexts to respond with appropriate savvy to (understanding) the use of the word "nigger" or "nigga." However, my concern is with those who have no cultural connection to the word (by this, I mean those who have not been chattel slaves, then deemed three-fifths of a human being, and now feel every day the vestiges of slavery and institutional racism) and those who do not have any exposure to vile and vicious American racial supremacy. There are whites who reside in Prague or Johannesburg who may hear the word constantly used in rap lyrics and feel that they too can address African Americans or any dark skinned people of African descent as "nigger" or "nigga." This, to me, represents a hermeneutical problem of immense magnitude and exemplifies the distanciation between the speaker and different listeners. Bakhtin postulates that the speaker's word

63. Ibid., 282.

is oriented toward a specific conceptual horizon that penetrates the world of the listener. He states,

> It is precisely such an understanding that the speaker counts on. Therefore, his orientation toward the listener is an orientation toward a specific conceptual horizon, toward the specific world of the listener; it is in this way, after all, that various different points of view, conceptual horizons, systems strive to get a reading on his word, and on his own conceptual system that determines this word, within the alien conceptual system of the understanding receiver; he enters into dialogical relationships with certain aspects of this system. The speaker breaks through, . . . constructs his own utterance on alien territory, against his, the listener's apperceptive background.[64]

This "orientation toward the listener" is very much akin to what the philosopher and literary theorist Kenneth Burke calls "identification." People are able to identify with hip-hop and rap music because the rhetoric has touched a nerve, a chord, a level of consciousness in them that lives and persuades. This is also like the magic that Burke describes, and I shall say more about that later.

Hip-hop and rap are intensely linguistic and stylistic. The language of much of the music is grounded in the art of storytelling—an oral and aural practice that engulfed the Black family and community as a language art. When I listen to rappers like Tupac and Notorious BIG along with Jay-Z and 50 Cent, I have come to conclude that their music indeed has a magic quality to it; mysterious, spiritual, living, tragic, and sad. Nevertheless, there is a tone and a cadence that signifies freedom and strength—both sometimes gone awry and warped or morphed into violence, misogyny, and patriarchy. This is the dual nature of rap seen vividly in the actual real lives of the artists, some of whom have gone to prison for murder, selling and using drugs, etc. On the issue of magic Burke is right when he states that,

> . . . there is an intrinsically rhetorical motive, situated in the persuasive use of language. And this persuasive use of language is not derived from "bad science," or "magic." On the contrary, "magic" was a faulty deviation from it, "word magic" being an attempt to produce linguistic responses in kinds of beings not accessible to the linguistic motive.[65]

64. Ibid.
65. Burke, *A Rhetoric of Motives*, 43.

Burke is suggesting that rhetoric itself is not tantamount to magic, but that rhetoric has a creative element that enables it to function like magic. It creates a magical experience in the hearer that enables her to identify with the realistic linguistic function of the rhetorical enterprise. Magic has a rhetorical ingredient in it. Burke writes:

> The term rhetoric is no substitute for "magic," "witchcraft," "socialization," "communication" and so on. But the term rhetoric designates a *function* which is present in the areas variously covered in those other terms. And we are asking only that this function be recognized for what it is: A linguistic function by nature as realistic as a proverb . . . For it is essentially a realism of the act: moral, persuasive—and acts are not "true" or "false." . . . It is different with the peculiarly rhetorical ingredient in magic, involving ways of identification that constitute variously to social cohesion . . .[66]

While Burke says that magic has a rhetorical ingredient in it, I am suggesting that the converse is also true, i.e., rhetoric has a magical ingredient in it. This means to me that if rhetoric is not magically constituted, it realistically has some semblance of that effect on the listeners. And, this is what I mean by magic, although I prefer to use the more theological or philosophical term "mystery." Burke seeks to turn rhetoric on its head while recognizing that it is the act of persuasion. It permeates the nature of being such that it cannot be relegated to a status that suggests that it is devoid of philosophy's first principles. The impact of hip-hop and rap music on the world's myriad cultures and races attests to the fact that people identify with some element of black culture and music. This identification may not be intentional or cultural—but basic to human nature. This is quite mysterious. Finally, Burke says:

> As for the relation between "identification" and "persuasion:" we might well keep it in mind that a speaker persuades an audience by the use of stylistic identification; his act of persuasion may be for the purpose of causing the audience to identify itself with the speaker's interests; and the speaker draws on identification of interests to establish rapport between himself and his audience. So, there is no chance of keeping apart the meanings of persuasion, identification (consubstantiality) and communication (the nature of rhetoric as "addressed"). But, in given instances, one

66. Ibid., 44.

or another of these elements may serve best for extending a line
of analysis in some particular direction.[67]

Apparently, there is something that enables the rap music and the ubiquitous use of the word "nigger" or "nigga" to be understandable to persons of
many different cultures. In some sense the music has accomplished what
the philosopher Hans Gadamer calls the "fusion of horizons" because
there seems to be some level of understanding and appreciation of the
music. Maybe it is the beat, the tempo, the cadence, the rhythm. I don't
really know. Nevertheless, there is an appetite for the music that is felt all
over the world among different races and cultures. Music, in general, has
the ability to speak to people on a level that no other medium can match.

A few months ago while sitting in the baggage claim area of Hous-
ton's Intercontinental Airport, I observed and overheard two Black and
two Latino youth conversing about their lives. Their discussion was laden
with the use of the word "nigger" as they laughed and fraternized with one
another. This was somewhat surprising to me because they used the word
so freely in referring to each other as well as others who were the subject of
their conversation. I realized that this usage was quite embedded in popular culture, and young African Americans and other minorities apparently
had a different understanding of the word than I did. They are products
of a postmodern culture where history has been eclipsed by subjectivity
and the privileging of nowness. Nevertheless, the use of the word "nigger"
or "nigga" has taken on Gadamarian overtones such that it has fused a
connection between persons of different cultural horizons. The usage has
been fused, but the meaning is still unclear when used by Japanese, Chinese, Afghans, Germans, Algerians, Egyptians, and others who have not
had the common historical experience of Blacks in America, experiences
I have previously enumerated.

Finally, Ernesto Grassi, the Italian rhetorical philosopher, argues that
rhetoric is as substantive as philosophy. This is unlike those Aristotelian
and Platonic idealists who postulate that *episteme* is grounded in proofs
rather than speech or rhetoric. Like Burke, Grassi recognizes that meaning
and action are integral to rhetorical discourse. In other words, form and
content are one. Stylistics is not devoid of essence, meaning, knowledge
or content, but language, i.e., rhetoric, is grounded in human experience.
This is as evident in Black preaching as it is in rap music and the poetics of Langston Hughes or Amiri Baraka. The wonder and astonishment
of words and language is the means by which reality is perceived and

67. Ibid., 46.

understood. Language is a prerequisite to defining and understanding the nature of reality. Rhetorical speech is not merely the art of persuasion but it constitutes a first principle or metaphysic of being. Grassi says, "But let it be remembered that it is only within the limits of human communication and the tasks that arise from it that the problems of philosophy and the function of rhetoric can be discussed."[68]

Grassi is arguing against the rationalist or logical notion that the human starting point is rationality. Instead he argues that language is the genesis of existential reality.[69] The hip-hop musicians and the rappers perform rhetorical and linguistic acrobatics almost every time they speak —often spewing out social commentary on racism, police brutality, capitalism, egoism, self-esteem, crime, education, etc. More often than not, these comments are grounded in and surrounded by the use of the word "nigga" and appreciation of the music. There is an appetite for the music that is felt all over the world among different races, cultures, and socioeconomic classes. This appetite extends into the Black church where there is a growing number of gospel rappers such as Kirk Franklin whose music has become a staple of youth choirs, steppers and other nontraditional elements of Black church liturgy.

SERMONIC DISCOURSE: "FOR THE SAKE OF THE GOSPEL"

"To the Jews I became like a Jew to win the Jews. To those under the law, I became like one under the law, so as to win those under the law. To those not having the law, I became like one not having the law, so as to win those not having the law. To the weak, I became weak, to win the weak. I have become all things to all men so that by all possible means, I might save some. I do all this for the sake of the gospel that I may share in its blessings." —1 Corinthians 9:19–23

My beloved, today we are in a pretty tough situation. Everything around us is under siege or "under construction"—like our Facebook pages or websites. I'm convinced that there has got to be a message in this coming to prominence of the absurd—Lady Gaga is the new Madonna and Li'l Wayne is the new Tupac, the Marvin Gaye and James Brown of Rap and Hip-hop. Li'l Wayne has replaced Lil Bow Wow and Lil Richard; he is now

68. Foss, et al., *Contemporary Perspectives on Rhetoric*, 51.

69. Grassi, *Rhetoric as Philosophy*.

a symbol. He is a sign. He is a metaphor for everything in the postmodern Black community. He is the metaphor for rap music. It's like you can't get on the Top 10 charts without Li'l Wayne on your album. He has a role in 3 of the top 10 rap songs: "I'm On One" by DJ Khaled—featuring Drake, Rick Ross and guess who—Li'l Wayne. This is the #1 Rap song on Billboard's Top 100 hits. And, then his own song "How to Love" by Li'l Wayne is number 2 and the number 7 song "Look At Me Now" by Chris Brown featuring Busta Rhymes and guess who, Li'l Wayne. The lyrics are explicit, not suggestive, but explicit: the f-word, the s-word, MF and drugs, getting high, getting sexed, getting money. And, the violence: "I'm So Hood." DJ Khaled and Rick Ross, "I wear my pants below my waist," "I'm out here grinding," "I don't care what nobody say, I'm gonna be me; we taking over." This is what parents, teachers, preachers, counselors are up against in the Black community. Yes, we got issues in our house, in our family, in our church, and in our community. This is where our people are—our young people are mesmerized by this multimedia craze and their behavior and actions are *simulations* of what we see on the videos and hear on the radios. They are imitating what they see others say and do: "I wear my pants below my waist" because DJ Khaled and Rick Ross and Li'l Wayne do it and they have glamorized it and they told me to do, and I do it. We are caught in the Matrix where we don't know what is the dream and what is the real. I can't read well, but I can text; I can't spell, but I can blog; I can't write a complete sentence or spell a word correctly because I have new language created by technology—the smart phone is my new partner, my friend. Oh, and now our youth have a thousand friends on Facebook—their friends are virtual friends—not really my friends, but I'm caught up in the Matrix like Neo or Orpheus and I don't really know who I am or what I'm doing. A lot of our youth are lost in a world that don't mean nothing. That's what they tell me. The profanity don't mean nothing. The drugs, the sex in the lyrics don't mean nothing. Well, I'm not so sure about that. This is what I am up against in church—everything is imitation. *Mime* from the Greek word mimesis means to imitate, to mimic, to copy. We don't want any new and innovative ideas because I can copy, imitate, and mimic somebody else and this is seen from praise and worship to the sermon. And thus lies the problem—my dilemma with this scriptural text today. At first glance, I'm troubled by Paul's desires to be all things to all people. It smells of inauthenticity and accomodationism. It reminds me of the imitation I'm talking about. It is a type of simulation. A ventriloquism. It's a mime, a mimesis, a mimetic act: "To the Jews I became as those under the law, so as to win those under the law. To the weak, I became weak, to win the weak." This indeed may be meeting people where they are. This is wearing my pants below my waist. This is "I'm so hood" to win the sagging pants youth to win the hood-acting Black youth of today.

So what should or will we do for the sake of the gospel?

We have to meet people where they are if we want to make the gospel real. Listen, Paul says "to the Jew, I became as a Jew," mind you he is already a Jew—a Pharisee of the Pharisees; to those under the law, I became like one under the law. To those not having the law, I became like those not having the law and to the weak, I became weak to win the weak." It is true that I listen to young people—split verbs and all. I talk to 'em and rap with them. I make them pull their pants up and pronounce their words. I correct their verb usage and teach them how to spell big words. And, it starts with people as young as Keon and as old as Allen and Stephan and Trey and Haywood and Kristina and Quanesha and Robin and Kaycie—thank you very much. I try to talk their language sometimes: "we done," "they was," "we been," "I seen," "they had went." I always say that I'm talking like Huck and Jim in Mark Twain's novel *Adventures of Huckleberry Finn*. But, I'm also talking like Li'l Wayne, Nicki Minaj, Big Sean, and Chris Brown. And, guess what, every time I try to talk like they *does*, the youth come down to my office and tell me that I got my subjects and verbs mixed up and they don't think it's a good idea for me to talk that way. "You don't say." If I'm supposed to know better and I do know better, then I say to them, that they are also supposed to know better. Paul knows better than to try to act like the lawless and the weak, but he does it to win those who need to be won over to his side of the faith. Do I like rap music with all the violence, the cussing, the demeaning of women and girls? No, I don't support that. Do I listen to it with tweeters and sub woofers and turned up loud? Yes, I do. Is that all I listen to everyday, seven days a week? No. So why do I listen? So I can know what the youth are listening to. I listen so that I can speak their language. I listen and watch what they watch, so that I can win them over to the church, so that I don't judge them, so that they can know that I don't just know big words and that my thinking is not just abstract and esoteric—but I can relate, I can talk their language and not only that, but, if you are highfalutin, I can be highfalutin. If you are uppity, I can act uppity, to win the uppity. If you are down and dirty, mean and ugly—I might not be able to help you.

Then Paul says, "I do it all, I do all this for the sake of the gospel, that I may share in its blessings." The gospel is more important than any of us.

The gospel is the motivating force for whatever we do. The gospel. The good news of Jesus Christ is the reason why I do what I do. Yes, Second Baptist, I listen to rap; yes, I want the kids to dance; yes, I want them to mime; yes, I allow them to dress in the styles they like—the Cargo shorts, the 2x shirts, the tennis and the backpacks. Not because I like or even encourage it, but it ain't about me and it ain't about you and your traditions, your family values and your church policies—it's about the gospel. The good news of Jesus Christ. Paul says: "To the weak, I became weak, to win the weak. I became all things to all men, so that by all possible means, I might save some. I do all this for the sake of the gospel that I may share in its blessing." I do it for the sake of the gospel—that I may share in its blessings—this gospel is a blessings bestowing gospel—I can feel the presence of the Lord, I'm gonna get my blessing . . .

Chapter 9

The Preacher as Interpreter
Words on Other Texts

*"Freedom is never voluntarily given by the oppressor;
it must be demanded by the oppressed."*
MARTIN LUTHER KING JR.

"Freedom lies in being bold."
ROBERT FROST

INTERTEXTUALITY AND THE SURPLUS OF MEANING

THE SERMON AS INTERPRETATION is an act of freedom and love grounded in the struggle for meaning and understanding. The interrelationship between texts, that is scripture and non-scriptural texts, is grounded in words and meaning. Literature of all types and genres, especially poetry and novels when read by the preacher contributes to her singular eloquence as a pulpiteer. While eloquence is not enough to constitute authenticity, it is necessary to maintain one's status as a noteworthy preacher in the Black church and community. Eloquence and poetic flair often serve to mediate moral and intellectual shortcomings. The goal is for the preacher to lead a balanced life of prayer, study, sermon writing, and leisure. These things, taken together, constitute the pleasure of reading and preaching.

Intertextuality is the framing of texts by other texts or the relationship of one text to another. It is the connections between a given text and other texts. This includes the writer as text, and context as text vis-à-vis the social, religious, political, and economic realities of particular texts. These elements are subcomponents of the broad understanding of context as text.

Intertextuality is the imbrication and/or obfuscation of boundaries between texts. This overlapping is often so ubiquitous that it is difficult to determine where one text ends and another begins. In scriptural texts this is seen most vividly in the Synoptic Gospels, where the writers of Matthew, Mark, and Luke constantly reference the Markan text. One text overlaps the other. That is the meaning of intertextuality. Moreover, intertextuality reflects on and analyzes how texts can impact other previously written texts to the point of transforming the understanding of the prior text. Sometimes this is more negative than positive or vice versa.

This section focuses on the idea of intertextuality of Jean Baudrillard's major book *Simulacra and Simulation,* with some references to two other works, *Radical Alterity* and *Carnival and Cannibal.* This last work is as Bakhtinian as it is Baudrillardian in the sense that carnival breaks down social barriers and equalizes self and Other. Inasmuch as the film *The Matrix* is about the difference between the real and the virtual, it is also a perversion of the real because the actors in the film are shown in what appears to be a catatonic state in one frame and in an active dream world state of existence in another. The film seems to focus on the absence of reality, except that the image of the actors bears an exact resemblance to the self in both the real and virtual worlds. And yet, the simulacrum is that which bears no relation to reality. Clearly there is a type of simulacrum evident in the film, but it falls short of what Jean Baudrillard seems to be advancing. He states his objection to the film in the following way: "The most embarrassing part of the film is that the new problem posed by the simulation is confused with the classical, Platonic treatment. This is a serious flaw. The radical illusion of the world is a problem faced by all great cultures, which they have solved through art and symbolization. What we have invented in order to support this suffering, is a simulated real, which henceforth supplants the real. And *The Matrix* is undeniably part of that."[1]

---

1. Baudrillard, "Interview for *Le Nouvel Observateur*," vol. 1.

No Longer Bound

The Matrix is a simulated real, a supplanting of the real according to Baudrillard. It is not a reality, but a simulacrum—a breakdown between representation and reality. This means, however, that it is hard to distinguish between what is real and what is not if we are caught in the matrix—caught between a dream world and the real world. And, isn't that the point of the film, to convince the viewer that the world, as we know and experience it, is a matrix and we participate in it rather unknowingly? The real world and the dream world are so overlapping that they appear to be one and the same.

Baudrillard addresses the simulacrum and simulation as well as hyper-reality when he writes:

> The real is produced from *miniaturized* cells, matrices, and memory banks, models of control—and it can be reproduced an indefinite number of times from these . . . It is no longer anything but operational. In fact, it is no longer really the real, because no imaginary *envelops* it anymore. It is a hyper-real . . . It is no longer a question of imitation, nor duplication, nor even parody. It is a question of substituting the signs of the real for the real, that is to say of an operation of deterring every real process via its operational double, a programmatic, metastable, perfectly descriptive machine that offers all the signs of the real and short circuits all its vicissitudes. Never again will the real have a chance to produce itself.[2]

The aforementioned description of the real morphs into a hyper reality that essentially is the death of the real. It is a dream that replaces the real. The obliteration of the real into a simulation of the real seems to be the point of Baudrillard. The self is diffracted into a code, which has power over the self, the mind, and the body.[3] That is exactly what seems to be going on in the film, *The Matrix,* and by implication in real life. What is real preaching or a real sermon today in the age of the worldwide web where the temptation to cut and paste information overwhelms the need to read widely. And, God forbid, some preachers and students never learn how to write a sermon because they focus their energies on imitating and copying that which they admire without considering the fact that what they are copying or imitating may also be a copy. Miles Jones's notion of the authenticity of the preacher is discarded for the sake of popularity and convenience.

2. Baudrillard, *Simulacra and Simulation*, 2.
3. Baudrillard and Guillame, *Radical Alterity*, 42–43.

MULTIMEDIA INTERPRETATION

In this section, I seek to interpret two films *Coming to America* and *The Matrix* and several poems as examples of how the preacher is called to interpret texts of all types and genres using the method of textual criticism to facilitate the analysis. My hope is that the preacher will understand that her major task as a preacher is one of interpreting texts. This interpretation is not limited to scriptural texts, but to all types of texts as I have said previously. My focus now on multimedia texts will hopefully broaden the horizon of the preacher's imagination and provide examples of literary criticism that may help the preacher to interpret scriptural texts. All texts beg to be interpreted. The reader may ask, why talk about multimedia—films and poems—to the preacher and the theologian? Well, because everything needs to be interpreted and to do so demands reading and more reading in the humanities and social sciences. The preacher can never read enough, much less read too much. Reading widely is an act of love toward God and the people of faith.

The film *Coming to America* is a reflective interpretation of culture and it parallels the work of the preacher in the sense that they both harbor elements of critique and entertainment. The sermon is compelled to address both cultural and scriptural issues, while film must be overwhelmingly entertaining. I am beginning to think more and more that the demands on the sermon and the film are almost the same. In order to hold the congregation's attention, the preacher has to display a little pizzazz.

Poems and sermons are more correlative than different because the preacher is striving to be a poet in language and style. The preacher often mimics the succinctness and clarity of the poet. Or, he should mimic these traits. The Black preacher's eloquence is heard in his alliteration, rhyme, rhythm, cadence, modulation, and elongation of words. My preaching professor Miles Jones could take a single word and massage it into meaning and make it devoid of any misunderstanding. He did this while synchronizing his hands and the particular word with rhyme, rhythm, cadence, modulation, and elongation. He was a wordsmith like so many other Black preachers of his era and today. He was a multimedia and multidimensional preacher before his time. Too often today, we have media preachers, i.e., television preachers who pay the networks so that they can be seen and heard. The focus is more on the personality of the preacher than the gospel. And yet, the public seems to love it. This may be the result of our love for the media rather than our love for the gospel message.

MEDIA REPRESENTATION

While the Black preacher in America has been historically one of the most well versed public intellectuals[4] produced on American soil, she/he is often portrayed in movies as an ignoramus. The art and craft of Black preaching is caricatured in a way that hyperbolizes the absurd and the irrational while sublimating any semblance of spiritual discipline and rational argument. A corollary to the ignoramus is the appetitive nature of the Black preacher as one who is greedy and driven by unrequited sexual desire. The film audience is expected to infer that the Black preacher is morally and ethically suspect and, by implication, Black religious practices represent a type of cultural depravity asynchronous with traditional Judeo–Christian practices and beliefs.[5]

THE PREACHER AS DUNCE AND BUFFOON IN HOLLYWOOD FILM: A TEXTUAL ANALYSIS OF *COMING TO AMERICA*

The movie *Coming to America,* with a predominantly Black cast starring Eddie Murphy, Arsenio Hall, John Amos, Madge Sinclair, Vanessa Bell, and Paul Bates, is laden with stereotypes and images of the vestiges of colonialism. The movie's title suggests that America is a panacea and harbinger of the world's most beautiful and independent minded Black women. The film is misogynistic to the core. Moreover, the entire African continent is lampooned. Its customs, traditions, and practices are somehow inferior to those persons and things found on African soil. The myths in the film are dominant and overwhelming. This may or may not be the intention of the writer.

The movie opens with a scene depicting an African prince living in luxury and opulence with a palace court full of servants who provide every need for "His Highness"—a hyperbolic and overused term to refer to the king and his heir, Prince Akeem, played by the comedian of *Saturday Night Live* fame, Eddie Murphy. The main character Akeem is bathed by a team of beautiful women. The father, King Joffe Joffer, is played by prominent

4. From Lemuel Haynes (1753–1833) and Richard Allen (1760–1831) to Henry McNeil Turner, Absolom Jones, Henry Highland Garnett, Martin Luther King Jr., Adam Clayton Powell, Sojourner Truth, Jarena Lee and James Weldon Johnson, the Black preacher has been organizer and community leader. Also, see Martha Simmons and Frank Thomas, editors, *Preaching With Fire.*

5. Baudrillard, *Simulacra and Simulation,* 3.

stage and screen actor James Earl Jones, who is King of the fictive African nation, Zamunda. Arsenio Hall plays Akeem's sidekick, Semmi. The movie begins on Akeem's twenty-first birthday when the king is to announce the name of the woman who has been selected to be his bride. The woman who has been groomed to marry the prince is interviewed by Akeem, who tries to get her to be self-expressive, but instead she responds as a robotic automaton. Akeem further establishes her lack of individuality by requesting that she perform a series of embarrassing and humiliating acts, to wit, "bark like a dog" and "hop on one leg." African women are portrayed in this important scene as thoughtless, mindless and servile. The patriarchal overtones inherent in this and other scenes are degrading to women and suggest that Africa is oppressive to women and even her own people. Even when the young prince is presented with the chosen bride-to-be, there is a wild African display of scantily clothed dancers performing ritualistically in celebration of the prince's engagement. This contrasts with the movie's closing scene, where Akeem's marriage to an American girl is presented in a more traditional, refined, and muted setting.

The absurdity of the film is exacerbated by the coin toss to determine whether the prince would travel to Los Angeles or New York to find himself a wife. And then to choose Queens, New York randomly further advances the absurdity. Akeem says he wants a woman who can "arouse my intellect as well as my loins." This "arousing" woman could only be found in America. The contrast of African wealth with American poverty in Queens is another motif that represents African naiveté and "backwater" intelligence regarding finances and monetary issues. One of the most distressing stereotypes of the Black preacher is presented in a scene during "Black Awareness Week" at a community center in Queens. The preacher is represented as a sex crazed, ignorant buffoon. Black Awareness Week is an opportunity for self-expression. It is hosted by Reverend Brown and his band "Sexual Chocolate." Sexuality permeates the movie and is a subtheme in the music and the language.

Reverend Brown, played by Arsenio Hall, gesticulates throughout his histrionic appeal for money: "I feel good because there's a god somewhere" and, "only God above can give that woman the kind of joy . . ." The focus on God and the Black preacher is an attempt to portray the Black community as an eschatological, pie-in-the-sky group of people who believe anything that the stupid preacher espouses. The preacher is a messageless entertainer who conflates religion and God into a form of desire such that the uttering of the sermon is a discourse in meaningless gibberish. The preacher is presented as a comedic figure, but he is, in fact, is a sad and insulting one.

The gratuitous appearance of Samuel L. Jackson as a thief and armed robber in the fast food restaurant scene reiterates the perception that the Black male is the architect of American violence and the archetype of criminality and dysfunction. That scene could have been easily left out— unless the entire film is intended to be a spoof of American hegemony on everything cultural and enlightened. I believe that the film perpetuates the representation of Blacks and Africans as barbaric, overlooking Africa's own resources. The best that the world can offer can only be found by leaving Africa and coming to America. America is the god of civilization, and Africa, by contrast, is the epitome of ignorance in need of understanding and transformation.

MEDIA LANGUAGE AND FORMS

The text of the film connotes a typical understanding of Africans and African Americans. Africans are backwards, hating their own traditions and practices, and African Americans are violent, schemers, hyper-religious, thieves, and robbers—those who will steal and parade the stolen booty in public without any semblance of moral responsibility. Profanity and sexual references are also constant to the dialogue and images—especially in the barbershop and in the relationship with the hustling landlord.

In many ways the film also expresses satire and irony. Blacks are represented by the actors as incompetent bumbling buffoons who are unable to negotiate the complex world of New York City. There is very little iconoclastic language, but some of the symbols, like the inordinate use of rose petals spread in front of the king and prince, and the clapping of hands as an unspoken order to move with haste, reinforce the notion of classism within Africa and the United States. America, in this film, is symbolic of "Savior and Lord."

INTERPRETATION OF THE FILM, "THE MATRIX"

The cyberthriller *The Matrix* is written and directed by the Wachowski Brothers and stars Keanu Reeves and Lawrence Fishburn. I was struck by the Baudrillardian notion of *alteritas* evident in the film. This diversity is represented by the film's characters Morpheus and the Oracle—both African American and even Neo, the protagonist, is also a person of color.

In the opening scene, a shady character says to Neo, "Hallelujah. You're my Savior. My own personal Jesus Christ." In another conversation the antagonist says to Thomas Anderson aka Neo, "In one life you are Thomas Anderson. The other life is lived in computers where you go by the name Neo." Thomas Anderson works for a respectable computer software company, but in his dreams he is often plagued by threats that simulate real world violence and death.

The film opens with a scene where the camera glimpses the book *Simulacra and Simulation* in an intentional effort to be unclear. The book's title is barely recognizable, but what is very recognizable is the fact that the essence of the book has been cut out to form a hiding place for various types of computer discs or chips. So, we see the cover of the book that is not a book. It is the form of a book—an image of a book. But, its "book-ness" is an illusion that bears resemblance to a real book such that the lack of distinction between the real and the imaginary is evident. In this scene the book *Simulacra and Simulation* is itself a simulation. Baudrillard explains the difference between to dissimulate and to simulate. He writes:

> To dissimulate is to pretend not to have what one has. To simu-
> late is to feign to have what one doesn't have. One implies a pres-
> ence, the other an absence. But it is more complicated than that
> because simulating is not pretending.[6]

Now, in one sense, the book in the film is not a book, but a "feigning to have what one doesn't have" because the book has a cover with a title; it has apparent depth, width and length. It has a body, but no substance because it lacks an essential element of bookness, i.e., pages. So, my previous assertion that the book is a simulation may not be totally true because simulating is not pretending. Pretending is dissimulating such that Baudrillard says that, it "leaves the principle of reality intact: the difference is always clear, it is simply masked, whereas simulation threatens the difference between the 'true' and the 'false,' the 'real' and the 'imaginary.'"[7] Because the book is both present and absent, i.e., present in form (cover) and absent in substance (pages), it is a riddle. It both simulates and dissimulates in the film which leads me to assert that it is a simulacrum (a breakdown between representation and reality) and a simulation. That particular camera shot in the film may be the most critical and important intertextual instance in the entire film because Baudrillard's influence is implied

6. Ibid.
7. Jung, *Psychological Types*.

by that split-second frame of reference. Other influences of theorists such as Sigmund Freud and Carl Jung are evident throughout the film because of their contribution to dream theory and interpretation vis-à-vis the collected unconscious. Jung, in particular, maintains that the unconscious is a structured world commensurate with the conscious (real) world.[8]

In the film, Thomas Anderson aka Neo, alternates between the real world and the dream world. He has two identities—two names, two personas that are both blurred and clear. While his body goes through a metamorphosis, it ultimately returns to its original state in form and appearance. He is the one who doesn't believe that he is the One. So, is he a simulation of the One while pretending not to be the One? The character Neo is not very self-aware, although he is encouraged by the Oracle to embrace the Socratic dictum, "know yourself." He struggles to believe that he is who Morpheus says he is.

In the film, the dream world is the real world where the matrix is everywhere. "It is in the room. You can feel it when you go to church . . ." says one character, suggesting its pandemic and ubiquitous presence. Another, character says, "It is in the world to blind you from the truth."

Morpheus, in a plot advancing moment, offers Neo a blue pill or a red pill and says, "Remember, all I'm offering is the truth." After Neo's journey deep into the truth or dream world, Morpheus says to him: "welcome to the real world."

"You wanted to know what the Matrix is, Neo? The matrix is a neural interaction simulation. You've been living in a dream world."

Again, Morpheus asks rhetorically, "What is the matrix? Control. It is a computer generated dream world."

Neo says. "I don't believe it, wake me up."

"Fear and doubt and disbelief have to be let go. Free your mind."
"The matrix is a system and the doctors and the lawyers, etc. will fight to protect it," says another character.

Religious symbolism permeates the film from names and terms extrapolated from the Judeo-Christian religion such as, "The Nebuchadnezzar" which is the name of Morpheus' ship to "Trinity" the female heroine and to "Zion," the last human city. And, towards the end of the film, a character says: "I'd like to share a revelation that I had." The use of apocalyptic language and symbols portend the eschaton when the world, as we perceive it, will be no more and there will be a "world without borders and

---

8. Guerin, et al., *A Handbook of Critical Approaches to Literature*, 159.

boundaries." These lines, probably more than any other verbalized words in the script, capture the meaning of semiotics and intertextuality.

Finally, a reference to room 303 opens and closes the film, suggesting to me that the dream world and the real world are overlapped. The boundaries between these worlds have been obfuscated or annihilated such that difference is indiscernible. Thus, the matrix is itself a simulation. And, a simulacrum.

A PSYCHOANALYTIC INTERPRETATION OF ADRIENNE RICH'S POEM, "DIVING INTO THE WRECK"

In this next section, I will offer interpretations of poetry by Adrienne Rich and Robert Frost. My goal throughout this book has been to show you why and how I read. I want you to see what I, a black minister, get out of these authors.

This poem seems to be about what I call the phenomenology of self. The first few stanzas suggest to me that the subject is experiencing a process of individuation and self-understanding contrary to the *Mythemes* of Claude Levi-Strauss. The language in the poem "book of myths" suggests that the author knows something about the "symbolic projections of a people's hopes, values, fears, and aspirations."[9] Her knowledge regarding the inherent assumptions of myths about women enables her to proceed to examine her own life with the same power and determination with which Jacques Cousteau, the French author and undersea explorer, examines the deep, dark, dangerous depths of the sea. Also, there are other images of the phallic symbol in the language of the third stanza, i.e., "edge of the knife-blade."

> First having read the book of myths,
> and loaded the camera,
> and checked the edge of the knife-blade,
> I put on
> the body-armor of black rubber
> the absurd flippers
> the grave and awkward mask.

According to Freudian psychoanalysis, sexual images leap forth from almost every line of the poem especially in the words "checked the edge of the knife-blade, I put on the body-armor of black rubber." All of this could

9. Ibid., 161.

be interpreted as symbolism for the preparation to commence a sexual act. For Freud, almost every act or object had a sexual meaning or interpretation; however, the language of this poem suggests that whatever the subject is doing is private and individualistic, and somewhat forced or against the will. This is an internal struggle with the self—a battle between the *id* and the *superego* being mediated by the rational, governing power of the *ego*. I believe the following lines attest to this introspective interpretation.

> *I am having to do this*
> *not like Cousteau with his*
> *assiduous team*
> *aboard the sun-flooded schooner*
> *but here alone.*

The subject's contrast with Cousteau suggests that this is not a literal voyage, but a figurative, symbolic search for the authentic self and no amount of armor is sufficient to protect one from the collateral damage from the wreck. Unlike Cousteau with a team of industrious, hard-working divers, and oceanographers on an open deck sailing vessel, she (the subject) is here alone in the dark depths of her own singular self, a place where there is no sunlight and maybe no hope. And yet, "there is a ladder," a symbol of rescue—a means to escape. This is a ubiquitous, omnipresent ladder, which is "always there hanging innocently; and, to say "we know what it is for, we who have used it" suggests to me that this ladder is indeed a vehicle, a means by which one can pierce the deep consciousness of the mind and body. This is not the first time that the subject has embarked on this journey toward knowledge of the inner self, and secondarily knowledge of others.

The language, "I go down rung after rung and still the oxygen immerses me" has a postmodern tone of oral sexuality to it, maybe the influence of Freud upon us all. Also, the words,

> *And there is no one*
> *to tell me when the ocean*
> *will begin.*

These words reflect a child-like spirit, a desire to be told by some authoritative voice the meaning of life. Psychologically, this poem seems to be about the quest for identity—particularly sexual identity inasmuch as there are hermaphroditic qualities clearly indicated in the following stanzas:

> *This is the place.*
> *And I am here, the mermaid whose dark hair*

streams black, the merman in his armored body.
We circle silently
about the wreck
we dive into the hold.
I am she: I am he

The mermaid and the merman vis-à-vis the dual ontology, "I am she, I am he" suggests in Jungian terms that the female is partially constituted by maleness, and conversely the male is likewise constituted by elements of femaleness. This is both Freudian and Jungian inasmuch as the issues of sexuality and consciousness permeate the symbolic language symbolizing what the philosopher William Desmond calls "being and univocity." This is certainly a union of the two entities as the "circle" suggests. Moreover, the final stanzas also reflect a collectivity, a unity within the individuated self: "We are, I am, you are . . . the one who find our way . . ."

AN ARCHETYPAL INTERPRETATION OF ADRIENNE RICH'S POEM, "DIVING INTO THE WRECK"

This poem is filled with archetypal images of water as seen in the ocean and the sea, and for Carl Jung, the master of archetypes, "water is the chief symbol of the unconscious as well as the harbinger of images of creation, purification, birth-death-resurrection, and fertility."[10]

The sea is another story
the sea is not a questioning power

Moreover, the very title of the poem "Diving into the Wreck" is filled with images of water. We often think of divers as deep sea divers, explorers of the oceans, seas, and rivers. The very act of diving conjures images of water. According to Jung's description, "The sea: the mother of all life, spiritual mystery and infinity; death and rebirth; timelessness and eternity; the unconscious."[11] While the sea is a symbol of mystery and the unconscious; the sun, on the other hand, is a symbol of consciousness, creative energy and spiritual vision. In this poem, Adrienne Rich uses the image of the sun: "aboard the sun-flooded schooner," and "the drowned face always staring toward the sun." The image of the sun is one that suggests creative energy, power and control, i.e., life. The language, "sun-flooded," is indicative of the explosive and overwhelming nature and power of life's creative energy.

10. Ibid.

11. Ibid.

Moreover, the poem is laden with colors: "black rubber" symbolizing mystery, chaos, the unknown, and the unconscious. The color "black" in Jung, like all Europeans, also symbolizes death and evil while the color white is, more often than not, a symbol of purity, light, innocence, etc. Guerin does point out that there are negative aspects to "white" as an image. It too is a symbol of death and terror. Too many African Americans, however, the color white represents the embodiment of negativity as reflected in the nature and practices of colonialism and racism in American democracy. Racism is often preceded by the color white as in "white racism."

Moreover, the Ku Klux Klan and the Knights of the Ku Klux Klan, were/are both American terrorist organizations whose sole purpose is to suppress the rights of Blacks through hangings, murder, and other forms of violence and intimidation. Their uniform garb used to cover their white skin is a white cloak that exposes only the eyes. So, in the consciousness of most African Americans "white" is very much a symbol of hate, evil, and terror.

Adrienne Rich's poem, "Diving into the Wreck" also makes reference to other colors such as blue and green.

> First the air is blue and then
> it is bluer and then green and then
> black and I am blacking out and yet
> my mask is powerful

Finally, this poem is about the quest for wholeness while surrounded by both death and life. Idealism has been shattered by the reality principle. The archetypal image of the circle suggests the nature of this struggle toward unity:

> We circle silently
> about the wreck
> We dive into the hold.
> I am she: I am he

The *yang-yin* image seems to be achieved in the preceding lines. The union of the opposite forces of the masculine (*yang*) and the feminine (*yin*), conscious mind and the unconscious, activity and passivity have been achieved. What a complex and powerful poem!

A DECONSTRUCTIVE INTERPRETATION OF ROBERT FROST'S POEM "MENDING WALL"

Robert Frost's poem "Mending Wall" implies brokenness and openness. To mend is to fix something that is broken and the nature of a wall implies that something needs to be barricaded, partitioned, separated, or broken down using Jacques Derrida's notion of "binary oppositions." And yet, why mend a wall that is not loved or wanted? To mend the unwanted is to restore that which is hated.

> *Something there is that doesn't love a wall,*
> *That sends the frozen-ground-swell under it,*
> *And spills the upper boulder in the sun,*
> *And make gaps even two can pass abreast.*

The central tension in the poem has to do with the existence and mending of a wall that by its very nature possesses something that is repugnant and repulsive. This is a wall that is not a wall because there is nothing to "wall in or wall out." Moreover, the wall has gaps in it "where even two can pass abreast." This wall is a symbol of separation because instead of it dividing the neighbors, i.e., keeping them from each other, it appears to create a sense of *communitas* between the neighbors, rather than enmity or discord.

> *I let my neighbor know beyond the hill;*
> *And on a day we meet to walk the line*
> *And set the wall between us once again.*
> *We keep the wall between us as we go.*

This is a wall that has no "wallness" to it. It serves the opposite purpose of a wall because it fosters unity and not division. This wall generates a type of love—a brotherly love or what the Greeks termed *philia*. This is the very opposite of the first line, "Something there is that doesn't love a wall." The rest of the poem suggests that the first line should read more like, "Something there is that *does* love a wall." Still, the narrator struggles against this conclusion. I say this because the reprise of the neighbor, "Good fences make good neighbors," is itself constituted by a binary opposition that ultimately holds the poem together. Good fences/good neighbors and bad fences/bad neighbors is a way of setting boundaries. A fence establishes territory and land ownership such that cows or any animal will not impinge upon another's property. And, while apple trees and pine trees will never be able to cross the wall, the fence—individual apples and individual pine cones could be blown by wind onto each other's property if it were not for the wall. Because of the wall, the fence, there is nothing to feud about and nothing to precipitate a violent confrontation between these two neighbors. The "mended" fence assures each neighbor of the others' independence and lack of liability—both anamnestically and proleptically.

As I said earlier, the wall/fence really does reverse itself in the poem. While there is tension between the speaker's voice and the voice of the neighbor:

> *". . . Something there is*
> *that doesn't love a wall,*   vs.
> *That wants it down. . ."*

> *"He says again,*
> *Good fences make*
> *good neighbors."*

Finally, the poem is an almost perfect example of Derrida's "binary oppositions." In this text, it is not the good fences that make good neighbors, but rather the gaps in the wall/fence.

> *The gaps I mean,*
> *No one has seen them made or heard them made,*
> *But at spring mending-time we find them there,*
> *I let my neighbor know beyond the hill;*

So, it appears to me, in some deconstructive sense, that the fact that the wall needed mending, i.e., repair at spring time, suggests that it is not the "good fences that make good neighbors," but rather the fences that are in need of repair each spring that brings the neighbors together. Without the need for repair, there would be no gathering, no conversation—no mending wall. In this poem, *bad* fences make good neighbors and gaps in need of mending ensure continuity and, more importantly, companionship.

A FEMINIST INTERPRETATION OF ROBERT FROST'S POEM "MENDING WALL"

The title of the poem represents both the feminine and the masculine: "Mending Wall." The language "to mend" sounds rather feminine to me, fostering images of the caring housewife who sews the family's clothing and repairs socks, shirts, etc. Wall, on the other hand, suggests strength, sturdiness, a towering protective device. The speaker in the poem seems to be more feminine, while the neighbor more assertive and masculine:

> *He is all pine and I am apple orchard.*
> *My apple trees will never get across*

> *And eat the cones under the pines, I tell him.*
> *He only says, "Good fences make good neighbors."*

The speaker's attitude is much more talkative which stereotypically suggests femininity, while the neighbor seldom speaks, and when he does, he has little to say. He repeats himself without elaboration. Moreover, the "apple trees" of the speaker is suggestive of the biblical "Garden of Eden" and Adam and Eve's eating the forbidden fruit, symbolized by the apple. (confer Genesis 3:5-6)

The outdoor setting of the poem suggests masculinity while "spring" is suggestive of the feminine. In spring time, there are flowers blossoming, the sprouting of grass and leaves indicative of creation and the birth of new life. The language of spring conjures images of softness, colors and delight and freshness of the air. Spring flowers also find bees sampling the nectar from their petals and birds chirping and singing joyously. Images of the "birds and the bees" as a metaphor for sexual desire are found in the following stanzas:

> *Spring is the mischief in me, and I wonder*
> *If I could put a notion in his head:*
> *'Why do they make good neighbors? Isn't it*
> *Where there are cows? But here there are no cows.*
> *Before I built a wall I'd ask to know*
> *What I was walling in or walling out,*
> *And to whom I was like to give offense.*

This entire section of the poem has a feminine tone of questioning, planning, and a measured approach to action, unlike the often thoughtless and impetuous action of the masculine persona. Moreover, the language of love as in "something there is that doesn't love a wall, that wants it down" is also indicative of the feminine.

I think the poem redefines gender stereotypes because the speaker and the neighbor appear to be masculine, but the speaker's language and the inherent symbolism of the language seem to be more feminine than masculine.

Finally, the speaker's voice is tentative—explorative because it lacks authority:

> *Something there is that doesn't love a wall,*
> *That sends the frozen-ground-swell under it*
> *And spills the upper boulder in the sun.*

The wording, "something" is indecisive, illusive, indefinite, and portrays the speaker as feminine, i.e., in the way that a patriarchal society perceives the feminine. Also, it is significant and indicative of masculine domination and desire to control that women are literally absent from the poem. Moreover, the fences in the poem conjure images of colonization for the Black person in America as well as images of cattle or hogs—animals that are caged, controlled, and oppressed.

SERMONIC DISCOURSE—"BEGINNING WITH THE WORD"

In the beginning was the Word, and Word was with God, and the Word was God. He was in the beginning with God. All things came into being through him, and without him not one thing came into being. What has come into being in him was life, and the life was the light of all people. The light shines in the darkness, and the darkness did not overcome it. (John 1:1–5)

Some of us may be more focused on the end than the beginning. We have heard that "it's not how you start, but how you end up that is important." The goal is important. This reminds me of Aristotle's ethics. Aristotle was born in 384 BC and at the age of seventeen he went to Athens to study under Plato—at his academy. Book one of Aristotle's *Ethics* begins with the end. "Thus it seems that happiness is something final and self-suffering and is the end of all that man does." In other words, Aristotle is saying that the goal of life is happiness—a type of living well and doing well. For Aristotle, a balanced life is critical to excellence. Both excess and deficiency contribute to the destruction of excellence. We all know what excess is, don't we? This is a season of excess for some and deficiency for others. Excess—drinking too much wine, beer, and whiskey. Excess—staying out too late. Excess—eating too much not just once in a while, but every day. Excess—lying perpetually. Excess—buying more than your cash or your charge cards can support. Excess—excessive force, excessive violence, excessive talking, excessive complaining, excessive working, never relaxing—just chilling. But then again you can spend too much time "chilling." Deficiency is the other side of excess. It is not doing enough. Deficiency in reading. Deficient means lacking something that would bring you up to par, up to snuff, up to the norm, up to the mean, up to the average. It seems to me that deficiency marks many of us, just as excess does. Deficient is like insufficient. Deficient means deficit. Deficient—insufficient funds in our account because of excess. Excessive spending leads to deficiency, a deficit balance. Ok, you see then that the goal in life is happiness and neither excess nor deficiency will make us happy. That's why today, I'm concerned about the beginning. It is how we begin our lives that determine to a great deal how we end up. Even before a child is born that child's chances of survival are determined to a large extent by the behavior, health, and habits of the mother. If the mother smokes and eats poorly or drinks alcohol and does drugs, then that child will be born with a deficit—behavior and attention deficit, physical and personality disorders. If you curse and denigrate your child every day instead of offering hopeful and encouraging words, then you are dooming that child's destiny to the dangerous dungeons of do-nothingness and despair. So, from my meager understanding of our text this morning, it seems that we have to look at how we get this life started. That's why my sermon title today, "Beginning With the Word," is so critical to the life of the church and the Black community. We are not beginning with science and technology—the new gods of postmodernity and before that the modern world. No, we are not beginning with the self, the ego or the mind and body. We are not beginning with an idea or a thought or an axiom, or a formula—no. The most appropriate starting point, the most transforming point of origin, the most potent part of this prologue to the Gospel of John is the *Word. The Creative Word. The incarnate Word. The Word as agency.* The Word as redemption. The Word as light of the world.

The scripture text states: "In the beginning was the Word, and the Word was with God and the Word was God." The word is eternal. From the start, the Word was. The Word of God is a speech act, but it's more than that. More than speech. This Word has power in the world. It creates life. "By the Word of the Lord the heavens were made, and all their host by the breath of his mouth . . . For he spoke, and it came to be; he commanded, and it stood firm" (Ps 33:6–9). The Word is essential to creation and yet it precedes creation. This Word is pre-existent Word. In the beginning was the Word, and the Word was with God, and the Word was God. The Divinity of the Logos is clear. The Word was God. God is identified as the Word. The isness of God is constituted by the Word. The oneness of God and the oneness of the Word are the same. So when one sees Jesus, one sees God; when one hears Jesus, one hears God. Let us see and hear what the Word has in store for us. Let us see the power of the Word in the work of the church and the community. Let us hear the majestic and sweet melodious word as it is read, as it is taught; as it is preached, and as it is lived.

Finally, the Word has a powerful life—giving character to it. Jesus Christ is the Word and the life of the Word. The text says, "what has come into being in him was life, and the life was the light of all people" (v. 4). Jesus Christ is the Word and the Word is life and light. The Word is life. The Word is healing. The Word is the Word that gives sight to the blind. The Word is the Word that touched blind Bartimaeus; the Word is the Word that gave healing to the lame, healing to the sick of mind and body; the Word is the Word that gives life in the midst of death and destruction. In the presence of war and violence, the Word is the intercessor. The Word is the life of Jesus Christ. The Word is the light of the world. There is life and light in the Word. The Word is the light of my pathway and the lamp unto my feet; The Word is the power of love and faith; the Word enables us to hope and to imagine a new world, a new being, a new life of transformation and peace.

Bibliography

Aristotle. *The Metaphysics,* Book Alpha V. New York: Penguin, 1998.

Augustine. *De Doctrina Christiana,* Book IV. New York: Oxford University Press, 1995.

Austin, J. L. *How to Do Things with Words,* 2nd edition. Cambridge, MA: Harvard University Press, 1975.

Bakhtin, Mikhail. *The Dialogic Imagination: Four Essays.* Austin: University of Texas Press, 1981.

Baldwin, James. *Another Country.* New York: Dial, 1962.

———. *The Fire Next Time.* New York: Vintage, 1963.

Barthes, Roland. *Image, Music, Text.* New York: Hill and Wang, 1977.

———. *The Pleasure of the Text.* Translated by Richard Miller. New York: Hill and Wang, 1975.

Baudrillard, Jean. "Interview for Le Nouvel Observateur." (June 19–25, 2003) by Aude Lancelin. Taken from the International Journal of Baudrillard Studies (2004) http://www.ubishops.ca/baudrillardstudies vol. 1.

———. *Simulacra and Simulation.* Translated by Sheila Faria Glaser. Ann Arbor: University of Michigan Press, 1994.

Baudrillard, Jean and Marc Guillame. *Radical Alterity.* Los Angeles: Semiotext (e) 2008. The Film, *The Matrix,* written and directed by the Wachowski Brothers.

Bonhoeffer, Dietrich. *Act and Being: Transcendental Philosophy and Ontology in Systematic Theology.* Minneapolis: Fortress, 1996.

———. *Ethics.* New York: Simon and Schuster, 1955/1995.

———. *Life Together.* New York: Harper and Row, 1954.

Bressler, Charles E. *Literary Criticism: An Introduction to Theory and Practice,* 3rd ed. Upper Saddle River, NJ: Prentice Hall, 2003.

Brody, Jennifer DeVere. "Black Cat Fever: Manifestations of Manet's *Olympia.*" *Theater Journal* 53:1 (March 2001) 95–118.

Brunner, Emil. *The Divine Imperative: A Study in Christian Ethics.* London: Lutterworth, 2002.

Burke, Kenneth. *A Rhetoric of Motives.* Berkeley: University of California Press, 1969.

Champion, Laurie, ed. *The Critical Response to Mark Twain's Huckleberry Finn.* New York: Greenwood, 1991.

Cone, James H. *God of the Oppressed.* New York: Seabury, 1975.

———. *Risks of Faith: The Emergence of a Black Theology of Liberation.* Boston: Beacon, 1999.

———. *Speaking Truth.* Grand Rapids: Eerdmans, 1986.

Bibliography

Connerton, Paul. *How Societies Remember.* Cambridge: Cambridge University Press, 1989.

Derrida, Jacques. *Learning to Live Finally: The Last Interview.* New York: Melville House, 2007.

————. *Of Grammatology.* Translated by Goyatri C. Spivak. Baltimore: The Johns Hopkins University Press, 1997.

Desmond, William. *Being and the Between.* Albany: SUNY Press, 1995.

Douglass, Frederick. *Narrative of the Life of Frederick Douglass, An American Slave.* New York: Barnes and Noble Classics, 2003.

Du Bois, W. E. B. *The Souls of Black Folk.* New York: Bantam, 1903/1989.

Ebeling, Gerhard. *Word and Faith.* Philadelphia: Fortress, 1963.

Eliot, T. S. *Christianity and Culture.* New York: Harcourt Brace, 1948.

Ellison, Ralph. *Invisible Man, Prologue.* In *The Norton Anthology of African America Literature*, edited by Henry Louis Gates and Nellie Y. McKay, 15–18. New York: Norton, 1997.

Fanon, Frantz. *Black Skin, White Masks.* New York: Grove, 1952.

Faulkner, William. *Requiem for a Nun.* New York: Random House, 1951.

Foss, Sonya J., et al. *Contemporary Perspectives on Rhetoric*, 3rd ed. Long Grove, IL: Waveland, 2001.

Gadamer, Hans-Georg. *Truth and Method.* New York: Continuum, 2004.

Gaines, Ernest. *A Lesson Before Dying.* New York: Vintage, 1994.

Gandhi, Leela. *Postcolonial Theory: A Critical Introduction.* New York: Columbia University Press, 1998.

Glaubman, Richard. *Life Is So Good.* New York: Penguin, 2000.

Gosse, Edmund. *Father and Son.* London: Penguin, 1989.

Grassi, Ernesto. *Rhetoric as Philosophy: The Humanist Tradition.* Carbondale: Southern Illinois University Press, 1980/2001.

Guerin, Wilfred L., et al. *A Handbook of Critical Approaches to Literature*, 4th ed. New York: Oxford University Press, 1999.

Habermas, Jürgen. *Religion and Rationality: Essays on Reason, God and Modernity.* Cambridge: The MIT Press, 1998.

————. *Theory and Practice.* Translated by John Viertel. Boston: Beacon, 1973.

Harris, James Henry. "Patriarchy in the Black Church." In *Walk Together Children*, edited by Dwight Hopkins and Linda Thomas, 67–83. Eugene, OR: Wipf and Stock, 2010.

————. *Preaching Liberation.* Minneapolis: Fortress, 1996.

————. *The Word Made Plain:The Power and Promise of Black Preaching.* Minneapolis: Fortress, 2004.

Heidegger, Martin. *Being and Time.* New York: Harper Collins, 1962.

hooks, bell. *Salvation: Black People and Love.* New York: Harper Collins, 2001.

Hopkins, Dwight. *Down, Up, and Over: Slave Religion and Black Theology.* Minneapolis: Fortress, 2000.

Husserl, Edmund. *Analyses Concerning Passive and Active Synthesis: Lectures on Transcendental Logic.* Translated by Anthony J. Steinbock. London: Kluwer Academy, 2001.

Isasi-Diaz, Ada Maria. *En la Lucha: A Hispanic Women's Liberation Theology.* Minneapolis: Fortress, 1993.

Iser, Wolfgang. "The Reading Process: A Phenomenological Approach." In *New Dimensions in Literary History*, edited by Ralph Cohen. Baltimore: The Johns Hopkins University Press, 1974.

Jüng, Carl. *Psychological Types*. Translation by H. G. Baynes. Princeton: Princeton University Press, 1971.

Kafka, Frantz. *The Metamorphosis and Other Stories*. Translated by Stanley Appelbaum. New York: Dover, 1996.

Kegley, Charles William. *The Theology of Emil Brunner*. New York: Macmillan, 1962.

Kierkegaard, Søren. *Works of Love*. New York: Harper and Row, 1964.

Kluckhohn, Clyde and A. L. Kroeber. *Culture: A Critical Review of Concepts and Definitions*. New York: Vintage, 1952.

LaRue, Cleophus. *The Heart of Black Preaching*. Louisville: Westminster, 2004.

Levine, Lawrence W. *Black Culture and Black Consciousness*. Oxford: Oxford University Press, 1977.

Lindbeck, George. *The Nature of Doctrine: Religion and Theology in a Postliberal Age*. Louisville: Westminster, 1984.

Lyotard, Jean-Francois. *Phenomenology*. Translated by Brian Beakley. New York: SUNY Press, 1991.

———. *The Postmodern Condition: A Report on Knowledge*. Minneapolis: University of Minnesota Press, 1984.

McLuhan, Marshall. *Understanding Media: The Extensions of Man*. New York: New American Library, 1964.

McLuhan, Marshall and Quentin Fiore. *The Medium Is the Message*. New York: Random House, 1967.

Mamiya, Lawrence H. and C. Eric Lincoln. *The Black Church in the African American Experience*. Durham, NC: Duke University Press, 1990.

Marsh, Charles. "Christ as the Mediation of the Other." In *Reclaiming Dietrich Bonhoeffer: The Promise of His Theology*, 81–110. New York: Oxford University Press, 1996.

Memmi, Albert. *The Colonizer and the Colonized*. New York: Orion, 1965.

Morris, Aldon D. *The Origins of the Civil Rights Movement: Black Communities Organizing for Change*. New York: Free Press, 1984.

Mueller-Vollmer, Kurt. *The Hermeneutics Reader*. New York: Continuum, 1985.

Musser, Donald W. and Joseph L. Price, eds., *The New Handbook of Christian Theology* Nashville: Abingdon, 1992.

Newton, K. M., ed. *Twentieth Century Literary Theory: A Reader*, 2nd ed. New York: Palgrave MacMillian, 1998.

Niebuhr, H. Richard. *The Meaning of Revelation*. Lousiville: Westminster, 2006.

Niebuhr, Reinhold. *Beyond Tragedy: Essays on the Christian Interpretation of History*. New York: Scribner's, 1937.

Ochs, Peter. *Peirce, Pragmatism and the Logic of Scripture*. Cambridge, UK: Cambridge University Press, 2005.

Proctor, Samuel DeWitt. *The Certain Sound of the Trumpet*. Valley Forge, PA: Judson, 2000.

Rice, Charles. *The Embodied Word: Preaching as Art and Liturgy*. Minneapolis: Fortress, 1992.

Richards, I. A. *The Principles of Literary Criticism*. London: Kegan Paul, Trench, Trubner, 1924.

Bibliography

Ricoeur, Paul. *Interpretation Theory: Discourse and the Surplus of Meaning*. Fort Worth: Texas Christian University Press, 1976.

Said, Edward W. *Orientalism*. New York: Vintage, 1978.

Simmons, Martha and Frank Thomas, eds. *Preaching With Fire*. New York: Norton, 2010.

Stuckey, Sterling. *Slave Culture: Nationalist Theory and the Foundation of Black America*. New York: Oxford University Press, 1987.

Tanner, Kathryn. *Theories of Culture*. Minneapolis: Fortress, 1997.

Taylor, Charles. *Multiculturalism and the Politics of Recognition*. Princeton: Princeton University Press, 1992.

———. *Sources of the Self: The Making of the Modern Identity*. Cambridge, MA: Harvard University Press, 1989.

———. *The Ethics of Authenticity*. Cambridge, MA: Harvard University Press, 1991.

Thompson, Audrey. "Til Earth and Heaven Ring: A Theological Theory of the Sense of Sound in the Black Preaching Event of the Word." PhD diss., Princeton Theological Seminary, 2010.

Thurman, Howard. *Deep Is The Hunger*. Richmond, IN: Friends United, 1978.

———. *Deep River*. Richmond, IN: Friends United, 1978.

Tillich, Paul. *Love, Power, and Justice: Ontological Analyses and Ethical Applications*. New York: Oxford University Press, 1954.

———. *Theology of Culture*. Minneapolis: Fortress, 1997.

Townes, Emile. *Womanist Ethics and the Cultural Production of Evil*. New York: Palgrave MacMillan, 2006.

Troeltsch, Ernst. *Ernst Troeltsch and Liberal Theology: Religion and Cultural Synthesis in Wilhelmine Germany*. New York: Oxford University Press, 2001.

Trouillot, Michel-Rolph. *Silencing The Past*. Boston: Beacon, 1995.

Twain, Mark. *Adventures of Huckleberry Finn*. Berkeley: University of California Press, 1985/2001.

Ward, Richard F. "Performance Turns In Homiletics." *Journal of Reformed Liturgy and Music* (1996) 30.

Williams, Melvin D. *Community in a Black Pentecostal Church: An Anthropological Study*. Pittsburgh: University of Pittsburgh Press, 1974.

Williams, Raymond. *Keywords: A Vocabulary of Culture and Society*. Oxford: Oxford University Press, 1985.

———. "The Technology and the Society." In *The New Media Reader*, edited by Noah Waldrip-Fruin and Nick Monfort. Cambridge: The MIT Press, 2003.

Wilmore, Gayraud. *Black Religion and Black Radicalism*. Maryknoll, NY: Orbis, 1983.

Scripture Index

Subject Index

representing Black church theology, 6
as speech act, 120–21
as statement of faith, 38–39
as text, 106
titles of, 30–31
understanding as prerequisite to, 106
as the Word of God, 24, 27, 73
writing of, 120–23
written and spoken, chasm between, 107
sexuality, language of, 39
signifying, 97–99
Silencing the Past (Trouillot), 168
Simulacra and Simulation (Baudrillard), 209, 215
simulacrum, 209–10
simulation, 205, 215
Sinclair, Madge, 212
skill, experience and, 104–5
slave preachers
eloquence of, 22, 24
experience of, 27
literacy of, 18
slavery, 1, 2, 6, 9, 99
condemnation of, attaining quasi-doctrinal status, 167
as dehumanizing of Blacks, 180
Douglass's depiction of, 17
history of, still alive, 188
language of, 133–34, 188
in Pauline writings, 42–43
Richmond's role in, 94
slave master as god in, 53–54
white church's complicity in, 43
slaves, religion of, 73–74
Socrates, 51, 113
SOLs (standards of learning), 16
Souls of Black Folk, The (Du Bois), 75, 136
sound
in Black preaching, 106–8
meaning and, 121
South (United States), memories of, 1–2
Speaking the Truth (Cone), 139
speech, as event, 96, 98–99

speechlessness, as communication, 96
Spirit, in community, 48–49
spirituality, personal, 158
Spivak, Gayatri, 183
spring, imagery of, 223
storytelling, art of, 201
Stranger, The (Camus), 67
Struggle for Recognition, The (Honneth), 108
studying. *See* education
subaltern peoples, 184
suffering, cross as visible symbol of, 48
suspicion, hermeneutic of, 26
Sykes, Wanda, 200
symbol, 127
Symposium (Plato), 61
systematic theology, 7–8, 26, 190
Systematic Theology (Tillich), 38, 103

talk, love lacking in, 61–62
Taylor, Charles, 108–10, 111, 112
Taylor, Meshach, 182–83
television preachers, 101, 211
tension, self-understanding and, 32
text
audience's response to, 120–22
as link in fusing horizons, 124
understanding of, 96–97
textual analysis, 4, 22, 29
textuality, 31, 79
theatre, participation in, 4
theology
freedom and, 8. *See also* liberation theology
liberal, 8, 166
philosophical, 25, 26. *See also* systematic theology
practical, 7, 8
preaching and, 7
responsibility of, 195–96
systematic, 7–8
theory, practice and, 104
this-worldly, 140
Thomas, Linda, 141
Thurman, Howard, 52, 60
Till, Emmett, 3, 169
Tillich, Paul, 23, 38, 43, 44–45, 52, 96, 103, 131

Subject Index